PLATE 4 *Peach Cloud* page 214

PLATE 5   *Blueberries Baked in Phyllo*   page 226

Gooey Desserts

Gooey Desserts

The Joy of Decadence

Elaine Corn

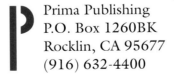

Prima Publishing
P.O. Box 1260BK
Rocklin, CA 95677
(916) 632-4400

Production: Robin Lockwood, Bookman
    Productions
Copyediting: Marcia Williamson
Typography: Bookman Productions
Interior design: Suzanne Montazer
Jacket design: The Dunlavey Studio, Sacramento
Indexing: Lois Shumaker and Susan Coerr
Cover photograph of Individual Caramel Lava
    Cakes (page 150): Kent Lacin
Interior photography: Kent Lacin
Food styling: Eréz
Floral Styling: Greta Lacin
Glass in photo plate 1 courtesy of Virginia Breier
    Gallery, San Francisco
Photo props courtesy of Macy's, Sacramento, and
    William Glen, Sacramento

Acknowledgments for recipes used:
For "Concord Cake": *The Best of Gaston Lenotre's Desserts,* by Gaston Lenotre. *Ice Cream and Candies* © Copyright 1978 by Flammarion. *Desserts and Pastries* © Copyright 1975 by Flammarion. Adapted by arrangement with Barron's Educational Series, Inc., Hauppauge, New York.

Narsai David for "Lips of the Beauty" from *Monday Night at Narsai's* by Narsai M. David and Doris Muscatine, New York: Simon & Schuster, 1987.

Camille Glenn for "Pineapple Upside-Down Cake" from *The Heritage of Southern Cooking.* New York: Workman Publishing, 1986.

The *Louisville Courier-Journal,* 1981–1986.

The Pillsbury Company for "Tunnel of Fudge Cake."

Barbara Gibbs Ostmann and Jane Baker for "Gooey Butter Coffee Cake" from *Food Editors' Hometown Favorites,* Maplewood, N.J., Hammond, Inc., 1984.

Library of Congress Cataloging-in-Publication Data

Corn, Elaine.
    Gooey desserts : the joy of decadence / by Elaine Corn.
        p.   cm.
    Includes bibliographical references and index.
    ISBN 1-55958-697-4 (pbk)
    1. Desserts.   I. Title.
TX773.C6344   1993
641.8′6—dc20   93-8071

94 95 96 97 98 RRD 10 9 8 7 6 5 4 3 2 1

Printed in the United States of America

Made primarily from recycled fibers

Dedication

I couldn't have written this book without my mother, Vivienne Corn. Her baking is so reliable that she, not a caterer, baked the entire buffet for my brother's bar mitzvah in 1965.

Nearly 30 years later, she opened up her files to me so I could research this book from a familiar perspective. For a solid autumn week, we sat in the den back in El Paso and leafed through old magazines, cookbooks, and favorite dessert recipes from our family. When my cookbook project neared its end, my mother called on her long experience in home baking. With the pride of a picky nonprofessional, she spent 50 hours editing the second of four drafts to prevent any part of this book from sounding elitist, unclear, or idiotic. Only a mother would do that, and do it so well. My dad figures in this peripherally—he tolerated the 50 hours.

This book never would have been completed had it not been for my husband, David SooHoo. He is a support staff embodied in a single person. For more than a year, he let me "shop" at the SooHoo family pantry, my name for the walk-in refrigerator at his Sacramento restaurant, Chinois East-West. He never charged me for all the eggs and cream; and he says he still loves me despite the fact that experiments for this book displaced pizza in our refrigerator at home. David also managed my occasional panic attacks with philosophy and tenderness. He is now in the habit of enjoying dessert at breakfast.

Our little boy, Robert, doesn't yet realize that his mommy is an author. He doesn't know what it means to have his name in the dedication of a book. When he's older, I'll tell him it was because of *Gooey Desserts* that he was introduced to Swedish Cream. Later I'll tell him why I made it three times in one day.

Contents

Acknowledgments

Cookbooks don't happen in a vacuum. I needed and demanded the interest and support of most of my friends. I am grateful the following lovers of dessert could help: Patricia Murakami, the talented and joyous pastry chef at Chinois East-West in Sacramento, who let me use her pastry kitchen, coached me, brainstormed with me, drove to San Francisco cooking classes with me, and had a seamless atta-girl approach to this endeavor; Andrea Litton, former bakery owner and now a nurse, who gave chemistry insight; Judy Parks, Sacramento pâtissière and culinary teacher, who dealt with endless questions about the properties of ingredients; Marcy Friedman, who spilleth over with recipes and stories of desserts enjoyed all over the world; Gloria Herbert, a master food preserver through the University of California-Davis, without whose lemon curd this book would have been incomplete; and Fred Teichert and Nancy Weaver, whose merged cookbook library offered old tomes from the South, which deepened and enriched this book's American viewpoint.

I am indebted also to my newspaper and food-writing friends: Gloria Glyer, food editor of the *Sacramento Union;* Jan Townsend, food writer at the *Sacramento Bee;* Susan Puckett, executive food editor of the *Atlanta Journal-Constitution;* Felicia Gressette, food editor of the *Miami Herald;* Cathy Barber, food writer for the *Dallas Morning News;* and Jan Hazard, food editor of *Ladies Home Journal.*

Professional chefs were eager to share their passion for gooey desserts: Rick Whitnah, Vince Alexander, Lina Fat, and Kevin Nichols, who probably has forgotten all about his contribution. It is a caramel sauce so perfect and thick I can only hope my version inspires the same ironic compliment the original drew from a customer who should have known better: "Kevin, why are you using bottled caramel sauce?"

My lineup of recipe testers represents all levels of skill and interest in cooking: Kathleen Abraham, Linda Ball, Eric and Jorey Beamesderfer, Brenda Bell, Leslie Bramlage, Tracey Broussard, Lauren Chatham, Lee Crisan, Melinie diLuck, Marcy Friedman, Jim Gentry, Gloria Herbert, Dixie Jew, Linda Jew, Andrea Litton, Patricia Murakami, Judy Parks, Bill Sailor, Carl Schubert and family, Fred Teichert, Shirley Wong, and Celeste Woo.

The following people have been drawn into my life by this book, and I am indebted to them: Martha Casselman, for being the agent and friend I most enjoy sharing ideas with; Jennifer Basye of Prima Publishing, for naming this book, asking me to write it, and giving me the recipe for Swedish Cream; Robin Lockwood for being a reassuring editor; Suzanne Montazer for not only designing the book but trying the recipes; Barbara Fitzpatrick, who turned the tangled roots of my computer files into a tree of life; Darrell Corti, who has never let me down when I needed help or needed to vent; Kent Lacin, Lindy

Dunlavey and Eréz for ooey gooey food photography; and Karen Ewing of Java City coffee roasters in Sacramento, whose advice is good to the last drop.

Special thanks go to all the people I interviewed while I was food editor at the *Austin American-Statesman, Louisville Courier-Journal,* and *Sacramento Bee.* Many recipes these people shared over nearly two decades fit the gooey category perfectly. They are gratefully used here to help explore this happy concept.

Introduction

In a cookbook market saturated with cakes, confections, pies, and puddings, no one has ever compiled desserts based on *how they feel in your mouth*. Although gooey as a goal might sound silly, this book represents a serious culinary search for texture. To put it bluntly, *Gooey Desserts* showcases a category of desserts that squishes out around the sides of your tongue.

The desire for "gooeyness" often is a secret, private longing that surfaces when dessert is served. A likely place to find goo-lovers is in recipe exchange columns in newspapers. As a food editor, I saw hundreds of recipe requests, and most were for desserts. Of those, the gooey factor was strong enough to warrant yearly printings of Better-Than-Sex Cake and Turtle Pie.

What exactly is gooey? The dictionary says it is sticky and sweet. That is too limiting. It helps to define it by describing what it isn't. Fruitcake isn't gooey. Date-nut bread isn't gooey. Most desserts you'd eat at Passover aren't gooey. The phrase "have your cake and eat it, too" does nothing for people interested in "gooeyness." Common cake is something a goo-lover would politely poke at, uninterested in the cake's tender crumb. Goo-lovers aren't interested in crumbs. They're interested in filling and frosting, cream and caramel. (The cakes in *Gooey Desserts* only look like cakes—underneath the disguise you'll find gooey layers.)

Gooey is really a state of mind. The word conjures up myriad meanings —soft, lush, rich, smooth, velvety, and slick. Some people associate gooey with the sensual, the pleasurable, the erotic. Picture a dessert that curls back where a fork went through—a truly gooey consistency, gently retracting. It's the looped tip of a Dairy Queen cone. It's the snowy peak of meringue.

In selecting recipes to showcase "gooeyness" best, I was surprised by what friends and professionals believed qualified:

"You're putting in bread pudding, aren't you?" It was fairly a command from Cathy Barber of the *Dallas Morning News*. My group of advisers in California hadn't mentioned bread pudding, and I had initially decided to leave it out. But I changed my mind when I discovered the two extremely wet, boozy bread puddings you'll find in these pages.

My agent, Martha Casselman, said, "You're putting an ice cream cake in, aren't you?" To my mind, ice cream isn't gooey. But the ice cream cake in Martha's dreams is surrounded by gooey complements. And so you'll find Martha's answer in Chapter 5, "Great Gooey Cakes"—a mocha ice cream cake with chocolate-flavored caramel and thick chocolate sauce on top. I am converted. This ice cream cake is definitely gooey.

Susan Puckett of the *Atlanta Journal-Constitution* nearly strong-armed me to include desserts from America's most lubricated zone, the South.

Those would be Better-Than-Sex Cake, Dump Cake, Dirt Cake, and Banana Pudding.

But no one had to convince me to include certain desserts. They were naturals. The essence of gooey resides in the finest chocolate mousse, and in handmade caramel pulling itself free of a chocolate coating. Lemon meringue pie with fresh lemon juice and frothy meringue may be the apotheosis of gooey desserts. Big Banana Cream Pie (with caramelized bananas) and Vanilla Pudding (made from scratch) compete for top honors in physical comeliness as well as gooey excess.

I am not a fan of mixes and do not use them in this book except in Chapter 7. I prefer making desserts the long way for quality, flavor, and principle. I enjoy the full process—I want to feel I have truly cooked something. Also, I always use pure ingredients. The choices we make—fresh cream and cheeses, unsalted butter, decent-quality chocolate, supple vanilla beans or pure extract, and really fresh eggs—affect the finished product.

While I generally avoid cake mixes and imitation whipped toppings, I do occasionally suggest shortcuts involving the use of commercial chocolate sauces, syrups, or glazes; storebought caramel or butterscotch sauces and toppings; frozen raspberries or strawberries (for purees); and evaporated milk (in Tres Leches Cake). Marshmallows and marshmallow cream are necessary for many recipes. And economical chocolate chips are used from time to time in place of more expensive chocolate.

As to the wisdom of producing a book about gooey desserts in an era when the message could be perceived as a metaphorical pie in the face of the contemporary American health movement, let's be realistic. Few of us eat dessert with every meal. Not many of us eat dessert every day. But when you really want dessert, you want the most satisfying experience, if not an exaggerated episode of dessert enjoyment. Personally speaking, if I know something gooey is waiting in the wings, it's all I can do to suffer through an entrée until dessert is wheeled out.

Most of us happen to adore dessert. Regard this as sin, and you've got yourself a web of psychological complications. Think of dessert as a work of beauty and art, and it becomes legitimate satisfaction. Eat only a little, and you'll enjoy it even more.

Dessert is a symbol of love and pleasure, part of the softness of life that shelters us temporarily from the hard edges. As proof, the next time you bring a gooey dessert to a pot luck, watch all the smiles.

Elaine Corn
Sacramento, 1993

Ingredients and Equipment for Gooey Desserts

Primary Ingredients

Gooey desserts owe their special properties to their ingredients. Besides fresh cream, butter, cheese, and eggs, you can get "gooeyness" from corn syrup, honey, marshmallows, maybe a little gelatin or pureed fruit. Quality ingredients deserve proper equipment, and the result begs a beautiful presentation.

Cream

Whipped cream swirled as big as a beehive is a tantalizing vision. The irony of whipped cream is that it's light and heavy at the same time. It may be 40 percent fat, yet it is folded into a mousse to "lighten" it.

Cream labeling is based on butterfat content. Names may vary throughout the country, but federal standards break down like this:

- *Heavy whipping cream* not less than 36 percent butterfat
- *Light whipping cream* (also called whipping cream) 30 to 36 percent butterfat
- *Light cream* (also called coffee cream or table cream) 18 to 30 percent butterfat
- *Half-and-half* 10.5 to 18 percent butterfat

Some manufacturers have an even higher butterfat content—and they advertise it. In Europe, Canada, and Australia, you'll find cream with a much higher fat content—after a day or two it must be spooned rather than poured. Even an unpracticed palate would notice the difference in flavor and density. *Crème fraîche*, which is commonly used in France, is heavy cream slightly acidified so that it thickens to the pourable consistency of cake batter. French pâtissier Gaston Lenotre thinks crème fraîche tastes vaguely like hazelnuts. You'll find instructions on how to make your own version in various recipes throughout this book. It will keep one week.

Most cream we buy in supermarkets is ultrapasteurized. It is no secret that ultrapasteurized cream is slow to whip and carries a charred taste. These flaws are annoying, but not unmanageable. I assure you, ultrapasteurization is intended to keep the food we eat safe, not to frustrate cooks. In fact, you will be seeing more, not less, ultrapasteurization in cream products in years ahead. It pays to know how to get the best whipped condition from our cream supply.

To whip cream Whipping-grade cream is the national standard. I, though, prefer heavy cream for most whipping. The higher the butterfat, the more stable the whipped product, and the quicker and more easily the cream will whip. Because this all comes down to a few percentage points of butterfat, heavy cream and whipping cream are used interchangeably throughout this book, except where noted for certain caramels or ganache.

To speed whipping, cream should be ice cold. Chill the bowl in the freezer a few minutes. Toss the beaters and the measured amount of cream into the freezer as well. After this easy preparatory step, you should have no problem whipping cream.

To counter any off-flavor, sugar is added to cream almost every time it is whipped.

Piping cream   Cream is often piped through a pastry bag to decorate a dessert. The tip you select should have a large opening. If the opening is too small, only liquid will make it out the hole.

Butter

Butter is one of my daily joys. In the height of cholesterol-panicking, calorie-counting, and fat-gramming, I never gave it up. I'd rather have a dot of butter on toast than a pat of margarine. My family plays tricks on me, but I can tell the difference every time (thinking, who couldn't?). To paraphrase one product's claim, "I *can* believe it's not butter."

Recipes in this book call for unsalted butter, period. Salted butter has a longer shelf life, but to me, it detracts from the butter flavor in dessert. If salt is used, add it separately.

Butter throughout the world must be at least 80 percent butterfat. With standardization, you'd expect all butter to cost the same and be the same. More expensive butter isn't necessarily better butter. Packaging and advertising have nothing to do with flavor and quality. Flavor depends on the feed and grasses eaten by cows. Butter graders check for acidity, malty flavors, and bitterness. Some say the butter in France's Normandy is the best in the world because of the type of grass that grows there. My personal favorites are the butters of New Zealand and Denmark. I can often find Danish butter in delicatessens specializing in European products.

Butter storage   Nothing absorbs odors like butter. Avoid icebox flavors by wrapping butter in plastic for refrigerator storage. If you need softened butter for a recipe, remove it from the refrigerator an hour before you need it. If you won't be using your butter for a few days after purchase, freeze it.

Chocolate

Good chocolate should have enough cocoa butter to make it look shiny and feel good in your mouth. If it has been refined well, it will have smooth flavor and lack astringency.

Chocolate's quality has nothing to do with where it's from—good chocolate is made in many places. I'm a fan of Guittard from Burlingame, California; Ghirardelli from San Francisco; Valrhona from France; and Callebaut from Belgium.

These endorsements are not to diminish the baking performance of such brand icons as Hershey's and Baker's. The amount of cocoa butter in these products is comparatively low, but the compromise has kept these brands economical. The price of chocolate, unfortunately, is almost always proportionate to its quality. Even so, when chocolate is the primary taste—as in ganache, a chocolate cup, a dense truffle torte, or a mousse—the chocolate you select should be excellent.

Most recipes in this book call for semisweet chocolate. Use it interchangeably with bittersweet chocolate. I occasionally call for milk chocolate or white chocolate. For easy measuring, use one-ounce squares. If you have a kitchen scale, buy bulk chocolate and chop off an amount and weigh it.

The fascination we have for food not in its usual color (blonde raspberries, purple bell peppers, white beets) is underscored by a love affair with white chocolate. Technically, white chocolate isn't true chocolate because it doesn't contain cocoa liquor. Inferior white chocolate tastes like wax (or is that the taste of raw shortening?). Good-quality white chocolate is subtle and smells like the beach. Reasonably priced white chocolate chips have excellent melting qualities.

To chop chocolate   You're hoping the food processor gets a big mention? As much as I love my food processor, it is a chaotic chocolate chopper. Pieces end up so uneven that you get both chunks and powder. This will not serve you well if you're melting the chocolate. It's a fact: chopping chocolate is one of baking's biggest hassles.

Chopping chocolate in preparation for melting reminds me of a basic tenet in Chinese cooking: ingredients must be of uniform size for even heating. If cut into pieces of comparable size, they will melt faster and more evenly.

A large chef's knife makes chopping chocolate easy (and we chop a lot of chocolate in this book). Set the chunk (or squares) of chocolate on a board or countertop, and hold the knife before you in your dominant hand, parallel to your body. Set your other palm on top of the blade, and lower the blade into the chocolate. Force the knife down in controlled slices, rocking it until you break through.

To melt chocolate   "Slow" and "low" are the bywords. Chocolate needs only enough heat to lose its shape, change molecular structure, and become liquid. If warmed too quickly or with too much heat, cocoa butter can come out of its bond, or the chocolate can burn. That's why most directions in this book ask you to melt chocolate in a double boiler over barely simmering water.

The microwave seems like a safe place to melt chocolate. In most cases, it is. But careless overheating is just as costly in microwave ovens as over direct heat. I've baked a brown crust on chocolate due to my microwave's hot spots. Use a medium setting and stir every 20 or 30 seconds after the first 1 or 2 minutes, depending on the amount of chocolate. Turn off the heat when only a small chunk is left unmelted, whether in a microwave or double boiler. Stir until the little chunk melts into the mass.

White chocolate needs especially gentle handling. Its milk solids can become grainy if melted too hot or too fast.

Save a seizure Regardless of how you melt chocolate, don't cover it as it melts. Condensation will drip into the chocolate, in which case a seizure most assuredly will occur. Your reflecting pool of chocolate will instantaneously contort into an unsightly mass of unstirrable graininess. (You can bring it back by adding a tablespoon or two of water and a few pats of butter—if your recipe can incorporate those additions. Continue slow, gentle melting and stirring. The rigid mass will relax into a smooth, glossy fluid.) Often, chocolate is melted with butter or water or both. These ingredients protect the warming chocolate and hasten the meltdown but can't in themselves prevent the chocolate from scorching.

To store chocolate Double-wrap your chocolate in plastic, and treat it as you would wine—meaning store it at temperatures of 55° to 60°, such as in a basement.

Eggs

Without eggs, there would be few gooey desserts. Yolks provide thickening, richness, and texture in custards, mousses, and pie fillings. Whites give poof, puff, stabilization, and aeration in mousses, meringues, soufflés, and various cakes.

In the past, recipes that called for raw yolks and raw whites were considered innocuous. But as a result of outbreaks of salmonellosis poisoning in 1989 traced to consumption of raw eggs, not many of us are eager to dare the odds anymore.

This—after the most famous consumer of raw eggs gulped four to prep for a prize fight in *Rocky*. This—after a legendary category of American desserts, the "icebox dessert," beat raw eggs with sugar and flavoring, topped them off with whipped cream, and called it a cake.

How we handle eggs becomes our best defense. Food-service situations (restaurants, hotels, hospitals) are far more susceptible to human error than home kitchens. At home, your eggs, no doubt, are in the refrigerator (well, they ought to be) until needed. Home cooks tend to be a staff of one or two, and complete one recipe at a time.

The actual risk from raw eggs is still being investigated by various government agencies. Meanwhile, advisories are still in place about not serving raw eggs to pregnant women, infants, the convalescent, and anyone with a compromised immune system.

As important as raw eggs have been to gooey desserts through many centuries, *most* recipes in this collection have managed to avoid them.

Yolks   Yolk-based custards cooked to 160° pose no safety problems. But the raw yolks that have always been part of the anatomy of classic chocolate mousse have had to go.

To my surprise, when my old mousse had its most luxuriant component excised and was implanted with a new, cooked-yolk base, the result—dare I say it—was even better!

I have developed two cooked-yolk mousses to replace forever mousse with raw yolks. They begin with hot sugar syrup added to yolks, which are then cooked over a double boiler about 5 to 8 minutes to 160°. In one recipe, the cooked yolks are combined with melted chocolate and butter. Beaten egg whites are folded in to intensify the chocolate flavor and create a slick, glossy mousse. This mousse can be found in the recipe for the Concord Cake (page 93).

The second mousse resembles buttercream. The cooked yolks are poured down the side of a mixer bowl while butter is beaten. Again, melted chocolate and egg whites are folded in. This mousse can be found in Triple Chocolate Polyester Mousse Cake (page 95).

Additionally, you may lighten the mousse with whipped cream rather than beaten egg whites. The mousse will then have a matte finish, with the cream slightly subduing the chocolate flavor and causing a firmer set.

Any use of raw yolks or raw whole eggs is noted in the recipes.

Egg whites   Egg whites are deemed a low safety risk but are not without problems.

For highest volume, egg whites should be warm. In the past, cooks left them out a number of hours at room temperature—a practice bacteria loved. Although lysozymes in egg whites help prevent the growth of bacteria, holding whites at room temperature for many hours courts risk.

To whip egg whites: Because properly stored egg whites are cold, remove refrigerator-chill by warming them in a bowl positioned over a pan of simmering water just as you begin to beat them. If you have a portable electric mixer, beat the egg whites at the stove to the foam stage. Add whatever sugar is called for once the foaming begins, then remove the bowl from the heat and finish beating to the appropriate stiffness.

If you prefer a safer white, the American Egg Board has found that with a ratio of **2 tablespoons sugar to 1 egg white**, egg whites may be beaten over very low heat until low peaks are formed and reach a temperature of 160° without loss of volume or texture.

What are stiff peaks? To test for stiffness, dip a beater into the beaten whites, draw it up, and turn the beater upside down. A "peaked" topknot should just hold its shape without falling over. If the whites look as though they've got a rash, they've been overbeaten.

Egg white storage: Remember, you can freeze egg whites. So the packages don't end up as mysterious baggings, freeze the same number (four, for example) at a time in zip-style plastic bags. Lay flat on a dish until frozen, then stack the packages.

One egg white = 1 measured liquid ounce.
All eggs used in this book are sized large.

Sugar

Question: What is dessert without sugar? Answer: Not dessert.

Sugar is the essence of all that's sweet. As a world commodity, it is traded for fortunes. It is a baby's fondest sensation, and it brings the same smile to adults.

Yet sugar has a technical side whose function is indispensable in everything from activating yeast to retaining moisture so cakes don't come out dry. Sugar provides the stick in sticky buns, the stretch in caramel, the glue in nougat. Without it, custard would coagulate too quickly and meringue wouldn't be as high, stable, or stiff. The quest for textural "gooeyness" would prove fruitless if not for sugar.

Note: In recipes where brown sugar is called for, use light brown sugar unless otherwise noted.

Caramel

No collection of gooey desserts would be complete without caramel. For tactile sensation as well as the appearance of a disgustingly rich texture, nothing better answers the call. Caramel taken just to the brink of amber-brown, with cream and butter, is the mozzarella cheese of the dessert kingdom. Perfect caramel resists parting with its dessert. The fork can't quite free itself.

Because you will use lots of caramel to improve the "gooeyness" of a dessert, it is axiomatic that you will be making your own caramel. You have to remember but one ingredient—sugar.

To create caramel, heat pure white sugar in a heavy pot over medium-high heat until it liquifies and almost burns. Technically, you are burning off water and carbon. The sugar melts to a clear liquid, then deepens to a mahogany brown. The color can change gradually or in a split second. The darker it gets, the less sweet it becomes. When cream and butter are added, you then have caramel sauce.

Caramel problems   Melting and cooking sugar sounds simple, but many pitfalls await you. If the caramel cooks too dark, it will burn, and you'll have to start over. More pesky is the crystallization of sugar into gritty granules in the midst of your caramel. Even when sugar is bubbling along nicely, the bubbles may splash against the sides of the pan, harden into crystals, and ruin your caramel.

There are many defenses against crystallization. Invert or high-fructose sugars, which you already know as honey or Karo syrup, keep caramel smooth. A number of caramel recipes in this book make use of these safeguards. Another preventative is to add acid in the form of vinegar, lemon juice, or cream of tartar. Acid should stabilize the sugar and keep it from crystallizing. At least that's how it's supposed to work. Don't count on it.

The best way to thwart crystals when you first observe them is to cover the pan with its lid and allow pent-up steam to melt the crystals back into the liquid sugar. Covering the pan does bog down the speed of the caramelization process, but more time spent on the project is better than a ruined batch.

It is impossible to leaf through recipes for gooey desserts without encountering a recipe for caramel. Learn how to make it. The results are definitely worth it. In an emergency, or if you are insecure about making caramel, check the shelf of ready-made caramel sauces (usually near the ice cream) in any supermarket.

Deciding when it's done   I have dispensed with thermometer readings for most of the caramel-making in this book. Instead, just look at it. Observe such colors as "pale honey," "gold," "amber," "amber brown," "iced tea," and "mahogany."

A thermometer reading is helpful when pulling sugar off the stove when the liquid sugar is still clear, as with the soft ball stage. A thermometer is *necessary* in candy-making. If you want the reassurance of a thermometer for all stages of sugar cooking, refer to the chart provided on page 9.

Candy thermometers, though, for all that they are depended upon, are notoriously inaccurate. I've used two at a time and gotten slightly different readings. To keep the thermometer as true as it will get, don't let it touch the bottom of the pan or the reading will be too high. Also, sugar with impurities will draw higher temperatures.

Caramel-in-progress is easier to see in a light-colored pot. Gray cookware is too dark to let you see clearly what's happening inside, and may be damaged by high heat. Heat eventually wore out the lining of a gray pot (I won't mention the brand) I used to cook sugar a few times, revealing a layer of raw aluminum. I now own a copper saucepan expressly for the rigors of sugar boiling. A stainless-steel saucepan won't let you down, either.

Cold-water test: A cold-water test is a sensory gauge of the sugar's progress. Here's how it works.

Boiling pt. temp	Candy	Cold-water test
230–234	Syrups	*Thread:* Pulls into a thread, but will not form a ball
235–240	Fudge, fondant	*Soft ball:* Forms a soft ball that flattens when removed from water
244–248	Soft caramel candy	*Firm ball:* Forms a firm ball that will not flatten when removed from water
250–266	Nougat, divinity	*Hard ball:* Forms a hard ball that will not flatten when removed from water, and feels like plastic (Italian meringue)
270–290	Taffy, butterscotch	*Soft crack:* Separates into threads that are not brittle
300–310	Brittle	*Hard crack:* Separates into threads that are hard and brittle (spun sugar)
320		*Clear liquid:* Liquefied sugar turns light amber, then pale honey in color—the light caramel stage (coating nuts)
338		*Brown liquid:* Caramel sugar turns from amber brown to the color of iced tea (some caramel-cream sauces, cream puff coating)
356		*Mahogany:* Liquefied caramel as dark as it can get and still be usable; pour onto an oiled baking or casserole dish or ramekin to cool (flan, caramel custard, caramel sauce)
374		*TOO LATE!* Caramel smokes

Source: Adapted from *A Handbook for Food Professionals: Sugar's Functional Roles in Cooking and Food Preparation*, The Sugar Association, Inc., 1101 15th Street NW, Washington, DC 20005.

Once the sugar begins to boil, stop stirring. Remove a little syrup with a spoon and let a drop fall into a bowl of ice water you've put next to the stove. The sugar blob will solidify into some sort of shape, mass, or (hopefully) a ball.

Hold the blob between your thumb and forefinger. Roll it around. Determine if it's soft or hard, flat or round. Does it stick to your teeth or not stick to your teeth? Does it spin a thread or break like glass?

To stir or not to stir? It's best not to stir caramel, but sometimes you have no choice. The sugar might decide to melt off to one side. Try tilting the pan to distribute the sugar. If you must stir, do it before boiling begins, and use a wooden spoon because the heat of the syrup will transfer up the handle of a metal spoon and burn your hand.

Vanilla

This complex flavoring is anything but plain. Vanilla is the most popular flavor in the world. It's my favorite in everything from ice cream to custard sauce to chocolate glaze.

The vanilla pod is native to eastern Mexico. In the late 1700s, its vine was smuggled to the French protectorate island of Réunion, where it now thrives.

The best-quality vanilla beans are pliant, moist, and strongly perfumed. Low-quality vanilla beans are brittle and weak in flavor. Anyone who has tried to split, butterfly, and scrape the seeds from a tough vanilla pod knows the frustration of spending too much money for bad quality.

Madagascar, off the east coast of Africa, is the largest producer of vanilla beans. The vanilla beans considered the best in the world come from where they began, in Mexico. Mexican vanilla extract is another matter.

I grew up in the border city of El Paso, Texas. I made regular trips to Juarez to buy Mexican vanilla. It has an odd, menthol-like taste that seeps deep into all baked goods. The appeal of Mexican vanilla comes from more than this unmistakable taste. It's sold in bottles bigger than beer bottles for only a couple of dollars.

The unforgettable flavor of Mexican vanilla comes from coumarin, which is extracted from the tonka bean—not the vanilla bean. You can imagine the glee when it was discovered that the pleasant aroma of coumarin mimics the fragrance of true vanilla. In the cheapest brands of Mexican "vanilla," coumarin may have partially or completely replaced the real thing. The reason I could find this product only in Mexico was because coumarin had long been banned in the United States as a carcinogen. I've stopped using Mexican vanilla, but I still long for the taste.

Vanilla beans   To use a vanilla bean, press the creased edges toward each other to make the bean round. Cut through but not to the other side of the bean. Slit the bean all the way down, as if to butterfly it. Open it carefully: a million microscopic black seeds are inside. Carefully draw the back edge of a paring knife down the length of the bean and scrape up the seeds. Flick them into the dessert preparation, along with the scraped pod.

After you've made the recipe, rinse and dry the pod and wrap it in plastic for reuse. Or put the used bean in your sugar bowl—in three weeks, you'll have vanilla sugar.

Vanilla extract   Vanilla beans are used liberally in this book for custards and some puddings, but I've also given an amount for the equally valid "pure vanilla extract." To be labeled "pure vanilla extract," the product must be at least 35 percent alcohol by volume. Imitation or artificial vanilla is made with vanillin, a by-product of the wood pulp industry. To confuse matters, vanilla-vanillin blends are common. End confusion by purchasing only "pure vanilla extract."

As much as I adore vanilla, it is but one flavor in a spectrum of possibilities. Try replacing vanilla with brandy, bourbon, rum, Kahlua, Grand Marnier, amaretto, Calvados, peach brandy, wine, or any favorite spirit or liqueur.

Basic Equipment

I'm both purist and equipment-crazed. I believe in using simple accessories as much as possible and in involving just enough gadgetry to get the job done. I don't consider the microwave integral to my kitchen. Interestingly, though, I took immediately to the food processor and I call on it frequently in these recipes.

Within these pages, you won't be called upon to use much equipment that is out of the ordinary. I do, however, have strong opinions about (1) owning a certain few tools to make your life easier and (2) getting desserts to the table in something prettier than a Pyrex dish.

Indispensable Tools

Rubber spatulas   Important in mixtures for baking, folding, and scraping out the last drop of batter. Use a wide rubber spatula for most jobs, small ones for stirring chocolate or custard. Do NOT use a rubber spatula in long-boiling mixtures, such as candy or fudge. The spatula will melt and distribute plastic specks into the mixture.

Strainers   A 7½-inch double-mesh or fine-mesh strainer you can rest over a large bowl is best for straining custards and puddings. Because a strainer drains liquid, I hang mine by the sink.

Wooden spatulas   An alternative to rubber spatulas for stirring over heat, particularly for candies and fudge, and for getting into the corners of a pot. May be used to stir custards. Wood provides good drag for folding egg whites into mixtures.

Wooden spoons   Have many on hand. Unlike metal spoons, they won't transfer heat up the handle and burn your hands. They're also quieter than metal spoons. The classic test for the doneness of custard involves coating a wooden spoon.

Whisks   A good one consists of at least 8 wires. A big balloon whisk, with a copper bowl, whips egg whites beautifully. Use narrower whisks for routine beating of eggs or batters. To store, stand whisks, balloon up, in a cannister. I use an old oatmeal tin. Another alternative is to hang them by their wires from hooks.

Measuring cups   Have many sets on hand. Measuring cups with pour spouts are for liquid ingredients. Those without are for leveling off dry ingredients.

Measuring spoons   Have two sets, or more. If you've measured out a sticky ingredient, such as honey, in your only spoon set, you'll have to wash and dry the spoon before using it for baking powder.

Pastry brush   For brushing food with butter or moistening cake layers. Especially good for greasing baking sheets with butter. Pastry brushes *are* still made with animal bristles, but most come with synthetic bristles.

Cutting board   Try to find a big one. You'll use it for chopping chocolate, slicing fruit. If you prefer wood over space-age plastic, make it walnut, beech, or maple, and clean it frequently and well.

Double boiler   Not necessary to buy a fitted set, but it's always nice. If you lack a double boiler, make one out of two pots or a metal bowl that fits snugly in a pot below it. The double boiler is used often in custard-making and chocolate-melting.

Heavy pot for sugar cooking   As was mentioned in the caramel section, use a pot with a light-colored interior so you can see the progress of your sugar's caramelization. Stainless steel is an adequate choice. Porcelain-lined enamel is fine for viewing, but the cast iron under the porcelain is so good at heat retention that even when you remove the pot from the heat, the sugar will be in contact with a very hot pot for a long time, unless transferred or set in cold water, and will continue to cook just when you want it to stop.

Bowls and Bakeware

Dark bakeware makes batters and crusts crisp and dark. Because this book is about gooey desserts, not crusty bread, don't use dark cookie sheets and baking dishes.

Bowls   I am the queen of bowls—rubber bowls, bowls with handles, trifle bowls, handmade bowls, metal bowls, ceramic bowls, copper bowls, and glass bowls. I have a friend who gauges the difficulty of a recipe by how many dirty bowls it makes: White Chocolate-Caramel Cheesecake with Macadamia Nuts hit an eight-bowl high. Owning too few bowls means you have to wash them before the recipe is finished. If you are unhappy with your bowls, a set of nested glass bowls will do much for your kitchen experiences. Easily found in supermarkets along the "cookware" aisle, a nested set is reasonably priced and guarantees a bowl at the ready. To expand your inventory, I recommend garage sales.

Bowls and Their Capacities
"Large" bowl	2 to 3-plus quarts
"Medium" bowl	1 to 2 quarts
"Small" bowl	up to 1 quart

Custard cups and ramekins   Custard cups resemble Asian teacups. Ramekins look like miniature soufflé dishes. Neither is necessary for success in baking individual custards; I've successfully substituted coffee cups for these specialty baking forms. With cups, you can serve custard on doily-lined saucers, and hold on to the handle as you eat. This method of custard consumption is much appreciated during television viewing.

Rectangular baking pans   The most common dimension for this piece of bakeware is 9 by 13 inches. Before writing this book, I did not own a baking pan of these dimensions. I now realize its importance in standardizing baking times, and use mine often. I confess, I object to its looks. I prefer pottery or bowls of comparable capacity for a beautiful presentation. If a dessert is unbaked, it's easy to transfer from the standard glass pan to a spectacular container. If you are bored with your glass baking pan, switch to a prettier one, guided by the chart on page 14 showing the volumes of typical baking pans.

Square baking pans   Whether 8 or 9 inches square, these are the baking pans most likely to hold a batch of brownies or fudge. A 9-inch square pan is a little more difficult to find.

Springform pans   If you want to bake cheesecake, you must own at least one springform pan. The side latches to a bottom with a fastener that is spring-loaded. At serving, the side is removed.

I suggest a 9-inch springform pan for general purposes. The batters for some cheesecakes are so large that a 10- or 12-inch springform pan is required. These can be found at restaurant-supply stores or stores that specialize in wedding cakes or cake-decorating.

Cookie sheets/jelly-roll pans   You should own a couple of jelly-roll pans (15- by 10- by 1-inch size) and, if possible, a half-sheet pan (17- by 12½-inch size), which is half the size of a commercial baking pan. Use them for cookies but also to place in the oven under other baked items to catch drips, or for baking sponge cake and flat meringue. Or use the pan as a tray you can decorate when you have nothing larger to hold a big presentation.

Water bath   Custards and other desserts may need to bake in a larger pan filled with water. This is known as a water bath, or *bain-marie*. Construct one with what you have on hand—a roasting pan or a 9- by 13-inch baking pan to hold water. If you lack these, you can buy an inexpensive disposable aluminum turkey-roasting pan. If used expressly for a water bath, it will hold up indefinitely.

Helpful Paraphernalia

Mixers   It is best to have (1) a big-job, heavy-duty countertop model with 2-, 4-, or 5-quart mixing bowls and (2) a cordless hand-held electric mixer for smaller mixtures. Having both makes you more efficient. For instance, when

Typical Baking Pans and Capacity Alternates

4-cup baking dish =	9-inch pie plate
8- by 1¼-inch layer cake pan =	7⅜- by 3⅝- by 2¼-inch loaf pan
6-cup baking dish =	8- or 9- by 1½-inch layer cake pan
	10-inch pie plate
	8½- by 3⅝- by 2⅝-inch loaf pan
8-cup baking dish =	8- by 8- by 2-inch square pan
	11- by 7- by 1½-inch baking pan
	9- by 5- by 3-inch loaf pan
10-cup baking dish =	9- by 9- by 2-inch square pan
	1¾- by 7½- by 1¾-inch baking pan
	15- by 10- by 1-inch jelly-roll pan
12-cup baking dish =	13½- by 8½- by 2-inch glass baking pan
15 cups =	13- by 9- by 2-inch glass baking pan
19 cups =	14- by 10½- by 2½-inch roasting pan

you bake sponge cake, beat the yolks with the hand-held mixer, then beat the whites with the heavy-duty mixer. You won't have to stop and wash a mixer.

Pastry bag and tips   Putting forth good gooey dessert presentations means you must have a pastry bag set, especially for the more Himalayan creations. The cone-shaped bags aren't expensive and come in plastic or plastic-lined cloth. Each type is washable and should be dried hanging up inside out.

Pastry bags are for decorating with whipped cream, piping out meringue disks, dropping macaroon batter easily onto cookie sheets. For whipped cream and meringue batter, in general, pastry tips should have large openings, whether plain or rippled. Whipped cream is difficult to force through a small tip—liquid, rather than fluff, squeezes out. In some cases—Russian Cream, for example—the cream may be piped straight from the pastry bag's opening, sans tip.

Plastic wrap   No pastry room is complete without it. Plastic wrap is indispensable for pressing on the surface of custards, puddings, and pie fillings; for covering bowls of whipped cream and ganache; for protecting chocolate; for rolling and freezing chocolate cookies; and for generally ensuring high-quality storage of your desserts. Restaurant-grade quality is thick and durable and prevents the intrusion of other refrigerator odors. Consider double-wrapping delicate mixtures, such as whipped cream, which are easily invaded by odors.

Parchment paper   Not completely necessary, but when used to line baking sheets, it prevents certain meringues and cakes from sticking. You can substitute with a brown paper bag cut to size.

Timer   Have many on hand. They should make a continuous noise, not beep just once. A kitchen sand timer (an hourglass) is cute but doesn't make a big enough fuss. Great bakers "feel" when something is done, or smell it. If you are forgetful or have a lousy sense of timing, a timer will warn you before your creation burns.

Optional cardboard liners   One of the handiest tricks of the trade. Cardboard circles perfectly fit the bottoms of just about any size springform pan and come sized for jelly-roll pans and other baking sheets.

Bake the liner along with the cheesecake (or whatever frozen or baked dessert you've placed in a springform pan). Serve the finished cake from the liner rather than from the pan's metal bottom. The pan is then available for another use. Additionally, if you'll be taking your dessert to a party, you can leave your pan at home. Cardboard circles can be found at restaurant-supply stores or where cake-decorating items are sold.

Icing spatula   A long, wide metal blade with flex, bent near the handle. It makes smooth, even strokes when you're icing/frosting.

Zester   A tiny grater with small, sharp holes. Rakes the colored part (zest), not the white (pith) from citrus peels.

Thermometer   Good to have when tempering chocolate or making caramel. See notes on caramel, page 7.

CHAPTER ONE

Creamy Dreamy Gooey Desserts

Cream and Sugar Slave

The basic elements of the primordial gooey dessert are cream and sugar. Here they are layered in glaring simplicity and plumped high in a dessert dish. If made a day in advance, the brown sugar sandwiched within the cream thickens into a faux caramel.

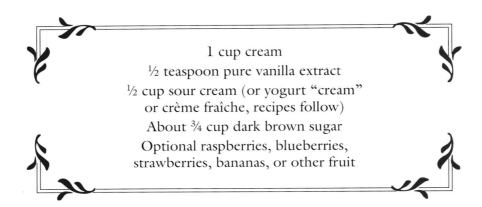

1 cup cream
½ teaspoon pure vanilla extract
½ cup sour cream (or yogurt "cream"
or crème fraîche, recipes follow)
About ¾ cup dark brown sugar
Optional raspberries, blueberries,
strawberries, bananas, or other fruit

In a cold bowl and using cold beaters, whip the cream and vanilla only to medium-stiff peaks. Fold in sour cream. Spoon half the cream mixture into individual dessert dishes or goblets, or into one 6-cup bowl, such as a soufflé dish.

Sieve half the brown sugar over the cream. Cover with remaining cream. Sieve the rest of the sugar on top. Refrigerate. In 24 hours, brown sugar will "caramelize." At serving, top with fruit, or eat plain.

Makes 4 servings.

Note: This cream is delicious plain as a dessert topping instead of sweetened whipped cream (Chantilly Cream). The slight tartness created by the sour cream is a balancing contrast for extremely sweet desserts.

Yogurt Cream

Not that calories, or lack of them, count
for much here, but you can tone them
down by using yogurt instead of some
of the cream. To make yogurt thick, it
must be drained.

Place 2 cups plain natural low-fat
yogurt (without gelatin or gum) in a
colander lined with cheesecloth or white
paper towels. Set colander in a pan (such
as a round cake pan), cover the entire
apparatus with a cloth or plastic wrap,
and put in the refrigerator to drain for
several days or up to 4 days. Discard
whey and use thick yogurt as you would
sour cream.

Yield: About 1 cup.

Crème Fraîche

Put 1 cup cream in a jar with a lid. Add
1 tablespoon buttermilk. Screw on the
lid and leave the jar at room temperature
for 24 hours. Then chill the thickened
cream. Crème fraîche should thicken. If
it doesn't, the room may have been too
chilly. Add a little more buttermilk and
place the jar in a slightly warmer
spot until cream is thick but
pourable.

Strawberries in Rebecca Sauce

Rebecca Sauce got its name at the Galt House Hotel in Louisville, Kentucky. It has become a standard during strawberry season (read: Derby Day) as a dipping sauce for fruit and has replaced my notions of what strawberries 'n' cream ought to be.

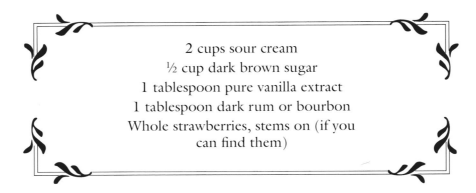

2 cups sour cream
½ cup dark brown sugar
1 tablespoon pure vanilla extract
1 tablespoon dark rum or bourbon
Whole strawberries, stems on (if you can find them)

Combine all ingredients, except strawberries, with a fork and stir until completely smooth. Chill before serving. Use for dipping with whole strawberries.

Alternatively, slice the strawberries, place them in the bottom of dessert goblets or bowls, and top with Rebecca Sauce. Chill well before serving. Garnish each with a whole strawberry, and because this is a spring dish, a sprig of mint.

Makes about 2¼ cups sauce for dip.

Note: For a pretty presentation, do a red-white motif. Place strawberries, stems up, on a plain white platter, or pile them in a huge white bowl. Put the Rebecca Sauce alongside in a red bowl.

Russian Cream
(Food of the Gods)

Even godlike comparisons fall short of fully describing this exquisite cream. In the Motherland, it might be swirled with pistachios or tinted green. I like it white and nut-free.

This is a tricky mixture that challenges fluid gelatin to remain lump-free when added to something cold. The hotter you can get the gelatin, the more you "catch it unawares" when it hits the cold cream. But you have to work quickly.

By this method, you can spoon the cream into place, or pipe spirals onto a plate, then top with a colorful fruit puree. It will look like a Dairy Queen cone—curled tip and all (see photo plate 1).

So overwhelming when plain, Vodka-ized Fruit (strawberries or orange sections) can be added for sympathetic balance, but it is completely optional.

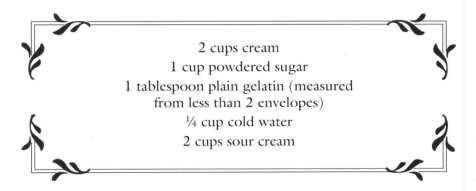

2 cups cream
1 cup powdered sugar
1 tablespoon plain gelatin (measured
from less than 2 envelopes)
¼ cup cold water
2 cups sour cream

Set aside ¼ cup of the cream. In a large bowl (not chilled), beat remaining cream to stiff peaks, gradually adding the powdered sugar. Set aside at room temperature while you prepare the gelatin.

Combine gelatin and water in a medium bowl you can place over heat. Set aside to soften for 5 minutes. Then, set the bowl directly over medium heat and swirl until gelatin is liquefied, about 1 minute.

Add the reserved ¼ cup cream and heat the mixture until it's hot.

Working quickly, fully blend a large "scoop" of the whipped cream into the hot gelatin-cream mixture by stirring and folding. *Immediately* fold the gelatin-cream back into the whipped cream—firmly and with fast strokes. The faster your motions, the less likelihood of lumps.

Fold in the sour cream. The mixture will glisten and mound. Spoon into individual dessert cups, or spiral high on plates from a nozzleless pastry bag. Chill about 3 hours before serving (see Notes).

Makes 5½ cups.

How to Use Gelatin

Careless wisdom equates 1 envelope of Knox gelatin with 1 tablespoon gelatin. This is short of the truth.

One envelope gelatin equals 2¼ teaspoons (¾ teaspoon shy of 1 tablespoon), and thickens 2 cups of liquid or 4 cups of semisolid mixture.

Two envelopes gelatin equal 1½ tablespoons and thicken 4 cups liquid or 8 cups semisolid mixture.

Note 1: To firm Russian Cream so it can be piped, chill mixture in a bowl about 30 minutes, stirring it every 10 minutes to prevent spotty sets.

Note 2: If you've mounded your Russian Cream high, you may be unable to cover it satisfactorily in the refrigerator. In this case, leave it uncovered.

Vodka-ized Fruit

Strawberries

Thinly slice 16 to 20 strawberries, mix with 2 tablespoons sugar and 2 to 3 tablespoons vodka, and set aside while you prepare the Russian Cream. Spoon berries, using a slotted spoon, into a dish or individual goblets, then top with cream.

Orange Sections

Slice top and bottom off an orange so it stands flat. With the orange standing on the counter and a sharp knife poised at the top, hold on with other hand. Saw off strips of skin, cutting between pulp and peel and using downward slices, all around the orange. With the peeled orange in your non-knife hand, hold it over a bowl to catch the juices. Cut along both sides of each membrane to free sections. Mix the captured juice with the orange sections, 1 tablespoon sugar, and 2 tablespoons vodka. Set aside while you prepare the Russian Cream, then add to goblets with a slotted spoon, and top with cream.

Swedish Cream

This recipe is much like a recipe for Russian Cream found in a national food magazine. What's more, the Russian Cream in this book is also known as Food of the Gods, the same title sometimes used for Date Pudding (page 190).

The ingredients for Swedish Cream and Russian Cream are essentially the same, but the techniques and results are different. Russian Cream is whipped, not cooked. Swedish Cream is heated, not whipped. Swedish Cream is smooth and pourable before setting. Russian Cream mounds and shines before chilling.

This recipe won $100,000 in a Washington State competition in 1979. It is gorgeous with Quick Blueberry Sauce, or with any puree of your favorite fruit.

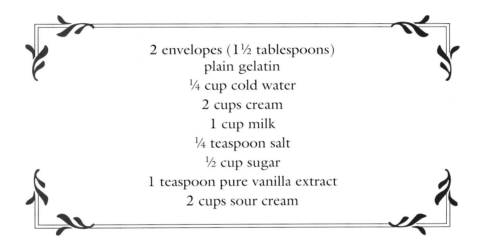

2 envelopes (1½ tablespoons)
plain gelatin
¼ cup cold water
2 cups cream
1 cup milk
¼ teaspoon salt
½ cup sugar
1 teaspoon pure vanilla extract
2 cups sour cream

Dissolve gelatin in water in a small bowl. In a heavy saucepan, combine the cream, milk, salt, and sugar over low heat. When sugar is dissolved, whisk in gelatin mixture and heat until smooth and gelatin is completely dissolved.

Pour from pot into a large bowl (preferably with a pour spout). Cool slightly, stirring occasionally, but do not allow to set. Add vanilla and sour cream, stirring and folding.

Pour the cream into individual dessert dishes, wine goblets, or an 8-cup mold. Chill covered at least 6 hours. Cream will set. Serve with Quick Blueberry Sauce (see Note) or with a fruit puree, or sin of all sins, eat it plain.

Makes 8 to 10 servings.

Note: You may also line the goblets with some of the Blueberry Sauce, then pour over cream.

Fruit Purees, Nature's Colors

In a puree, fruit is broken down to form a smooth liquid which may be flavored, thickened, gelled, or sweetened. Purees can be made in a food processor or blender. They should be strained of any seeds and solids.

Fruit puree can be the basis for many desserts and dessert components, including mousses, custards, creams, and pies.

As garnish, the decorative dot, swirl, or swizzle of fruit puree has become the darling of the dessert set. Its current vogue is nothing compared to the elevation of the humble plastic squirt bottle, from which such purees are forced.

In addition to adding beauty, a touch of color tastes good. If it's not sour or too tart, the puree can refresh an otherwise plain dessert or mitigate an overly sweet or rich one. The darkest depths of chocolate benefit by these spashes of color only when the chosen puree doesn't blot out the taste of the main attraction. The whitest creams are a stark backdrop for a shock of fruit color.

Strawberry Puree

Of the "reds," this is my favorite garnish flavor. Its sweetness is mild and refreshing, particularly when paired with chocolate or cream.

1-pint basket strawberries
1 tablespoon sugar

Wash strawberries, then core out stems. (Merely plucking the stems won't remove the woody core. Use a paring knife and cut a cone out of the top of the berry.) Puree strawberries and sugar in a food processor until completely smooth. Strain, discarding solids. The puree comes out the other side of the strainer. Pour into a plastic squirt bottle and chill.

Yield: About ¾–1 cup.

Raspberry Puree

Though raspberry puree is favored by many professional chefs, I've grown weary of seeing it on everything. However, the tart notes of raspberry flavor hold up well to very sweet desserts. It is a longtime companion of chocolate. With a hue deeper than strawberry's, it is beautiful on plain creams. You can adjust the tartness by adding more sugar. The amount added here merely augments the raspberry flavor without distorting its true tones. Please, strain out the seeds. They're small enough to be a real annoyance in most anyone's dental parts.

Quick Blueberry Sauce

2 cups blueberries (fresh or frozen)
½ cup orange juice
¼ cup water
2 tablespoons sugar
1 tablespoon cornstarch
¼ teaspoon grated orange peel
Pinch salt

Wash the blueberries. Combine all ingredients in a medium saucepan. Bring to a simmer. Cook and stir over medium-low heat 4 to 5 minutes, or until thickened. Serve warm or at room temperature. Store in the refrigerator.

Yield: 2 cups.

1½-pint basket raspberries
2 teaspoons (approximately) sugar

Puree raspberries and sugar in a food processor or blender until completely smooth. Strain, discarding solids. The puree comes out the other side of the strainer. Pour into a plastic squirt bottle and chill.

Yield: About ½ cup.

Blackberry Puree

If any fruit needs its seeds removed, it is the blackberry. When seeds stick, they can stick for days, welded into a molar so deeply as to vanish into grooves no toothbrush can find.

This puree is very dark and looks best on a white background, such as Crème Anglaise, Swedish Cream, Russian Cream, plain yogurt "cream," white chocolate, or white frosting.

Blackberries are tart and can handle sugar. If you've picked them yourself, you don't need to be told about the spiderwebs and bugs on the brambles you wished hadn't overtaken your yard: please wash blackberries.

1-pint basket blackberries
1 tablespoon sugar

Wash blackberries and drain in a colander. Pick off stems. Puree in a food processor or blender with the sugar until the mixture is as smooth as you can get it. Strain, discarding solids. The puree comes out the other side of the strainer. Pour into a plastic squirt bottle and chill.

Yield: About 1¼ cups.

For a decorative puree presentation, you can form it as feathers, curves, or webbing.

Feathering—Zigzag the puree on a plate, or into another sauce, going north-south. Draw a toothpick, knife, or index card back and forth across the zigzags, going east-west.

Curves—Squirt a dot. Draw a card through it in a curve, leaving a larger "head" and fading out with a tail.

Webbing—Squirt parallel lines. Draw a card through the lines in the same direction, so each line appears to drip into the next line.

Five Minutes and Counting
(Broiled Sour Cream with Fruit)

After broiling, the top is hot, the middle is warm, and the bottom, where the fruit lies, is cool. (See Getting the Goo Without the Gotcha' for the low-fat version, page 229.) This is a great make-ahead dish, as quick as they come.

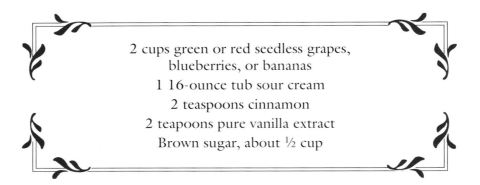

2 cups green or red seedless grapes,
blueberries, or bananas
1 16-ounce tub sour cream
2 teaspoons cinnamon
2 teapoons pure vanilla extract
Brown sugar, about ½ cup

Layer fruit evenly on bottom of 6 oven-proof dessert bowls or ramekins or a 6-cup baking dish (such as a soufflé dish).

Mix sour cream, cinnamon, and vanilla. Spoon over fruit. Sprinkle with brown sugar. Chill until serving time, then run under broiler until sugar is mostly melted, about 1 minute or less. Keep checking. Serve immediately.

Other fruits to try Strawberries, peaches, canned or fresh pineapple, nectarines, or strawberry-banana.

Makes 6 servings.

There's nothing more delicate than cream you've slightly soured yourself. If you have the time and want the mellow taste, try this simple procedure the day before you'll need the sour cream.

Homemade Sour Cream

1¾ cups cream
2 tablespoons buttermilk

Stir cream and buttermilk in a pint jar. Cover and shake. Let stand at room temperature, uncovered, 6 hours to overnight. Then chill well.

When ready to serve soured cream, beat to medium-stiff peaks—not stiff. Serve immediately. Whipped mixture should double in volume. If using with above recipe, whip softly before measuring.

Makes a scant 4 cups, whipped.

Chocolate-topped Berry Parfait

Guests will be asked to rap a protective layer of hardened chocolate to get to the cream and fruit below. The black topping gives this easy dessert a bit of grandeur.

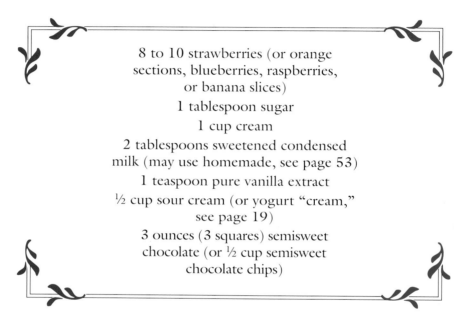

8 to 10 strawberries (or orange sections, blueberries, raspberries, or banana slices)

1 tablespoon sugar

1 cup cream

2 tablespoons sweetened condensed milk (may use homemade, see page 53)

1 teaspoon pure vanilla extract

½ cup sour cream (or yogurt "cream," see page 19)

3 ounces (3 squares) semisweet chocolate (or ½ cup semisweet chocolate chips)

Wash, hull, and thinly slice strawberries. Mix with sugar and allow to stand while you beat the cream.

In a cold bowl with cold beaters, whip cream, condensed milk, and vanilla to stiff peaks. Fold in sour cream (or yogurt).

Spoon strawberries into the bottoms of 4 parfait glasses or wine goblets. Top with dollops of cream mixture, making top surface level by twirling the glass while you smooth the top with the back of a spoon.

Chop the chocolate and melt in a double boiler over barely simmering water. (Or microwave on Medium, stirring every 20 or 30 seconds after the first minute, until only a small chunk remains.) Remove from heat and stir until melted and smooth.

Pour the chocolate in even amounts over the cream, tilting to coat entire surface. Let harden 1 hour at room temperature. Chill at least 2 hours before serving. At serving, tell guests to rap the chocolate seal with a spoon to shatter it.

Makes 4 servings.

Note: If you are out of sweetened condensed milk, whip the cream with 2 tablespoons powdered sugar.

Scotch Parfait
(Atholl Brose)

From Scotland comes a lush classic called Atholl Brose. Crunchy toasted oats are layered in parfait glasses with cream sweetened with honey, and then made a tad boozy from Scotch whiskey. Instead of toasting oats, as called for in the original style, use granola. Way off the original path is the addition of chocolate chips.

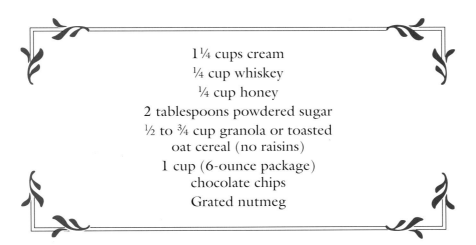

1¼ cups cream
¼ cup whiskey
¼ cup honey
2 tablespoons powdered sugar
½ to ¾ cup granola or toasted oat cereal (no raisins)
1 cup (6-ounce package) chocolate chips
Grated nutmeg

Place mixing bowl in freezer. Measure the cream and set it in the freezer while you prepare the whiskey and honey (see Note 1).

Stir whiskey and honey together and let sit a few minutes. Beat the cream and whiskey-honey mixture together in the very cold bowl, using cold beaters, just to medium-stiff peaks.

Layer cream mixture, granola, and chocolate chips in dessert goblets or parfait glasses, reserving some granola for topping. The final layer should be cream. Dust with nutmeg and reserved granola. Chill about 2 hours.

Makes 4 to 6 servings.

Note 1: Be sure your whipping bowl is ice cold, or better yet, *in* another bowl of ice. If the cream is too warm when combined with whiskey and honey, it just won't whip up.

Note 2: You can de-Scotch this dessert by replacing the whiskey with Chambord or any other liqueur or spirit.

Raspberry Fool

Given the word's real-world meaning as someone lacking in judgment, "fool" may have broader implications in politics than dessert. All that's here is sweetened cream mixed with pureed fruit.

The Scots' favorite fool is light green, from the tart puree of gooseberries. Who can find gooseberries these days? (Or ever?) Instead, prepare fool with strawberries, blueberries, even cranberries. Stone fruits, such as peaches, nectarines, and apricots, don't provide quite as dreamy a texture.

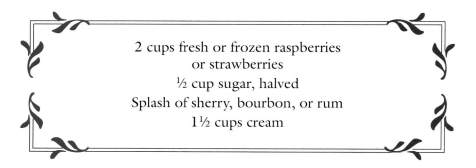

2 cups fresh or frozen raspberries
or strawberries
½ cup sugar, halved
Splash of sherry, bourbon, or rum
1½ cups cream

With a food processor or blender, puree the fruit with half the sugar. Strain out seeds. Combine puree with spirits.

In a cold bowl with cold beaters, whip the cream and remaining sugar to stiff peaks. Gently fold in fruit puree, leaving streaks. Spoon into individual dessert glasses or bowls.

Makes 4 to 6 servings.

This fool rushed in to my life the day after Thanksgiving. I had made my usual cranberry sauce with star anise and orange juice for the big feast. About 1 cup of it was left over. With a quick whipping of cream and a folding in of the cranberry sauce, a new family favorite was adopted: Nobody's Fool.

Nobody's Fool

2 cups cranberries
½ cup sugar
½ cup brown sugar
Juice of 2 oranges
Zest of 1 orange
2 whole star anise
1½ cups cream

Combine all ingredients except cream in a saucepan. Bring to a boil over medium heat, stirring now and then to prevent sticking. Reduce heat and simmer, uncovered, for 20 minutes. Chill.

In a cold bowl with cold beaters, whip the cream to stiff peaks. Fold in ¾ cup of the chilled cranberry sauce, leaving streaks.

Makes 4 to 6 servings.

Jam Whip

I consider this an idea for leftovers. Stray egg whites and whipped cream work a delicate transformation on any pantry's jam.

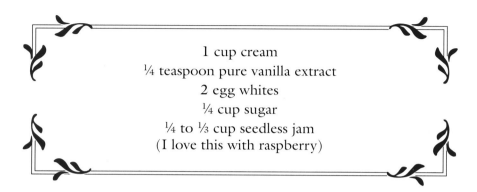

1 cup cream
¼ teaspoon pure vanilla extract
2 egg whites
¼ cup sugar
¼ to ⅓ cup seedless jam
(I love this with raspberry)

In a cold bowl and using cold beaters, whip the cream and vanilla to medium-stiff peaks.

Beat the egg whites to stiff peaks, gradually adding sugar halfway through.

Quickly fold in the whipped cream, then the jam, creating streaks and swirls.

Spoon into 4 individual dessert goblets or bowls, or a 6-cup serving dish. Decorate with a few fresh berries or mint.

To show you how easily Jam Whip re-invents itself, take my annual crusade, U.P.S.—Use Persimmons Soon.

Every autumn, my brother-in-law, Alvin, expects my creativity to deal humanely with the politically incorrect birthrate of his persimmon trees. And so I make Jam Whip with persimmon pulp instead of jam. The texture is fluffy, like a mousse.

Persimmon Whip

2 Hachiya persimmons (see Note)
1 cup cream
¼ teaspoon pure vanilla extract
2 egg whites
¼ cup sugar
Optional garnish: store-bought
nut brittle or Sticky Pecan
Praline Crumble (page 122)

Scoop the pulp from the jelly-ripe persimmons, discarding skin, core, and leaves. In a food processor or blender, puree pulp.

In a cold bowl and using cold beaters, whip the cream and vanilla to medium-stiff peaks.

Beat the egg whites until stiff, gradually adding sugar halfway through. Quickly fold in the whipped cream, then the persimmon pulp, creating streaks and swirls.

Spoon into 4 individual dessert goblets or bowls or into a 6-cup serving dish. Garnish with crumbled store-bought peanut brittle or with Sticky Pecan Praline Crumble.

Makes 4 servings.

Note: The beautiful orange Hachiya persimmon is recognized by its elongated shape and a tip at the bottom. By the time persimmons lose their trademark astringency, the fruit is so ugly they are easily mistaken for rotten. When persimmons look too mushy to eat, they're perfect.

Chantilly Cream

It's got a fancy name, but it's simply cream whipped with sugar and barely scented with vanilla. This is the cream to use with any recipe that says, "top with whipped cream."

Chantilly Cream is whipped to medium-stiff peaks, not stiff ones. Flavor it with cocoa, coffee, or liqueur.

Have all ingredients and your bowl and beaters extremely cold to avoid the risk of your cream quickly turning into butter.

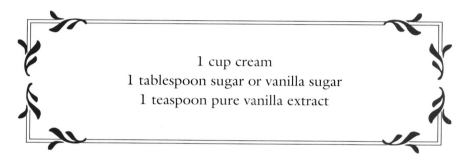

1 cup cream
1 tablespoon sugar or vanilla sugar
1 teaspoon pure vanilla extract

In a cold bowl and using cold beaters, whip cream, sugar, and vanilla on high speed to medium-stiff peaks. Store, covered with plastic wrap, in the refrigerator until ready for use, up to 24 hours.

Yield: 2 cups.

Chocolate Chantilly Cream
(with Cocoa)

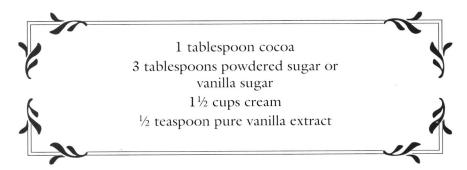

1 tablespoon cocoa
3 tablespoons powdered sugar or
vanilla sugar
1½ cups cream
½ teaspoon pure vanilla extract

Sift together cocoa and powdered sugar. Mix into ¼ cup of the cream, stirring until cocoa is completely dissolved.

In a cold bowl and using cold beaters, whip remaining cream on high speed to stiff peaks while slowly pouring in the cocoa mixture and vanilla. The resulting whipped mixture will have medium-stiff peaks. Store covered with plastic wrap in the refrigerator until ready for use, up to 24 hours.

Yield: 3 cups.

Vanilla Sugar

Many recipes in this book call for the use of a vanilla bean. Dry it, save it, and add it to your sugar bowl. Its essence will permeate your supply of sugar. In a couple of weeks, you will have vanilla sugar.

Use vanilla sugar whenever you whip up Chantilly Cream. Use as many vanilla beans in your sugar bowl as you like.

Custards

Crème Anglaise, stirred custard, boiled custard, baked custard, crème caramel, pots de crème, crème brulée, pastry cream, even pudding, are a maddeningly similar array of sublimely dissimilar entities—all subjectively gooey or necessary in gooey pursuits.

Some are soft, lush billows of creamy richness. Some tremble and cut clean with a spoon. Some are thick enough to fill other desserts and leave tooth marks. Others are made thin for pouring.

One thing is common to all: each can be considered a kind of custard. Bridging all forms of custard are three things—milk, eggs, and sugar. The milk

Tips for Great Custards

- For custard with body and richness, use yolks. For safety, cook custard to at least 160°. When done, custard will be able to coat the back of a wooden spoon, leaving no bare spots.

- The hotter the milk when it hits the yolks, the thicker the custard.

- Whisk the yolks and sugar up to 1 minute, but not longer. This mixture should be well blended. If overbeaten, custard may be tough.

- Once yolks and cream are combined in the saucepan, switch to a rubber spatula or wooden spoon. This prevents foaming and keeps the custard smooth so you can see what's happening.

- Impatient cooks, read this. If you think stirring custard in a saucepan directly over the heat is an effective shortcut that can bypass filling up another pot to create a double boiler, think how long it will take you to remake the custard.

  Chances of success, especially if you are easily distracted, rise considerably with the double boiler. Your custard will almost always come out curdle-free, yet will cook quickly and hot enough to get a good set. If you don't have a double boiler, use a bowl placed over a pot of simmering water or two pots stacked up, even if it's an awkward fit.

may in fact be cream, and the eggs may in fact be just yolks. Flavorings, such as vanilla, may add a fourth component.

Many formulas act as ratios, but really, a custard is made to suit a purpose. Do you want something custardy simply to spoon over cake, or do you want to eat the richest custard imaginable plain from a bowl? Are you filling cream puffs or layering a trifle?

To untangle custard nomenclature, the custards in this book are arranged in an order based on structure, from the loosest to the firmest, the pouringest to the most independent.

- The French edict to strain everything must have been written for custards. Beside you at the stove is a cool bowl, preferably sitting in ice, with a large fine-mesh strainer waiting for hot custard to be poured through. Particularly if you are using a vanilla bean with woody shards that can come loose during stirring, straining is a must.

- Icing down the custard is part of the custard process. It begins an immediate cooling effect necessary to hasten thickening while stopping any more effects from heat. If you took custard off the stove, left it in the pot, and didn't stir, the custard would still be so hot that it could continue to cook *and possibly curdle all by itself!*

In these days of competent ice-making refrigerators, filling a bowl with ice isn't a lot to ask. If you don't have an ice-maker, or your ice-maker hasn't coughed up much ice lately, fill the larger bowl with very cold tap water. Anything to stop the cooking.

- Vanilla beans are a wonderful perfumey flavorant, but expensive. You're in good company with pure vanilla extract or any of the spirits in your liquor cabinet. Remember, when adding delicate extracts, coldness will mask their flavor. In most cases, I think it's okay to exaggerate. If you're calling it "rum custard," don't make your guests go on a hunting party with their palate in search of the flavor "rum."

Crème Anglaise

Crème Anglaise is the dessert world's basic pouring custard. It can be made with cream, milk, or half-and-half. For ultimate richness, use cream.

Crème Anglaise often gets its flavor from infusing an entire vanilla bean in heated cream. For that reason, it may also be called Vanilla Sauce. It is also known as English Custard and as Custard Sauce.

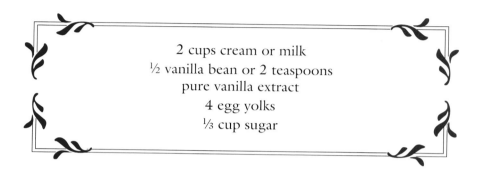

2 cups cream or milk
½ vanilla bean or 2 teaspoons
pure vanilla extract
4 egg yolks
⅓ cup sugar

In a heavy medium-size saucepan, barely boil the cream (see Note 1) and the vanilla bean, which has been split lengthwise, scraped with the back edge of a knife and added to the cream—seeds, pod and all. (If using vanilla extract, add it after cooking.)

Meanwhile, set a large fine-mesh strainer over a bowl set in a larger bowl of ice.

In the top of a double boiler, whisk the yolks and sugar by hand or with a portable electric mixer until thick and smooth, about 30 seconds. Slowly whisk in the hot cream and vanilla bean. Cook in the double boiler set over simmering water, stirring gently and constantly all around the bottom and corners with a rubber or wooden spatula. In time, foam will subside. The Crème Anglaise is done when it coats a wooden spoon without bare spots, 12 to 15 minutes.

Immediately pour through the strainer. (If using vanilla extract, add now.) Remove, wash, and save the vanilla bean. Keep stirring to cool the custard.

To store, cover with plastic wrap pressed directly onto surface of the Crème Anglaise, and refrigerate (see Note 3).

Makes 2 cups.

Note 1: You may heat cream (or milk) and vanilla bean in a glass quart-measure, uncovered, in the microwave on High for 3 to 5 minutes, until bubbles form around the edge.

Note 2: To vary flavor, add 1 teaspoon cinnamon to vanilla-flavored cream, or replace vanilla with 2 teaspoons brandy, rum, amaretto, Grand Marnier, or Kahlua.

Note 3: To keep Crème Anglaise warm for serving, place it in a bowl set in a larger pot of hot water.

How to Get the Most Out of a Vanilla Bean

Press the creased edges toward each other to make the slender bean round. Cut through but not to the other side of the bean, slitting the bean all the way down, as if to butterfly it. Open carefully. A million microscopic black seeds are inside. Carefully draw the back edge of a paring knife down the length of the bean, scrape up the seeds, and flick them into the cream or milk. Now add the scraped bean pod.

After the bean has been used, rinse it lightly, air-dry it, and store it with sugar in your sugar bowl.

Classic Soft, Stirred Custard

This is Custard Sauce or Vanilla Custard. It also gets mentioned as Boiled Custard, though it truly is not boiled. The only custards that can withstand boiling contain flour or cornstarch, which technically moves them up the scale of custard nomenclature to pastry cream.

If this isn't rich enough for you, I refer you to Custard Obsession (page 42) made with cream. This custard sets up nicely, with soft, billowy tufts you can scoop up by spoon either warm or cold. This is a good all-around custard with countless possible flavor modifications.

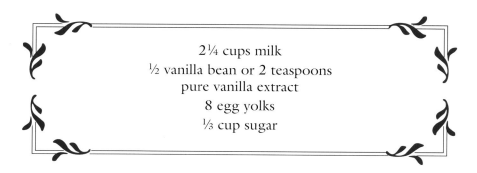

2¼ cups milk
½ vanilla bean or 2 teaspoons
pure vanilla extract
8 egg yolks
⅓ cup sugar

In a heavy medium-size saucepan, barely boil the milk (see Note) and the vanilla bean, which has been split lengthwise, scraped with the back edge of a knife and added to the cream—seeds, pod, and all. (If using vanilla extract, add it after cooking.)

Meanwhile, place a large fine-mesh strainer over a bowl set in a larger bowl of ice.

In the top of a double boiler, whisk the yolks and sugar by hand or with a portable electric mixer until thick and smooth, about 30 seconds. Slowly whisk in the hot milk and vanilla bean. Set mixture to cook in the double boiler over simmering water. Stir gently and constantly all around the bottom and corners, using a wooden or rubber spatula. In time, foam will subside. The custard is done when it can coat a wooden spoon without bare spots, 12 to 15 minutes.

Immediately pour through the strainer. (If using vanilla extract, add now.) Remove, wash, and save the vanilla bean. Keep stirring to cool the custard.

Pour custard into individual dessert bowls or into a large serving bowl. Cover bowls with plastic wrap and chill. Custard sets in 4 to 6 hours, depending on the size of the container. Serve warm or cold.

Makes 2¼ cups.

Note: You may heat milk and vanilla bean in a glass quart-measure, uncovered, in the microwave on High for 3 to 5 minutes, until bubbles form around the edge.

Presenting Custard

Custard may be comfort food for the homebound, or in regal simplicity, it's an elegant ending to a meal. It's all in the presentation.

Pour into ramekins, then allow to firm up, covered, in the refrigerator. Set each ramekin on a doily-lined plate. Sprinkle the top of the custard with cinnamon or cocoa or garnish with a mint sprig.

It's Not Just Vanilla Custard

Most of the time, custard is flavored with vanilla. But this certainly isn't the only possibility.

Almond Custard

Instead of using vanilla, use an equal amount of almond extract.

Rum Custard

Halve or omit vanilla flavoring and gently stir in 2 teaspoons dark rum if serving warm, 1 tablespoon dark rum if serving cold.

Brandy Custard

Halve or omit vanilla flavoring and gently stir in 2 teaspoons brandy if serving warm, 1 tablespoon brandy if serving cold.

Bourbon Custard

Halve or omit vanilla flavoring and gently stir in 2 teaspoons Kentucky bourbon if serving warm, 1 tablespoon if serving cold. Serve with mint-chocolate cookies. Garnish custard with a mint sprig and call it Mint Julep Custard. (Bourbon isn't bourbon unless it's made at least from 51 percent corn. Otherwise, it's just whiskey.)

Liqueur of Choice

Use any of the following, as above: Grand Marnier, amaretto, Southern Comfort, Kahlua, Crème de Menthe, Crème de Banana.

Custard Obsession

(Extra-rich Custard)

For those who crave the extravagance of cream, you've met your maker here. The extra fat content of the cream helps this custard set up with a silken bouyancy.

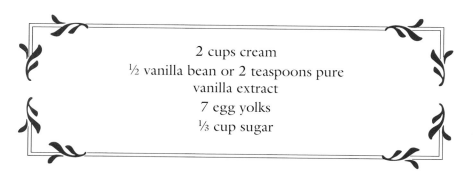

2 cups cream
½ vanilla bean or 2 teaspoons pure
vanilla extract
7 egg yolks
⅓ cup sugar

In a heavy medium-size saucepan, barely boil the cream (see Note) and the vanilla bean, which has been split lengthwise, scraped with the back edge of a knife and added to the cream—seeds, pod, and all. (If using vanilla extract, add it after cooking.)

Meanwhile, place a large fine-mesh strainer over a bowl set in a larger bowl of ice.

In the top of a double boiler, whisk the yolks and sugar by hand or with a portable electric mixer until thick and smooth, about 30 seconds. Slowly whisk in the hot cream and vanilla bean.

Set mixture to cook in the double boiler over simmering water. Cook and stir gently and constantly all around the bottom and corners, using a wooden or rubber spatula. In time, foam will subside. The custard is done when it can coat a wooden spoon without bare spots, 12 to 15 minutes.

Immediately pour through the strainer. (If using vanilla extract, add now.) Remove, wash, and save the vanilla bean. Keep stirring to cool the custard.

Pour custard into individual dessert bowls or into a large serving bowl. Cover with plastic wrap and chill. Custard sets in 4 to 6 hours, depending on the size of the container. Serve warm or cold.

Makes 2 cups.

Note: You may heat cream and vanilla bean in a glass quart-measure, uncovered, in the microwave on High for 3 to 5 minutes, until bubbles form around the edge.

Baked Classic Custard

Instead of being stirred on top of the stove, this custard bakes into a consistency that jiggles, shimmies, and slices softly. This is comfort food equal to that of stirred custard, but without requiring the close attention.

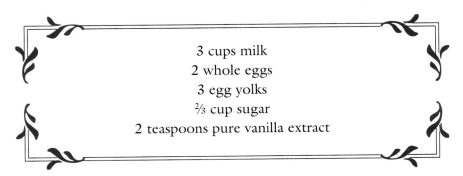

3 cups milk
2 whole eggs
3 egg yolks
⅔ cup sugar
2 teaspoons pure vanilla extract

Arrange 6 1-cup custard cups (or coffee cups) in a shallow roasting pan large enough to hold the cups without touching. Set rack in lower third of the oven. Preheat oven to 350°.

In a heavy medium-size saucepan, barely boil the milk (see Note 1).

In a large bowl (preferably with a pour spout) whisk the eggs, yolks, and sugar until pale and thick, about 30 seconds. Slowly pour in the hot milk, whisking.

Add vanilla and pour mixture into the cups, then place the roasting pan in oven. Fill pan with very hot tap water to within ½ inch of the top of the custard.

Bake about 1 hour. To test doneness, insert a knife 1 inch from the custard's edge; it should come out clean. The center will still be jiggly, but residual heat will finish cooking the custard after it's out of the oven. Remove some of the hot water with a turkey baster, then remove custards, cool and chill.

Makes 6 servings.

Note 1: You may heat milk in a glass quart-measure, uncovered, in the microwave on High for 3 to 5 minutes, until bubbles form around the edge.

Note 2: You may also bake this in a 1½-quart casserole dish, placed in a larger pan with hot water poured halfway up the sides. Bake 1 hour.

Espresso-Caramel Pots de Crème

A combination of espresso and caramel is the embodiment of rich flavor carried by rich texture. Present these little cups of custard on a doily-lined plate with plain chocolate or coffee-flavored cookies.

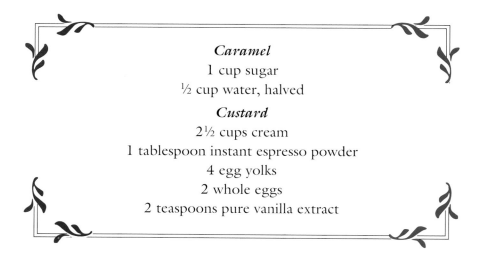

Caramel
1 cup sugar

½ cup water, halved

Custard
2½ cups cream

1 tablespoon instant espresso powder

4 egg yolks

2 whole eggs

2 teaspoons pure vanilla extract

Arrange 6 1-cup custard cups (or coffee cups) in a shallow baking pan large enough to hold the cups without touching. Set rack in lower third of the oven. Preheat oven to 350°.

For caramel In a heavy saucepan, bring the sugar and ¼ cup water to a boil over medium-high heat. If crystals form on the sides of the pan, cover the pan for 30 seconds or as long as 5 minutes, so steam rinses off the sides. When the sugar begins to darken, you may swirl the pan to even the color. When sugar is the color of iced tea (see Note 1), add remaining ¼ cup water, wait for sputtering to subside, then stir to smooth out the caramel. Remove from heat and cool slightly.

For custard Meanwhile, barely boil the cream (see Note 2). Slowly whisk the cooled caramel into the cream. On low heat, stir until caramel and cream smooth out and heat through. Remove from heat and whisk in espresso powder.

In a large bowl (preferably with a pour spout), whisk the yolks and eggs. Gradually add the caramel-cream, stirring well with a rubber spatula.

Add vanilla and pour custard into cups, then place in oven. Pour very hot tap water into the pan to come to within ½ inch of the top of the custard.

Bake about 35 to 40 minutes. To test for doneness, insert a knife 1 inch from the edge of the custard; it should come out clean. The center will still be jiggly, but residual heat will finish cooking the custard after it's out of the oven. The top may develop a dark skin. Remove some of the hot water with a turkey baster, then remove custards.

Makes 6 servings.

Note 1: Once sugar turns very brown, it is no longer sweet. Don't let it get this far.

Note 2: You may heat cream in a glass quart-measure, uncovered, in the microwave on High for 3 to 5 minutes, until bubbles form around the edge.

Snow Eggs in Espresso-Caramel Custard

Typically, this dessert (sometimes called Oeufs à la Neige) is an economical effort that makes use of egg whites after the custard has used the yolks. The dish was initially popularized in America by the country's first starry-eyed foodie, Thomas Jefferson. It remains a bistro favorite in France. It is also one of the all-time mouth-melting desserts.

The whites are beaten glossy-smooth with powdered sugar, which helps hold the "eggs" together as they poach in a hot sea of *barely* moving milk.

However, be careful. If the poaching milk gets too hot, its sugars will caramelize and form an amber-colored skin on the bottom of the skillet. This unsightly thick layer of burned sugar breaks up and floats around in the milk. If you keep the temperature of the poaching milk at 170°—no more!—you won't run this risk. That means no boiling. You may also poach in water, but the islands won't be as milky in color.

Snow eggs expand as they cook, shrink as they cool. If they come out tasting and smelling sulphury, your poaching liquid was too hot and the whites overcooked. To avoid discoloration, don't poach in aluminum or cast iron.

Espresso-caramel custard
1 cup sugar, divided
½ cup water, divided
2½ cups milk,
half-and-half, or cream
2 teaspoons instant
espresso powder
6 egg yolks
2 teaspoons pure vanilla extract

Snow eggs
8 egg whites
3 cups powdered sugar, sifted
1 quart whole or lowfat milk

Spun sugar, optional
⅓ cup sugar
2 tablespoons water

For espresso-caramel custard In a heavy saucepan, boil ¾ cup sugar and ¼ cup water over medium-high heat. If crystals form on the sides of the pan, cover the pan for 30 seconds or as long as 5 minutes, so steam rinses off the sides. When the sugar begins to darken, you may swirl the pan to even the color. When sugar is the color of iced tea, add remaining ¼ cup water, wait for sputtering to subside, then stir to smooth out the caramel. Remove from heat and cool slightly.

Meanwhile, place a large fine-mesh strainer over a bowl set in a larger bowl of ice.

Bring the milk barely to a boil (see Note). Whisk in cooled caramel and espresso powder.

In the top of a double boiler, whisk the yolks and remaining ¼ cup sugar by hand or with a portable electric mixer until thick and smooth, about 30 seconds. Slowly whisk in the hot caramel-espresso mixture. Set to cook in the double boiler over simmering water. Stir gently and constantly all around the bottom and corners, using a wooden or rubber spatula. In time, foam will subside. The custard is done when it can coat a wooden spoon without bare spots, 12 to 15 minutes. Strain, stirring to cool. Add vanilla.

To store, refrigerate with plastic wrap pressed directly onto surface of the custard until ready to serve. Makes 3¼ to 3½ cups.

For snow eggs Have ready a cookie sheet or tray loosely lined with dampened waxed paper. Have ready another tray lined with paper towels.

Beat the egg whites to stiff peaks. Gradually add the powdered sugar and beat until stiff again. Pipe whites into egg shapes or spoon into big balls onto the moistened waxed paper.

In a wide skillet, bring milk barely to a simmer. Carefully lower "eggs" into milk. Don't crowd. Poach about three or four at a time. After 2 minutes on each side, carefully lift out, using a slotted spoon, onto the towel-lined tray.

To serve Pour caramel-espresso custard into a large bowl (a clear bowl makes a beautiful presentation). Arrange the cooled snow eggs on top. Serve a snow egg with a big spoonful of custard around it. Decorate with optional Spun Sugar.

Another way Spoon custard into wine goblets. Top with a snow egg and decorate as above.

For spun sugar Bring sugar and water to a boil over medium-high heat, as above, until amber-colored. Remove from heat for a minute or two, then use a fork to dribble the caramel all over the snow eggs.

Makes 8 servings, depending on how big your "eggs" are.

Note: You may heat milk in a glass quart-measure, uncovered, in the microwave on High for 3 to 5 minutes, until bubbles form around the edge.

Melinie's Burnt Cream
(Crème Brulée)

Crème brulée is French for burnt cream. But if you chill custard, sprinkle it with sugar, and run it under a broiler until the sugar melts into a shiny, crackling sheet of caramel—that's English. Very old English.

The dish is a specialty of Trinity College in Cambridge, where the locals refer to it as Cambridge Cream. In the American Northeast, it's called Vermont Baked Custard. Burnt desserts, silken and smooth underneath, snappy-brittle on top, made a comeback in the mid-'80s in an unlikely locale. They swept California's restaurants in a bizarre gastronomic contrast to an otherwise health-conscious cuisine. Maybe the rationale was that an occasional transgression into cream and eggs was okay after all the light entrées from the sprouts-and-chèvre set wandered to the table. Looked at another way, this dish may not make the low-cholesterol list, but acid stomachs love it.

At serving, the custard must be very cold, which is probably the best argument for calling this a make-ahead dish. It is sprinkled as evenly as possible with a thickness of sugar. The broiler does the rest.

It is important to watch this "burning" process very carefully. Despite its name, you really don't want it to burn. Sugar is extremely tricky under or over heat. It can become perfect caramel one second and a scorched piece of useless brittle the next.

This is my friend Melinie's "died-and-gone-to-heaven" dessert. She's always said that when her cholesterol level is slipping dangerously low, she cooks up a batch of Burnt Cream and hides it in the back of the refrigerator. Within a day or two it is gone without a trace. Her cholesterol returns to normal, and no one is the wiser.

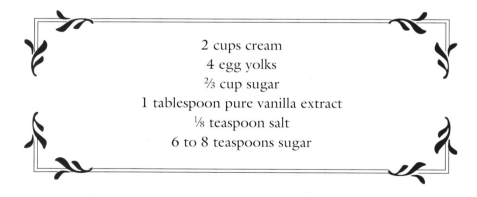

2 cups cream
4 egg yolks
⅔ cup sugar
1 tablespoon pure vanilla extract
⅛ teaspoon salt
6 to 8 teaspoons sugar

Arrange 4 1-cup custard cups or (coffee cups) in a shallow roasting pan large enough to hold the cups without touching. Set rack in lower third of the oven. Preheat oven to 350°.

In a heavy saucepan, heat the cream over medium-high heat until almost boiling (see Note). Remove from heat.

In a medium-size bowl, whisk the yolks and sugar until thickened, about 30 seconds. Slowly and continuously whisk in the hot cream, vanilla, and salt. Whisk for 1 minute.

Pour the mixture into the custard cups, then place in oven. Pour very hot tap water around the cups to come to within ½ inch of the top of the custard. Bake for 45 minutes.

Carefully slide the oven rack out. Using a turkey baster, remove some of the hot water. Remove the cups from the pan and chill custards for up to 6 hours.

Two to three hours before serving, preheat the broiler. Sprinkle each custard with 1½ to 2 teaspoons sugar. Broil, close to the heat source, until the sugar melts and the tops brown. Watch that the sugar does not truly burn, despite the name of this recipe. Refrigerate and serve well chilled.

Makes 4 servings.

Note: You may heat cream in a glass quart-measure, uncovered, in the microwave on High for 3 to 5 minutes, until bubbles form around the edge.

Spiced Burnt Cream with Hard Crack Topping

Besides having baby-skin texture, this dessert yields a gentle perfume, wafting from the mingling cinnamon and citrus. In this recipe, vanilla extract is less desirable than the essence from vanilla bean. (As always, if you do not have a vanilla bean, use vanilla extract after the custard is cooked.)

The hard crack topping is the ultimate "burn" that's smooth as an ice-skating rink and shatters like glass when rapped with a spoon. When caramel reaches the color of iced tea, pour it on top of the cold custard for an immediate set.

Burnt cream
3½ cups cream
1 vanilla bean or 2 teaspoons
pure vanilla extract
½ cup sugar
1½ tablespoons cornstarch
5 egg yolks
1 2-inch piece cinnamon stick

1 long strip of peel from
entire orange
1 long strip of peel from
entire lemon

Hard crack topping
1 cup sugar
¼ cup water

For burnt cream   In a heavy medium-size saucepan, barely boil the cream and vanilla bean, which has been split lengthwise, scraped with the back edge of a knife and added to the cream—seeds, pod, and all. (If using vanilla extract, add it after custard is cooked.)

Meanwhile, place a strainer over a bowl set in a larger bowl of ice.

In another heavy saucepan, beat the sugar, cornstarch, and yolks by hand or with a portable electric mixer, breaking up the balls of yolk until the mixture is thick, smooth, and pale, about 1 minute. Slowly whisk in the hot cream and vanilla bean. When smooth, add cinnamon stick and citrus peels.

Set over medium-high heat and cook, stirring gently and constantly with a wooden or rubber spatula, just until custard reaches a boil. Immediately pour through the strainer and stir to cool. Discard cinnamon and peels. Remove, wash, and save vanilla bean.

Pour custard into 6 custard cups or bowls (or use coffee cups). Chill at least 6 hours. Top with Hard Crack Topping.

For hard crack topping   In a heavy saucepan, bring sugar and water to a boil over medium-high heat. If crystals form on the sides of the pan, cover the pan for 30 seconds to 5 minutes, so the steam rinses off the sides. When the sugar darkens, you may swirl the pan to even the color. Take the caramel to a rich mahogany. Immediately pour it over tops of cold custards, tilting custard to evenly distribute a thin layer of caramel over each.

Chill another 30 minutes. The tops of the burnt creams will be slick as a rink.

Makes 6 servings.

Guanajuato Flan

From the state of Guanajuato in the interior of Mexico, and from the Hotel Santa Fe across from the city of Guanajuato's beautiful square, comes this dessert. It was part of a continuing discovery of the local specialties, all based on beans, pork, chilies, hot sauce, chicken, and Orange Crush.

I spied it on a dessert table, much to my distraction, during the required entrée segment of a meal. I stared at it from tortilla soup to chicken móle. Finally, it would be mine.

The dessert was flan. It was shown not in individual portions from inverted ramekins, but was displayed in its entirety, having been flipped from a tube pan onto a large platter. It was in a glorious pool of plain caramel the color of sorghum. My Spanish wasn't great, but they'd heard the request before. A waiter gave me the recipe, which I took from him, giddy with anticipation.

When I got home, I pulled this recipe together, and it has become a family standard ever since.

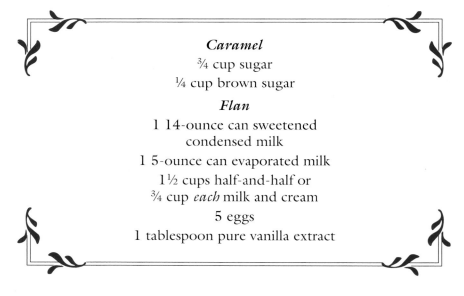

Caramel
¾ cup sugar
¼ cup brown sugar

Flan
1 14-ounce can sweetened
condensed milk
1 5-ounce can evaporated milk
1½ cups half-and-half or
¾ cup *each* milk and cream
5 eggs
1 tablespoon pure vanilla extract

For caramel In a heavy saucepan, bring the sugars to a boil over medium-high heat. If crystals form on the sides of the pan, cover the pan for 30 seconds or as long as 5 minutes, so steam rinses off the sides. When the sugar begins to darken, you may swirl the pan to even the color. When sugar is the color of iced tea, immediately pour it into a tube pan, casserole, or shallow, rounded bowl. Swirl to coat (use pot-holders!), then set aside to harden.

Have ready a large roasting pan to use for a water bath. Place rack in lower third of the oven and set oven to 300°.

For flan Empty the milks into a large mixing bowl. Beat in the eggs, one at a time. Add vanilla. When the mixture is somewhat frothy, pour it into the prepared pan over the hardened caramel. (If the caramel is still hot, you'll hear it pop.)

Cover the flan with buttered aluminum foil. Place it in the roasting pan and set in the oven. Fill with very hot tap water to within 1 inch of the top of the flan.

Bake 1 hour, 30 minutes. A knife inserted in the center should come out clean. If not, continue baking another 5 to 10 minutes, checking with the knife for doneness.

Remove from water bath. Cool 5 minutes. Carefully invert flan onto a large, round platter (see Note). The liquefied caramel will fall out with the flan and pool all around it.

Serve by the wedge, warm or cold.

Makes 14 servings.

Note: Use a platter with a definite rim to contain the caramel.

Sweetened Condensed Milk

Commercial sweetened condensed milk is nothing more than milk reduced to a creamy consistency by evaporation. Hopefully nothing has been added except sugar.

Gail Borden developed the milk after a voyage to London, where he saw babies dying from drinking milk from diseased cows. He used as inspiration a Shaker method of vacuum-sealing fruits to preserve them. Borden added sugar to act as a preservative. By 1853, he perfected the formula still essentially in use today. He patented it in 1856, and the next year founded the company that would become Borden, Inc.

In the absence of refrigeration for fresh milk, canned milk has become an authentic ingredient in many parts of the world. It adds a dimension to custard texture that plain milk and sugar can't offer. It thickens even more with the addition of an acid such as lemon juice. It also thickens if chocolate is added, or if it is heated.

Many brands of sweetened condensed milk appear everywhere, from traditional grocery stores to ethnic markets. In Mexico, Nestle's is the dominant brand of sweetened condensed milk. In America, some labels imply that the cans of milk have come from as far away as Vietnam or Holland. Most likely, they've been manufactured by a large American company. Longevity brand, with its Vietnamese labeling and Chinese lettering embossed on the can's top, for example, and Black & White brand, are made in Holland at the Cooperative Condensfabrick, a Borden plant. It is interesting to note that Eagle Brand is also sold under the product names Magnolia Brand, Meadow Gold, and Star Brand.

How to Make Your Own Sweetened Condensed Milk

Homemade "condensed" milk is easy to make. Milk is cooked long enough for natural sugars to become concentrated and mix with sugar you add. The thicker it gets, the browner it gets. For every 1 cup milk, use ¾ cup sugar.

6 cups whole milk
4½ cups sugar
½ vanilla bean

Heat the milk and sugar in a heavy saucepan over medium-low heat with the vanilla bean, which has been split lengthwise, scraped with the back edge of a knife and added to the milk—pod, seeds, and all.

When the sugar is dissolved, raise the heat to medium-high and hold between a simmer and a boil, stirring occasionally, for about 1 hour. Be sure the milk doesn't stick to the bottom of the pan. The milk will thicken, turn beige, and darken to light tan.

Strain into a bowl and cool. The "condensed" milk will have reduced to 4½ cups. It will keep several weeks, covered, in the refrigerator.

How to use your sweetened condensed milk:

- Use in equal amounts in recipes that call for canned sweetened condensed milk, particularly in baked custards.
- Try in hot coffee, in the Latin American tradition, or in iced coffee, in the Southeast Asian tradition.
- Use over fruits, as sauce, and in other desserts that call for sweetened condensed milk.

Yield: 4½ cups.

Brenda's Chocolate Pudding

I have Brenda Bell to thank for teaching me that one may cook a batch of chocolate pudding at any time of day, on any day, for no reason. She made this for me in the heat of summer back in Austin, Texas. We ate it still warm, sitting cross-legged on the floor. I believe at some point while we ate, we used our fingers.

Brenda's note card for this recipe calls for a "lump" of butter. We like butter a lot, so our lump, when measured accurately for this book, comes to 3 tablespoons.

Brenda's recipe also says to cool the pudding slightly before adding the vanilla and butter, to better preserve the essence of the extract. I can assure you that we did not wait.

Pudding
3 egg yolks
1 whole egg
1 cup sugar
3 tablespoons flour
3 rounded tablespoons cocoa
2 cups whole milk

2 teaspoons pure vanilla extract
3 tablespoons unsalted butter

Chocolate glaze
2 ounces (2 squares) semisweet chocolate
2 tablespoons unsalted butter
½ teaspoon pure vanilla extract

For pudding Beat the yolks and whole egg and set aside in a place convenient to the stove.

Whisk the sugar, flour, cocoa, and milk in a medium saucepan until free of lumps. Set over medium heat and cook mixture, stirring constantly with a wooden spatula, until just under a boil.

Remove from heat and whisk a little of the hot, thick chocolate mixture into the beaten eggs, then pour the egg mixture back into the main chocolate mixture, whisking really well. Continue to cook and stir over medium heat another 30 seconds to 1 minute, stirring constantly, until thick.

Remove from heat and stir in vanilla and butter. If lumps form, strain into a bowl. Divide among dessert bowls or goblets, cool, and cover. Eat warm or chill a few hours. Serve each portion drizzled with chocolate glaze or store-bought chocolate syrup.

For chocolate glaze Melt chocolate and butter over low heat, stirring until smooth and completely melted. Remove from heat and stir in vanilla. Use immediately. Yield: About ⅝ cup.

Makes 4 to 6 servings.

Pudding Parfait

This piling up of layers of pudding in parfait glasses or goblets really overdoes things nicely. These puddings are base recipes for all puddings used in this book.

Thick vanilla pudding
3 egg yolks
½ cup sugar
3 tablespoons flour
2 cups milk
1 vanilla bean or 2 teaspoons
pure vanilla extract
2 tablespoons unsalted butter

Butterscotch pudding
3 egg yolks
¼ cup sugar
3 tablespoons flour
2 cups milk
2 tablespoons unsalted butter
½ cup packed dark brown sugar
2 teaspoons pure vanilla extract
1 additional tablespoon
unsalted butter
*1 recipe Brenda's Chocolate
Pudding, page 55*

For vanilla pudding Beat the yolks and set aside, convenient to the stove.

Whisk the sugar, flour, and milk in a medium saucepan until free of lumps. Split the vanilla bean lengthwise, scrape it with the back edge of a paring knife, and add it to the milk mixture—pod, seeds, and all. (If using vanilla extract, add after the pudding is cooked.)

Set mixture over medium heat and cook, stirring constantly with a wooden spatula, just to a boil.

Remove from heat and whisk a little of the hot, thick pudding into the beaten yolks, then pour the yolk mixture into the main pudding mixture, whisking really well. Continue to cook 1 to 2 minutes more on medium heat, stirring constantly until thick.

Pour into a bowl. (If using vanilla extract, add it now.) Add the butter, stirring until it melts. If pudding has lumps, pour through a large fine-mesh strainer.

To store, press plastic wrap directly onto the surface of the pudding and refrigerate.

For butterscotch pudding Beat the yolks and set aside in a place convenient to the stove.

Whisk the sugar, flour, and milk in a medium saucepan until free of lumps. Set over medium heat and cook, stirring with a wooden spatula, just to a boil.

Meanwhile, use a small skillet to melt the butter and brown sugar over low heat. Slowly pour the hot brown sugar into the hot milk, whisking constantly. Continue cooking, stirring with a wooden spatula.

Remove from heat and whisk a little of the hot butterscotch mixture into the beaten yolks, then pour the yolk mixture back into the main butterscotch mixture, whisking really well. Continue to cook 2 minutes more on medium heat, stirring constantly with a wooden spatula, until thick.

Pour into a bowl and add vanilla and butter, stirring until butter melts. If pudding has lumps, pour through a large fine-mesh strainer.

To store, press plastic wrap directly onto the surface of the pudding and refrigerate.

To assemble parfaits Aerate the chilled puddings with a couple of good stirs. Spoon alternating layers into goblets, wine glasses, or parfait glasses, in the following order: chocolate pudding, vanilla pudding, butterscotch pudding.

Top with Chantilly Cream (page 34) or Chocolate Chantilly Cream (page 35). Drizzle all over with store-bought or homemade Chocolate Sauce (page 107) or Quick Caramel Sauce (page 216).

Makes 6 1-cup parfaits.

Note: Eat warm, or divide pudding among dessert bowls or goblets, cool, cover, and chill a few hours.

Danish Trifle with Macaroons

This quintessential make-ahead dessert won't be at its best until at least 12 hours after assembly. It gets even better after 24 hours.

Once you've snipped up the apricots and made (or purchased) the macaroons, the layers go quickly and make a gasp-inspiring dessert presentation.

The macaroons are airy, then chewy, upon entering your mouth.

---

1 recipe Almond Paste
Macaroons (or 4 dozen small
store-bought macaroons)
1¼ pounds dried apricots
2½ cups cream
¼ cup sugar
½ cup good-quality sherry
2 10-ounce jars excellent-quality
red raspberry jam

Almond paste macaroons
2 egg whites
½ pound almond paste
⅞ cup superfine sugar

Syrup
½ cup sugar
½ cup water

For assembly Prepare Almond Paste Macaroons, below. If you like, you can freeze them until assembly.

Snip apricots into little pieces with floured scissors. Place in a saucepan with water to cover. Bring to a boil and boil 5 to 8 minutes. Drain and set aside.

In a cold bowl and using cold beaters, whip the cream and sugar to stiff peaks. Set aside half the cream, covered, in the refrigerator for the crowning layer.

Just before assembling the trifle, soak the macaroons in sherry for 1 minute—but no longer! In the bottom of a trifle bowl or other clear glass bowl, arrange a layer of macaroons. Stir the jam well and spoon a ¼-inch layer over the macaroons, spreading evenly. Top jam with a layer of apricots and one of whipped cream. Make sure each layer touches the edge of the clear bowl for attractive, discernible layers, and keep an eye on the *sides* of the trifle to make sure layers are evenly placed.

Continue layering in this order macaroons, jam, apricots, and cream—but end with a final layer of apricots. At this point, cover the trifle with plastic wrap and refrigerate at least 12 hours before serving.

At serving, place reserved whipped cream in a pastry bag with a ruffled tip with a large opening. Pipe outrageously exaggerated swirls all over the top of the trifle and serve.

For macaroons Lightly oil 2 cookie sheets. Set rack in middle of oven and preheat oven to 325°.

Beat egg whites just until foamy. Stir in almond paste with a fork until well blended. While mixing, gradually add sugar. Drop by the teaspoonful onto cookie sheet. Bake 12 minutes, until light brown.

Cool on pan 30 seconds then remove to a rack. Makes about 4 dozen macaroons.

For syrup Meanwhile, simmer the sugar and water for 5 minutes. Remove macaroons while still hot, setting them on a cooling rack with waxed paper underneath to catch drips. Brush them with sugar syrup and let cool.

Makes 16 to 20 servings.

Note: Thinner layers throughout the trifle allow flavors to mingle better.

California Summer Fruit Trifle

Hyperbole is part of the allure of gooey desserts. They're bigger, taller, lusher, richer. Sometimes, if you hadn't noticed, they lack discretion. This beautiful trifle is no exception. It can serve as a glorious dumping ground for whatever fresh fruit is in season or on hand. I got carried away one summer and ended up with a trifle with more layers than the Pentagon—but a lot prettier.

Sponge cake
1 cup flour
2 teaspoons baking powder
5 egg yolks
¾ cup sugar
1½ tablespoons lemon zest
(from about 3 lemons)
¼ cup lemon juice
(from about 2 lemons)
2 teaspoons pure vanilla extract
5 egg whites
3 tablespoons sugar

Custard
2½ cups milk
6 egg yolks
4 tablespoons cornstarch
½ cup sugar

2 teaspoons pure vanilla extract
1½ tablespoons sherry
1 cup cream

Fig layer
1¼ pounds very ripe figs

Cherry layer
4 cups whole fresh Bing,
Lambert, or Ranier cherries
2 tablespoons sugar
1 teaspoon cornstarch mixed
with 1 tablespoon water

Peach layer
8 to 10 medium
freestone peaches
2 tablespoons sugar
Sherry or rum, for sprinkling

For sponge cake   Grease a 15- by 10- by 2-inch jelly-roll pan, line with waxed paper, grease again, and dust with flour, tapping out excess. Set oven rack in the middle of the oven, and heat oven to 350°.

Sift together the flour and baking powder. In a medium bowl, beat the yolks, sugar, and zest until smooth, about 1 minute. Add lemon juice and vanilla and beat until batter drops from beaters in a discernible ribbon, a full 2 minutes more.

Add the flour mixture, beating on low just until combined.

Beat the egg whites to stiff peaks, gradually adding the sugar halfway through. With a big rubber spatula, gently fold one-third of the whites into the yolk-flour base, using wide strokes. Very gently add in the remaining whites, folding them in until no whites show.

Spread batter in the pan. Use a flexible icing spreader to smooth the top. Bake 15 to 17 minutes, until lightly browned. A toothpick should come out clean.

Cool cake in the pan 5 minutes. Run a thin knife around the edges to loosen stuck areas. Invert onto the back of another jelly-roll pan. Slowly peel off the waxed paper. Then invert again onto a cake rack so cake is right side up and let cool competely.

For custard   In a medium-size saucepan, bring the milk to just under a boil.

Place a large fine-mesh strainer over a large bowl set in a larger bowl of ice.

In a bowl (preferably with a pour spout), beat the yolks, cornstarch, and sugar until smooth and ribbony, about 1 minute. Slowly whisk in half the hot milk, then pour the egg mixture back into the plain hot milk and bring it slowly to a boil.

Whisking constantly, boil mixture 1 minute; custard will become thick and tight. Immediately strain, then stir in vanilla and sherry. Stir custard to cool it down.

To store, press plastic wrap directly onto the surface of the custard, then chill 2 hours.

In a cold bowl and using cold beaters, whip the cream to medium-stiff peaks. Fold into chilled custard. Chill at least 3 hours more.

For figs   Rinse figs very well in a colander. Remove stems, puree fruit in a food processor or blender, and chill until use. (Peeling figs is optional. If figs are very ripe, skins will have nearly melted into the pulp and will be impossible to peel.)

Note: If you don't have fresh figs, use 1 10-ounce jar fig jam or 10 ounces dried figs reconstituted in water to cover for 2 hours, then drained.

For cherries   Wash cherries, then remove stems and pits. Measure 1½ cups cherries into a food processor or blender and puree until fruit is very smooth and no signs of skin remain. Reserve remaining whole cherries.

Pour puree into a saucepan and bring to a boil. Stir cornstarch mixture and add it to the boiling puree. Bring to a boil and simmer 2 minutes, stirring. Pour thickened sauce over reserved whole cherries. Mix well, then chill until use.

For peaches   Drop peaches into a large pot of boiling water for 30 seconds to 1 minute. Pierce one with a knife tip: if skin curls back, the peaches are ready to peel. (Do not boil longer than 1 minute, or peach pulp will begin to cook.) Remove peaches from water, using a slotted spoon or wide Chinese strainer, and place in a bowl of ice water until all peaches are peeled and pitted. Skins *should* slip off. If skins stick to flesh, peel with a knife.

Slice very thinly. Remove 1½ cups of peach slices and puree in a food processor or blender with the sugar. Combine this puree with remaining slices and chill until use.

To assemble Slice off any overcooked edges of the sponge cake. Cut cake into ¾-inch cubes. In the bottom of a trifle bowl or other clear glass bowl, arrange a layer of sponge cake, and sprinkle cake with sherry.

Spoon a ¼-inch layer of fig puree (or jam, stirred well) over the cubes, spreading evenly. Top fig layer with a layer of cherries, then a layer of peaches. Ladle a layer of custard over the peaches.

Make sure each layer touches the bowl so layers will be discernible. Rather than look down into the trifle bowl as you go, make sure the view from the *sides* is attractive.

Continue layering cake, sherry, figs, cherries, peaches, and custard twice more, ending with custard. At this point, cover trifle with plastic wrap and refrigerate at least 12 hours or overnight.

Makes up to 20 servings.

Note: If you do not have room in your trifle bowl for the last layer of custard, serve it separately when you spoon out the dessert to individual plates.

Tropical Tapioca

Are we in Hawaii or Thailand? Quick-cooking tapioca, mixed with coconut milk, provides a quick transport.

Babies and children love tapioca, so pour this into small lidded containers and send it off to school. The ingredients cost less than half the price of packaged mini-containers of tapioca. Adding pineapple and shredded coconut can make Piña Colada Tapioca. Or keep it simple with raisins and bananas.

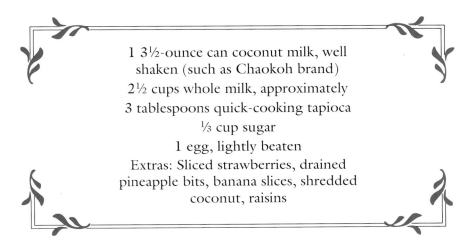

1 3½-ounce can coconut milk, well
shaken (such as Chaokoh brand)
2½ cups whole milk, approximately
3 tablespoons quick-cooking tapioca
⅓ cup sugar
1 egg, lightly beaten
Extras: Sliced strawberries, drained
pineapple bits, banana slices, shredded
coconut, raisins

Pour coconut milk into a 1-quart measure. Add whole milk to make 3 cups.

Pour milk into a saucepan and add tapioca, sugar, and egg. Stir gently just to combine, then let sit 5 minutes.

Over medium heat, bring tapioca mixture slowly to a full boil, stirring constantly with a rubber or wooden spatula.

At the boil, remove from heat. Fold in fruit of choice. Pour into ramekins, dessert bowls, or lidded containers. Cool 20 minutes. Stir tapioca well in each container, then chill. Tapioca will thicken as it cools.

Makes 4 or 5 servings.

Tapioca Caramel with Bananas

Made like flan, this tapioca gets gussied up in individual ramekins coated with brown sugar and bananas. In place of ramekins or custard cups, you could use coffee cups.

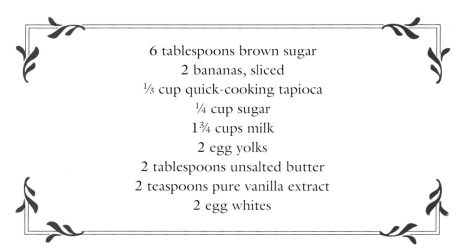

6 tablespoons brown sugar
2 bananas, sliced
⅓ cup quick-cooking tapioca
¼ cup sugar
1¾ cups milk
2 egg yolks
2 tablespoons unsalted butter
2 teaspoons pure vanilla extract
2 egg whites

For tapioca Set 6 buttered ramekins aside in a shallow roasting pan large enough to hold them without touching. Add brown sugar and bananas. Set oven rack in the bottom third of the oven and preheat oven to 325°.

Bring tapioca, sugar, and milk to a boil, stirring constantly with a wooden or rubber spatula. Remove pan from heat and stir in yolks, butter, and vanilla.

Beat whites to moderately stiff peaks and fold into tapioca. Spoon mixture over bananas. Set pan with ramekins in the oven and fill pan with very hot tap water to half-way up the sides of the tapioca. Bake 25 minutes.

Cool out of pan 10 minutes. Run a thin knife around edges of ramekins to loosen tapioca. While still warm, invert ramekins onto individual dessert plates, allowing syrup to spill out. Serve warm or chilled.

Makes 6 servings.

Note: Instead of using bananas, you can place crushed pineapple over brown sugar in the bottom of the ramekins.

New Orleans-Style Bread Pudding

My mother goes to conferences now and then with my father. When the men sequester themselves, she and some other spouses attend cooking classes. During one such confab in New Orleans, she took a class from Joe Cahn at the New Orleans School of Cooking, and brought home this incomparable recipe.

My friend Kathleen, who is also my chief bread-pudding tester, warns anyone who has just partaken of this dessert to wait a while before driving. "God forbid you might have to take a Breathalyzer test! Whew!"

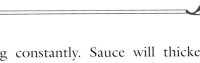

Bread pudding
1 10-ounce loaf stale French bread, crumbled, or 6 to 8 cups any type crumbled bread (see Note 1)
2 cups sugar
1 stick (½ cup) unsalted butter, melted
3 eggs
2 tablespoons pure vanilla extract
1 cup raisins

1 cup shredded coconut
1 cup chopped pecans
1 teaspoon cinnamon
1 teaspoon nutmeg
4 cups milk

Joe's whiskey sauce
1 stick (½ cup) unsalted butter
1½ cups powdered sugar
2 egg yolks
½ cup bourbon

For bread pudding Butter a 9- by 13-inch baking pan. Set oven rack in lower third of oven and preheat oven to 350°.

Combine all ingredients. Mixture should be very moist but not soupy. Pour into the buttered dish and bake 1 hour and 15 minutes, until top is golden brown. Serve warm with Joe's Whiskey Sauce.

For whiskey sauce Using a hand-held mixer, cream butter and sugar in a saucepan over medium heat, beating until all butter is absorbed. Remove from heat and blend in yolks. Pour in bourbon gradually, stir-ring constantly. Sauce will thicken as it cools. Serve warm on warm bread pudding. (This sauce contains uncooked egg yolks.)

Makes 16 to 20 servings.

Note 1: If you want to use fresh bread, reduce milk to 3 cups.

Note 2: My mother dislikes coconut and omits it from this recipe, with delicious results just the same.

Note 3: You can freeze this pudding to thaw and warm when ready to serve.

Brown-Sugar Bread Pudding with Amaretto Sauce

Using brown sugar instead of white and fresh bread instead of stale enhances the character of this tooth-tingling concoction. Dress it up by serving it in a tall goblet.

Bread pudding
4 to 5 cups fresh French bread, cut in 1-inch cubes (from an 8- or 10-ounce loaf)
4 eggs
1 cup brown sugar
2 teaspoons cinnamon
2 teaspoons pure vanilla extract
½ teaspoon salt
4½ cups milk

1 cup golden raisins
8 Bing or maraschino cherries

Warm amaretto sauce
2 cups sugar
2 sticks (1 cup) unsalted butter
½ teaspoon cinnamon
¼ teaspoon nutmeg
½ cup amaretto

For bread pudding Butter a 9-inch square baking pan. Set oven rack in lower third of the oven and preheat oven to 350°.

Place bread cubes in a large mixing bowl. In a separate bowl, beat the eggs and brown sugar until thick and smooth, then blend in cinnamon, vanilla, salt, milk, and raisins. Pour egg mixture over bread and gently combine. Transfer to buttered baking pan, set in a roasting pan, and place both pans in the oven. Fill the pan with very hot tap water up the sides of bread pudding. Bake for 1½ hours.

Spoon pudding into wine glasses or goblets. Ladle Warm Amaretto Sauce over pudding and top each serving with a Bing or maraschino cherry.

For amaretto sauce Make while pudding bakes. In a heavy saucepan, combine sugar and butter over medium heat. Cook and stir constantly to the soft ball stage (235° to 240° on a candy thermometer). Add cinnamon, nutmeg, and amaretto (see Note). Serve warm over still-warm bread pudding.

Makes 8 servings.

Note: You may use rum, bourbon, or a favorite liqueur, such as Grand Marnier, a coffee-flavored liqueur, or hazelnut liqueur, in which case this will not be Warm Amaretto Sauce, but something new and different.

Extra-Rich Rice Pudding

Make this recipe when you're in the kitchen doing other things, so you can keep an eye on the rice. You'll love watching the transformation of hard, pebbly grains into soft little cushions suspended in the milk. If you use a heavy, thick-bottomed pan, the double boiler most recipes specify for stove-top rice pudding isn't necessary.

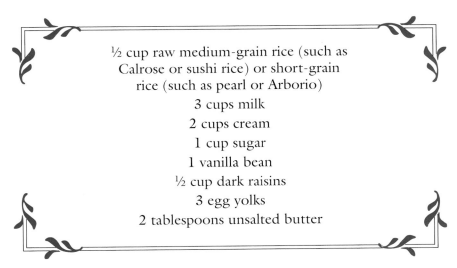

½ cup raw medium-grain rice (such as Calrose or sushi rice) or short-grain rice (such as pearl or Arborio)

3 cups milk

2 cups cream

1 cup sugar

1 vanilla bean

½ cup dark raisins

3 egg yolks

2 tablespoons unsalted butter

Add rice to boiling water and blanch 5 minutes. Drain, then return to pan and add the milk, cream, and sugar. Add the vanilla bean, which has been split, scraped and added to the rice—seeds, pod, and all (see Note 1).

Simmer uncovered so the milk is visibly but very gently bubbling, about 45 minutes total. After rice has simmered about 20 minutes, add raisins (see Note 2). Stir frequently with a wooden spatula, or pudding will stick.

Lightly beat the yolks. Remove about ½ cup hot rice pudding and mix it with the yolks. When well combined, return mixture to the rice pudding, turn off the heat, and stir well. Add the butter and stir until melted. Remove, rinse, and dry the vanilla bean for another use.

Spoon rice pudding into small bowls or dessert cups. Refrigerate until serving.

Makes 6 servings.

Note 1: Vanilla extract is not mentioned here as an alternate for the vanilla bean. The pudding benefits so much from this bean that I am reluctant to substitute extract. If you must, add 2 teaspoons vanilla extract when you add the butter.

Note 2: The addition of 1 teaspoon of microscopically minced lemon zest does wonders for this rice pudding. Add with the raisins.

The Long and Short of Rice

Medium- or short-grain rice produces the creamiest rice pudding of all, just as it makes the most luscious, creamiest risotto, because it is the most absorbent.

If you can't find anything except regular long-grain rice, you may use it with no adjustments to the recipe. The pudding will still come out creamy, but without the added dimension of richness produced by the shorter, thirstier rice.

Rice used for sushi is definitely shorter than long-grain rice, but agriculturally, it is considered a medium grain. Truly short-grain rice is nearly as wide as it is short. Grown in California's Sacramento Valley, it goes by the term "pearl" rice. American pearl rice is similar to Italian Arborio rice.

Rice Flan

The rice base for this flan has several lives. Its first stage is a lush, creamy mixture you can eat as is. As it bakes, it grows denser and richer, preparing for a second life as a cooked dessert.

If you use mascarpone cheese, you'll have a full-fledged gooey dessert richly deserving of inclusion in this book. If you use ricotta cheese, you'll chip away at the calories a bit without losing too much in gooey satisfaction.

My friend Andrea, a baking expert, made this in a deep-sided soufflé dish and crisscrossed strips of dough on top. The folks who sampled this at one of our tasting parties were stunned at the refreshing flavor and rich texture.

Pastry
15 tablespoons (2 sticks less
1 tablespoon) unsalted
butter, softened
¼ cup sugar
1 egg
2½ cups flour

Filling
¼ cup currants (or raisins)
2 tablespoons rum
2 cups milk
1 teaspoon pure vanilla extract
½ cup Arborio or other short-
grained white rice, such as pearl
(see page 68)

4 egg yolks
6 tablespoons sugar
1 teaspoon finely grated
orange zest
¼ cup chopped almonds,
optional
1 cup mascarpone cheese or
drained ricotta cheese
(see page 72)

Garnishes
Apricot jam
Powdered sugar

For pastry Cream butter and sugar just until soft and well combined. Add the egg and mix well again. Add flour and mix until dough forms a ball. Wrap in plastic or foil and chill 2 hours.

Roll out half the dough into a circle to line the bottom of an 8- or 9-inch springform pan. (You may refrigerate the dough-lined pan until ready to assemble the flan.)

For filling Soak currants in rum. In a medium saucepan, bring milk to a boil. Add vanilla and rice and cook, stirring, uncovered, until rice is double its original volume and has absorbed all the milk, about 30 minutes. Remove from heat and cool a few minutes.

Set oven rack in the middle of the oven and preheat oven to 400°.

In a medium bowl, beat the yolks and sugar. Add the orange zest, the almonds, and the currants with their rum. Blend in cheese, then fold mixture into rice. Pour rice into the pastry-lined springform pan.

Roll out remaining dough, and cut it into strips to form a lattice on top of the rice. Place the springform pan on a cookie sheet and bake for 35 minutes, or until set. (If browning occurs, cover top with foil.) Baking may take as long as 50 minutes. Cool cake in the pan.

To serve   Remove springform sides. Serve wedges drizzled with apricot jam heated to a simmer, and dust with powdered sugar.

Makes 8 to 10 servings.

Mascarpone Cheesecake in Mexican-Chocolate Crust with Pecans

(No Bake)

The variations of cheesecake from New York to California had become almost silly until America discovered Italy's mascarpone cheese. The thinking goes that if cheesecake is wonderful with cream cheese, it would be incredible with mascarpone.

Because of mascarpone's density and expense, cream cheese is added as economical filler. The mixture chills to extraordinary richness and creaminess.

Use your largest springform pan—at least 10 or 12 inches in diameter. Or, have a second smaller springform pan ready to catch the excess.

Chocolate-pecan crumb crust

1 round tablet Mexican table chocolate, or 2 ounces (2 squares) semisweet chocolate
10 double graham crackers (from 1 wrapped package from box)
1 cup pecan halves
2 teaspoons cinnamon
3 tablespoons brown sugar
4 tablespoons (½ stick) unsalted butter

Mascarpone filling

1 tablespoon gelatin (measured from less than 2 envelopes)

¼ cup cold water
1½ pounds mascarpone cheese
1½ pounds cream cheese (3 8-ounce packages), softened
1 cup sugar
2 tablespoons lemon juice
1½ tablespoons pure vanilla extract
1½ cups cream

Garnish

Chocolate shavings (see page 88)
Additional whipped cream (optional)

For crust Set oven rack in the middle of the oven and preheat oven to 400°.

Chop chocolate and drop through feed tube of an activated food processor or blender. Add graham crackers and pecans and process until fine crumbs (or crush crackers between sheets of waxed paper with a rolling pin).

Pour crumbs into springform pan. Stir in cinnamon and brown sugar. Add melted butter and, using your fingers, quickly mash the mixture until the crumbs hold together. Use your knuckles to press up the sides, then press over bottom of pan. Bake 10 minutes. Cool.

For filling Dissolve gelatin in water in a little bowl, then set aside to soften for 5 minutes. To keep gelatin liquefied, set bowl in a larger bowl of hot water.

Beat the mascarpone and cream cheese at high speed with an electric mixer (use paddle attachment, if you have one) until fluffy. Gradually pour in sugar while continuing to beat. At medium speed, beat in lemon juice and vanilla. Remove bowl from mixer and, using a big rubber spatula, *quickly* fold gelatin into cheese mixture.

In a cold bowl and with cold beaters, whip cream to stiff peaks. Fold a scoop of cream into the mascarpone mixture to lighten it and make it easier to blend with the cream. Then fold remaining cream into the cheese base. Pour into cooled crust. Cover well with plastic wrap and chill at least 4 hours.

Decorate with shaved chocolate and, if you like, with more whipped cream piped at intervals around the rim of the cake. Slice wedges with a knife dipped in a tall glass of hot water, then wiped dry.

Makes 16 servings.

Make Your Own Mascarpone Cheese

This cheese was not named for a San Francisco mayor, though "George Mascarpone" is a favorite malapropism for George Moscone.

Nothing could have made me happier than discovering that an incomparably smooth, rich cheese such as mascarpone could be made at home. It's done by curdling heavy cream with a sprinkling of store-bought citric acid. Commercially, this cheese is one of the priciest on the retail market. If made at home, it only costs you the price of a quart of cream.

1 quart heavy cream
½ teaspoon citric acid, such as Manischewitz sour salt (see Note 1)

Have ready a heavy Dutch kettle, a slotted spoon, some cheesecloth, a strainer, and a candy thermometer.

Pour the cream into the kettle and set over low heat. Slowly heat the cream to 180° to 190°. (At 175°, start to keep a close watch.) You can stir a little.

When the cream is ready, remove from heat. Sprinkle in the citric acid, stirring gently twice. Wait until liquid stops moving and stir gently a few more times. Cover the pot and let the curds form for 30 to 40 minutes. The curds will firm up, but may not be obviously separated from the whey.

Meanwhile, line a strainer with damp cheesecloth and rest the strainer over a large bowl.

Pour the cream through the strainer. Drain until mascarpone is room temperature (see Note 2). Cover the strainer, bowl and all, with plastic wrap to prevent refrigerator odors from assaulting the delicate cheese and chill for 24 hours, to finish firming the cheese.

The mascarpone left in the strainer will be thick and creamy and ready to use. Transfer to a bowl and peel off cheesecloth. Keep refrigerated. Use within a week.

Makes ⅞ pound.

Note 1: Sour salt is a very effective acid for mascarpone making. It is the essential flavorant in the classic Hungarian sauce for stuffed cabbage. It is also used in Jewish-style cabbage soup. You may find it at a supermarket, but you are all but guaranteed to find it at an ethnic European market or delicatessen. If you don't, use 2 tablespoons lemon juice or vinegar for every quart of cream.

Note 2: Drainage from the mascarpone is nice and creamy with a great deal of body. Don't let it go to waste. It may be whipped and served on top of fruit, cake, or pudding. It tastes like tangy sour cream or crème fraîche.

White Chocolate-Caramel Cheesecake with Macadamia Nuts

This was a big winner in a dessert competition in my area. It was made by Vince Alexander, chef at Slocum House restaurant in Fair Oaks, California. He devised a technique to keep caramel afloat in cheesecake batter during baking: a heavy mixture on the bottom, made with white chocolate ganache, supports the weight of the caramel and cheesecake on top.

Make this cheesecake a day in advance. A 10- or 12-inch springform is mandatory! There is just too much batter for a pan any smaller. However, two 8-inch springform pans also work well.

Because of its delicacy, the cheesecake bakes in a water bath. Protect your cake from leakage by wrapping outside the bottom and sides of the pan with heavy-duty aluminum foil. You'll get some seepage, but no damage.

White chocolate ganache
1 cup white chocolate chips
2 tablespoons unsalted butter
1½ cups cream
⅓ cup sugar

Crust
15 double graham crackers
(about 1½ wrapped
packages from box)
⅓ cup dark brown sugar
4 tablespoons unsalted butter

Caramel
1 cup sugar
½ cup water

Few drops vinegar or lemon juice
1½ tablespoons cornstarch
½ cup cream
1 tablespoon unsalted butter

Cheesecake batter
2½ pounds cream
cheese, very soft
2½ cups sugar
5 eggs
2 teaspoons pure vanilla extract
1 cup whole macadamia nuts

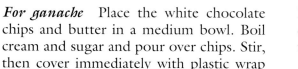

For ganache Place the white chocolate chips and butter in a medium bowl. Boil cream and sugar and pour over chips. Stir, then cover immediately with plastic wrap for 3 to 5 minutes to let the chocolate melt.

Remove wrap, stir again to smooth, and chill until ready to use—but not longer than 1 hour, or mixture may set too much.

For crust   Set oven rack in the middle of the oven and preheat oven to 350°. Double-wrap the outside of a 10- or 12-inch springform pan with heavy-duty aluminum foil, covering bottom and up sides, to catch any batter leakage.

In a food processor or blender, process graham crackers to fine crumbs. Pour crumbs into the springform pan. With your hands, mix in melted butter and brown sugar until crumbs hold together; use your knuckles to press crumb mixture up the sides and over bottom of pan. Bake 10 minutes. Cool.

For caramel   In a heavy saucepan, bring sugar, water, and vinegar to a boil over medium-high heat. If crystals form on the sides of the pan, cover the pan for 30 seconds or as long as 5 minutes so steam rinses off the sides. When caramel darkens you may swirl the pan to even the color. Take the caramel to an amber gold color.

Meanwhile, dissolve cornstarch in cream. When caramel is the desired color, remove from heat and quickly add cornstarch-cream mixture. Caramel will bubble up. When foaming subsides, stir in butter. Reheat a minute to even out the mixture to a smooth, thick texture. Cool by setting saucepan of caramel in a bowl of cool water; caramel will thicken even more.

For cheesecake batter   Set oven rack in the lower third of the oven and reduce temperature to 325°.

With an electric mixer, beat cream cheese for 2 or 3 minutes on medium speed (use a paddle attachment, if you have one). Scrape down when necessary. Still on medium speed, gradually add sugar. Add eggs one by one, mixing each only until absorbed. Don't overmix during these intervals or batter could "break." On slow speed, add vanilla and mix a few turns.

To assemble   Set aside 1 cup cheesecake batter in a measuring cup. In addition, set aside ½ cup caramel for top of cake.

Mix ⅔ of the remaining cheesecake batter with all of the ganache. Pour into the baked crust.

Mix the larger amount of caramel with remaining ⅓ of cheesecake batter. Pour over ganache, to within ½ inch of sides.

Top caramel layer with 1 cup reserved cheesecake batter, smoothing to edge of pan. Set cake in a shallow roasting pan and place in the oven. Carefully pour hot tap water into the roasting pan so it comes to within an inch of the top of the cheesecake.

Bake 1 hour, 45 minutes. The top will still jiggle slightly, but a knife should come out clean. Take cake from water. If necessary, use a bulb baster to remove some of the hot water. Cool in the pan on a rack.

For topping   Toast macadamia nuts on a baking sheet at 350° for 5 to 8 minutes, tossing a little, until you can smell them. They won't darken very much. Pour onto a cutting board and chop to the size of corn kernels.

Heat and stir the reserved ½ cup caramel on low heat, just to make it pourable. Stir in macadamias and spread over the top of the cooled cheesecake. Wrap tightly in plastic wrap and chill overnight. Cut with a knife dipped in tall glass of hot water, then wiped dry.

Before serving, set cake out at room temperature for 45 minutes.

Makes 14 slices.

Mexican Sour Cream Soufflé with Blueberry Sauce

Mexican sour cream is tart, thick, and slow-moving, much like crème fraîche. If you cannot find *crema Mexicana*, make crème fraîche yourself (page 77), then proceed with this soufflé. Of course, instead of Mexican Sour Cream Soufflé you'll have Crème Fraîche Soufflé, equally *bueno*.

Soufflé
½ cup milk, divided
in ¼-cup portions
3 tablespoons unsalted butter
½ cup sugar
½ cup flour
3 egg yolks
1 8-ounce jar Mexican sour
cream, crème fraîche,
or regular sour cream
Finely grated zest of ½ lemon
1 teaspoon pure vanilla extract

4 egg whites
1½ tablespoons
additional sugar

Quick blueberry sauce
2 cups blueberries
(fresh or frozen)
½ cup orange juice
¼ cup water
2 tablespoons sugar
1 tablespoon cornstarch
¼ teaspoon grated orange peel
Pinch salt

Generously butter an 8-cup soufflé dish. Additionally, generously butter a wide band of waxed paper and tie it around the dish with kitchen string, making a 2-inch-high collar. Sprinkle sugar all around the inside of the dish and collar, tapping out excess.

Set oven rack in lower third of oven and remove any other racks. Preheat oven to 350°.

For soufflé In a small saucepan, heat ¼ cup of the milk with the butter (or microwave on High in a glass measure for about 1 minute).

In a medium bowl, beat the remaining milk, sugar, and flour at low speed. Pour the hot milk into the flour mixture and beat well. Beat in the yolks, one by one. Stir in the cream, lemon zest, and vanilla.

In a large bowl, beat the egg whites to stiff peaks, gradually adding the additional sugar halfway through. Fold ⅓ of the whites into the sour cream base, using a wide rubber spatula. Gently fold in remaining whites. A few streaks of white may show.

Pour soufflé mixture into the prepared dish. Bake 30 to 35 minutes, until almost set on top, but with a wiggly middle.

Immediately, but carefully, remove the waxed paper collar. Scoop the servings of soufflé, collecting any partially cooked soufflé with each serving. Accompany with Quick Blueberry Sauce.

For blueberry sauce Wash the blueberries. Combine all ingredients in a medium saucepan, bring to a simmer, and cook, stirring, over medium heat 4 to 5 minutes or until thickened. Serve warm or at room temperature. Store in the refrigerator. Yield: 2 cups.

Makes 4 to 6 servings.

Crème Fraîche

Put 1 cup cream in a jar with a lid. Add 1 tablespoon buttermilk. Screw on the lid and leave the jar at room temperature for 24 hours. Then chill the thickened cream. Cream should thicken. If it doesn't, the room may have been too chilly; to remedy, add a little more buttermilk and set jar in a slightly warmer spot. Once "set," this can substitute for the Mexican sour cream.

Hot Vanilla-Tangerine Soufflé with Orange Sauce

During winter, nothing refreshes like citrus. This soufflé, served hot and sluicing, surprises all with its high-impact flavor. Treat your guests as if they were ingredients: assemble them (the guests) *before* you pull this from the oven.

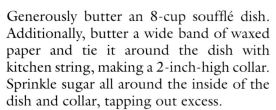

Soufflé

1 vanilla bean
¾ cup milk
6 egg yolks
3 tablespoons cornstarch
dissolved in ¼ cup milk
¼ cup flour
¼ cup sugar
Pinch salt
1 tablespoon finely
grated tangerine zest
1 cup strained
fresh tangerine juice

1 to 2 tablespoons Grand
Marnier or Cointreau
5 egg whites
¼ cup additional sugar

Orange sauce

1 cup orange juice
½ cup sugar
1 tablespoon cornstarch
3 tablespoons butter
1 tablespoon Grand Marnier
or Cointreau

Generously butter an 8-cup soufflé dish. Additionally, butter a wide band of waxed paper and tie it around the dish with kitchen string, making a 2-inch-high collar. Sprinkle sugar all around the inside of the dish and collar, tapping out excess.

Set oven rack in the lower third of the oven and remove any other racks. Preheat the oven to 400°.

For soufflé Split vanilla bean lengthwise, scrape it with the back edge of a paring knife, and add it to the milk—seeds, pod, and all. In a heavy medium-size saucepan, barely boil the milk and vanilla. (If using vanilla extract, it will be added after soufflé base is cooked.)

In a medium saucepan, beat yolks, cornstarch mixture, flour, sugar, and salt until smooth and pale, about 2 minutes. Whisk in warmed vanilla-milk, stirring until no lumps remain. Finally, add tangerine zest.

Cook on medium heat, stirring, until hot and thick, about 12 to 15 minutes. Whisk out any lumps. Scrape custard into a mixing bowl. (Remove, rinse, and save vanilla bean.) Whisk in tangerine juice and liqueur. Cool slightly.

Beat egg whites to stiff peaks, gradually adding the additional ¼ cup sugar halfway through. With a big rubber spatula, fold whites into the tangerine base, using wide strokes.

Pour mixture into the soufflé dish. Draw a deep circle in the center of the mixture with a spatula, to make a "crown."

Bake for 25 minutes. Soufflé will be dark on top and slightly runny in the center. Serve immediately with warm Orange Sauce.

For orange sauce Combine orange juice, sugar, and cornstarch in a saucepan. Bring to a boil, then boil 5 to 6 minutes, until thick and clear. Off the heat, whisk in butter and liqueur until smooth. Makes 1 cup sauce.

Makes 8 servings.

Tiramisu

Translated, this means "pick-me-up." After you eat it, you'll call it "weigh-me-down." This trendy dessert has a contemporary following in America, where it has been recently popularized in restaurants, but it comes from Venice, where it is old.

Many versions abound, and almost all of them are delicious. This one is rich with mascarpone cheese, full of coffee flavor, and overflowing with chocolate.

Mascarpone zabaglione

5 egg yolks
6 tablespoons sugar
⅓ cup Marsala
½ cup cream
1 pound mascarpone cheese,
softened to room temperature
(see Make Your Own Mascarpone
Cheese, page 73)

For the assembly

1 cup strong black coffee
(espresso, if possible)
2 tablespoons sugar
2 tablespoons rum
1 tablespoon pure vanilla extract
1 sponge cake (store-bought is
okay, or use the recipe
on page 60)
6 ounces grated
semisweet chocolate

For zabaglione Beat the yolks and sugar in a large bowl until pale and thick, about 1 minute.

Add Marsala and place the bowl over a pan of simmering water, beating all the while by hand or with an electric mixer on low, until the mixture thickens and triples in volume, about 12 minutes. The yolks should be very fluffy and soft, like a whipped custard. Be careful not to overcook, or the yolks will curdle. Remove from heat, stirring occasionally, to cool for 15 minutes. Transfer to a clean bowl, cover, and chill.

In a cold bowl and with cold beaters, whip the cream to stiff peaks. Fold a "scoop" of the cream into the mascarpone cheese to lighten the cheese so it will blend easily. Fold in remaining cream, then the chilled zabaglione.

To assemble Make a dipping liquid of the coffee, sugar, rum, and vanilla. Cut the sponge cake into 3- by 1½-inch rectangular strips (they don't have to be perfect).

Dunk the pieces of cake into the coffee liquid, then arrange them in a single layer in the bottom of a shallow bowl or baking dish (approximate volume of 8 to 10 cups). When the bottom is covered with cake, spoon half the mascarpone custard on top and smooth over. Top with half the grated chocolate (see Note 2).

Top with another layer of coffee-dunked cake, then with remaining mascarpone custard. Cover decoratively with remaining grated chocolate. Chill at least 3 hours, or overnight. To serve, cut into squares or wedges.

Makes 8 to 10 servings.

Note 1: I like to build Tiramisu in a big pasta bowl, for grandeur!

Note 2: See How to Shave Chocolate (page 88).

Almendrado

Almendrado is an almond meringue pudding. It is rich and sticky. It is also full of ingredients and techniques not favored by health practitioners or culinary purists.

Almendrado is tinted red, green, and white with food coloring, symbolizing the flag of Mexico. You may have a philosophy that opposes the use of food coloring. (Because today's coloring is not chemical, I've changed my reaction to the mere mention of food coloring, at which I used to wince.) After I made this uncooked meringue stabilized with gelatin, I stepped back and said to myself, "I think I just had some fun."

This is a great recipe for children—it's easy and fun and the result can be dipped in hot chocolate!

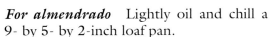

Almendrado
1 envelope plain gelatin
¼ cup cold water
6 egg whites
¾ cup sugar
1 teaspoon almond extract
Red and green food coloring
½ cup blanched, slivered almonds

Custard sauce
6 egg yolks
⅓ cup sugar
1 cup milk
1 cup evaporated milk
½ teaspoon pure vanilla extract

Garnish
1 cup cream
½ cup blanched, slivered almonds

For almendrado Lightly oil and chill a 9- by 5- by 2-inch loaf pan.

Dissolve gelatin in cold water in a little bowl, then set aside to soften for 5 minutes. Set in a larger pan of hot water to keep gelatin liquefied.

Beat the egg whites to stiff peaks, gradually adding the sugar halfway through. Beat in the gelatin and the almond flavoring.

Divide the whites into thirds. Tint one-third red and one-third green, leaving the remaining third white. Spread the egg whites in the chilled pan, starting with red, then plain, then green. Sprinkle with the almonds. Cover with plastic wrap to prevent gummy scum from forming and chill at least 2 hours, until firm.

For custard sauce Beat egg yolks and sugar directly in the top of a double boiler until light in color, about 1 minute. Add milk and evaporated milk. Cook over barely simmering water, stirring constantly, until thick, about 20 minutes. (If sauce becomes too thick, pour it into a bowl to stop the cooking.) Remove sauce from heat and add vanilla. If the sauce has any lumps, pour it through a strainer.

Keep the sauce in a pitcher for easy pouring at serving. Cover and chill.

To assemble In a cold bowl and using cold beaters, whip the cream to medium-stiff peaks and set aside.

Run a thin knife around the mold. Dip mold into pan of hot water, then unmold almendrado onto a plate. Slice almendrado in ¾-inch slices. Lay each slice on a plate to show off the colorful stripes. Pour custard down the middle of a stripe so as not to obscure the "flag." Garnish with whipped cream and an additional sprinkling of slivered almonds.

Makes 12 servings.

This recipe is adapted from a dessert at a restaurant called El Charro in Tuscon, Arizona. It was passed down from pioneer woman Yndia Smalley Moore, who gave it to her niece, who gave it to the chef.

Somehow, it fell into the hands of my best friend, Elinor Brecher, when she was a waitress at El Charro in the mid-'70s. I did not know Ellie yet, but this was to be her closest affiliation with a place where food is cooked. We met in 1981 when I rounded the corner of the newsroom at the *Courier-Journal* in Louisville. We stood eye to eye, exactly 4 feet, 11 inches from the ground. We were wearing the same shoes (Pappagallos, size 5½—hers brown, mine taupe). Our hair was frizzy and we both had punctured our ear lobes more times than was necessary for an era of understated pearl studs. Our professional attire tended to Indian gauze. Neither of us had lived too long in a world where men wore ties to work and women who dressed in cotton duck wrap-skirts were considered fashion plates.

Today, Ellie is a columnist for the *Miami Herald,* where she continues to write, wear shorts to work, and never cook —anything. Her own kitchen is a place for a refrigerator to cool nail polish and batteries. I was so shocked she had a recipe collection (this was on the back of a calendar) that, in her honor, I am including Almendrado so I can say I got a recipe from my friend Ellie. Ain't no more recipes where this came from.

CHAPTER TWO

Chocolate Goo

Great Gobs of Ganache on a Mudslide Cookie with a Surprise in the Middle

Two ganaches make a gob, dark chocolate on the outside and white in the middle. A gob of ganache rests on a settee known as the Mudslide Cookie.

A batch of Mudslides surprised the 16 bridesmaids and groomsmen at my wedding. Within five minutes of the vows exchanged in my backyard, we ate them in the kitchen with champagne and didn't offer them to anyone else.

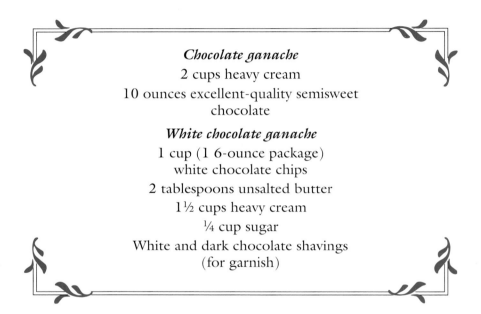

Chocolate ganache
2 cups heavy cream
10 ounces excellent-quality semisweet chocolate

White chocolate ganache
1 cup (1 6-ounce package) white chocolate chips
2 tablespoons unsalted butter
1½ cups heavy cream
¼ cup sugar
White and dark chocolate shavings (for garnish)

For gobs Make chocolate ganache. Heat cream to boiling. Meanwhile, chop chocolate fine and place in a mixing bowl (see Note). Pour hot cream over chocolate, stir, and immediately cover with plastic wrap. Let chocolate melt about 15 minutes.

Remove wrapping and stir mixture until chocolate is completely melted and smooth. Be sure to stir up the bits from the bottom of the bowl. The mixture will resemble thick soup.

Pour into a shallow pan to cool fast, pressing plastic wrap on the surface to prevent a skin from forming. Chill at least 6 hours, or up to 2 days.

Transfer cold ganache to the bowl of an electric mixer. Beat in quick bursts (use a paddle attachment, if you have one) 30 seconds to 1 minute, or until mixture is the consistency of sour cream. (Overbeating will "break" consistency.) The filling should be firm enough to slice, but soft enough to mound. Refrigerate an additional night, if you like.

Make white chocolate ganache   Place the white chocolate chips and butter in a medium bowl. Boil cream and sugar together and pour over chips. Stir, then immediately cover with plastic wrap for 3 to 5 minutes, letting the chips melt.

   Remove wrap and stir again to make smooth. Pour into a shallow pan to cool fast. Press plastic wrap on surface to prevent a skin from forming, then chill 2 hours or overnight.

   Transfer white ganache to the bowl of an electric mixer. Beat in quick bursts (use a paddle attachment, if you have one) 30 seconds to 1 minute, or until mixture is consistency of sour cream. (Overbeating will "break" consistency.) This ganache will be a little looser than the dark chocolate ganache. Refrigerate an additional night, if you like.

To assemble   Make white chocolate centers first. To shape, use a melon baller, then roll small white chocolate scoops into balls the size of marbles. Reserve.

   Using an ice cream scoop, form rounded "gobs" of dark chocolate ganache about the size of Ping-Pong balls. Turn scoop over and push a white chocolate ball into the center of each gob, then set each atop a Mudslide Cookie (see page 88).

   Arrange on individual dessert plates or on a platter. Cover loosely with plastic and chill until serving.

To serve   Present plain or with a pitcher of Crème Anglaise (page 38).

   At serving, drop white and dark chocolate shavings from on high, letting them fall where they may.

   Note: See How to Shave Chocolate on page 88.

Makes 12 to 16 gobs.

Mudslide Cookies

1 12-ounce package (2 cups) semisweet
chocolate chips, divided into equal parts

2 tablespoons unsalted butter

2 ounces (2 squares)
unsweetened chocolate

¼ cup sifted flour

¼ teaspoon baking powder

2 eggs

¾ cup sugar

½ teaspoon pure vanilla extract

In the top of a double boiler over barely
simmering water, melt half the chocolate
chips, butter, and unsweetened chocolate.
(Or microwave on Medium, stirring every
20 to 30 seconds after the first minute,
until only a small solid chunk of chocolate
remains.) Remove and stir until completely
melted. Set aside.

Sift dry ingredients and set aside. In a
small bowl, beat eggs, sugar, and vanilla for
1 minute. Add the cooled chocolate, then
the dry ingredients. Stir in the remaining
chocolate chips. Batter will be runny. (If
it's too runny to handle, chill it before pro-
ceeding.)

Lay out a sheet of plastic wrap. Pour
dough onto plastic and form it into a
tightly packed log 2½ inches thick and
about 12 inches long. Wrap and set in
freezer overnight.

Preheat oven to 350°. Cut log into ¾-
inch-thick slices. Place on an ungreased
cookie sheet and bake 12 minutes. Cookies
should be barely set and will have lost their
gloss in center. (If still glossy, leave pan in
30 seconds longer.)

Let set 1 minute, and then remove to a
rack to cool.

Makes 16.

Note: Ganache, as it is used in the
"gobs," really shows off chocolate.
Poor-quality chocolate can't hide.

How to Shave Chocolate

Use a good-quality bulk chocolate. The
bigger the bar, the easier shaving it will be.
It is most difficult with chocolate squares.

Set a chunk of chocolate in the microwave on Low for 30 to 45 seconds. Only
the outside of the chocolate should soften
(not melt).

Remove the chunk and set it before you.
Hold a large chef's knife parallel to your
body and over the chunk of chocolate.

With movements *away* from you, scrape
shavings off the soft areas of the chocolate.
They should be of all sizes and resemble
broken bits of cinnamon bark.

Continue microwaving and scraping for
as much decoration as you like.

The process is the same for white or
dark chocolate. Alternatively, you may
shave chocolate with:

- a vegetable peeler drawn down the
  narrow side of a chocolate bar
- a biscuit cutter scraped toward you
- a melon baller's spoon drawn over
  a soft chocolate surface

Gooey Chocolate Deliverance
(Andrea's Truffle Torte)

This is one of the most defiantly gooey desserts anywhere. We are not talking light and airy. We are not talking tender crumb. From my friend Andrea, what we really have here is a big batch of frosting. Two-thirds of it bakes into cake. The rest acts truly as frosting.

Put the Deliverance on the plate you intend to keep it on. Truffle torte sort of lodges on the surface it sticks to first.

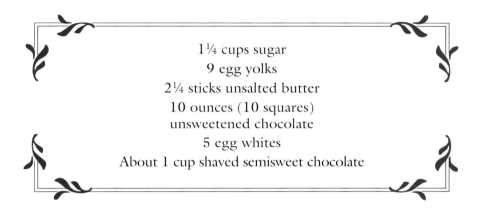

1¼ cups sugar

9 egg yolks

2¼ sticks unsalted butter

10 ounces (10 squares)
unsweetened chocolate

5 egg whites

About 1 cup shaved semisweet chocolate

Butter the bottom only of a round 8-inch pan. Set oven rack in the center of the oven and preheat the oven to 350°.

With electric beaters, slowly beat sugar and yolks for 3 to 4 minutes. It is important to dissolve the sugar completely.

Melt the butter and cool. In the top of a double boiler over barely simmering water, melt the chocolate (or microwave, uncovered, on Medium, stirring every 20 to 30 seconds after the first 2½ minutes, until only a small solid chunk of remains). Remove from heat and stir until smooth and cooled.

Cream the melted butter into the yolk-sugar mixture. Then stir in the melted chocolate.

Beat the egg whites to soft peaks. With a big rubber spatula, fold ¼ of the whites into the chocolate batter, then gently fold in the remaining whites, using wide strokes, until no white lumps remain.

Put ⅔ of the batter into the buttered pan and bake for 15 to 20 minutes. Refrigerate the remaining batter.

Remove cake from oven and cool in pan 5 minutes. Run a knife around the edge of the cake to loosen. Invert onto a platter or cake pedestal.

Frost with remaining batter by spreading most of it evenly all over the cake, then piping decorations around the rim and top. Sprinkle all over with shaved chocolate.

Cut into wedges, using a knife dipped in hot water, then wiped dry.

Makes 12 to 16 servings.

Note 1: Due to the intensity of the chocolate and its muddy-bottom texture, the wedges you cut should be smaller than anything you'll see on a Duncan Hines box.

Note 2: The frosting contains uncooked egg yolks.

On Chocolate

I had the amazing luck as a newspaper columnist to have written an article for the *Austin American-Statesman* that a lot of people liked.

It was about chocolate.

From January 4, 1979
NO CHOCOLATE MESS TO FACE

It's so easy to fix blame. Take chocolate, the scapegoat of unattractive skin, double chins, and allergic maladies. It is a food so coveted that it is hidden under beds and licked off beaters despite its visual penalties. For some reason the popularity of chocolate to those addicted to it has always been wrapped up in its repercussions.

[Now] a story is clearing up the complexion of chocolate's reputation to build a case—or, if you like, a torte—in its favor. A report released [last week] declares chocolate is not a major cause of allergic reactions. Further, chocolate is not to be accused as a universal cause of acne or obesity.

Dr. Joseph Fries, a New York researcher and the Mr. Goodbar of the American Academy of Allergies, has studied the effects of chocolate on the human body for 35 years and says there is no basis for any "pervasive mistrust of chocolate. Chocolate has been unfairly branded the culprit for a wide range of maladies, often with little justification."

Instead, Fries concluded, chocolate is a highly nutritious food whose virtues have been recognized where high energy in small bulk is critical.

As for pimples, it's no use fudging. Fries said: "Diet plays no role in acne treatment in most patients . . . even large amounts of chocolate have not clinically exacerbated acnes."

Although Fries does not indicate what foods if any are behind blemishes and flab, he comes to his conclusions after reviewing 150 scientific studies on chocolate's and cocoa's relationship to health conducted over 60 years.

Naturally, this news comes to the Chocolate Manufacturers Association like a bonbon in Bangladesh.

"The Fries report should reassure the American people that chocolate is a safe food which contains nutritive benefits," said CMA president Richard T. O'Connell. "This demonstrates that chocolate and chocolate-containing products have their place in the nation's diet."

Chocolate Bondage with Lush Chocolate Sauce

This is the cake cousin of Gooey Chocolate Deliverance. It's not as gooey inside. But outside, a naturally occurring basin in the top of the cooled cake becomes a perfect receptacle for Lush Chocolate Sauce.

Cake
1 pound excellent-quality semisweet chocolate
4 tablespoons water
2 teaspoons pure vanilla extract
1 tablespoon flour
3 tablespoons sugar
10 tablespoons unsalted butter, softened
4 egg yolks
4 egg whites

Lush chocolate sauce
8 ounces (8 squares) semisweet chocolate
1 cup heavy cream
½ cup sugar

Framboise chantilly cream
1 cup cream
1 tablespoon powdered sugar
1½ teaspoons Framboise, Chambord, or raspberry liqueur (see Note)

For cake Butter an 8-inch springform pan. Line with waxed paper and butter the paper. Set oven rack in center of the oven and preheat oven to 425°.

Chop the chocolate fine. Melt it, with the water, in the top of a double boiler over barely simmering water (or microwave, uncovered, on Medium, stirring every 20 to 30 seconds after the first 3 minutes, until only a small solid chunk of chocolate remains). Remove from heat and stir until completely melted and smooth. Add vanilla.

Whisk in flour, sugar, and butter. Whisk in egg yolks, one by one. Batter should be the consistency of frosting.

Beat the egg whites to stiff peaks. Fold into chocolate base. Pour into prepared pan and bake 15 minutes. Let cool in the oven with the door ajar.

Run knife around cake to loosen sides. Remove springform sides. Invert cake onto a serving platter or cake pedestal. Carefully lift off pan bottom and peel away waxed paper. The top will sink, forming a basin, as it cools completely. Fill basin with Lush Chocolate Sauce.

For lush chocolate sauce Chop the chocolate evenly. In a saucepan, heat half the cream with the sugar until it boils. Remove from heat. Add chocolate and stir until it melts and mixture is smooth. Add remaining cream and stir patiently until thick and smooth.

Decorate by piping Framboise Chantilly Cream around the base of the cake. Chill immediately.

To serve, remove from refrigerator 30 minutes before serving. Slice with a knife dipped in hot water, then wiped dry.

For Framboise chantilly cream In a cold bowl and with cold beaters, whip the cream, sugar, and Framboise to stiff peaks. Store, covered with plastic wrap, in the refrigerator until ready for use, up to 24 hours. Makes 2 cups.

Makes at least 10 servings.

Note: If you do not have a raspberry liqueur, whip the cream, then fold in about 1 tablespoon raspberry jam.

Concord Cake

I've been making this recipe since the early '80s, when two separate incidents connected me permanently to the Concord.

One was eating it at Café Metro in Louisville, Kentucky. The staff made the Concord only on Tuesdays, Thursdays, and Saturdays, and displayed it in the dining room in a ruthlessly tempting manner.

The second was when *The Best of Gaston Lenotre's Desserts* crossed my food editor's desk at the *Courier-Journal*. I recognized the cake in a picture in the book. When I finally met and interviewed Lenotre, the supreme pâtissier of France, he told me he had created the "Concord" cake to commemorate the maiden voyage of the French high-speed airplane, the Concorde. Maybe it does appear to lift in flight. But I think it looks like a chocolate porcupine —still a showstopper.

I no longer wait for a Tuesday, Thursday, or Saturday, or even to travel back to Louisville to eat this cake. Now I can control my own supply. The sensation from meringue and mousse is poof and slide.

Meringue disks
3½ tablespoons cocoa
1 cup powdered sugar
5 egg whites
⅔ cup sugar

Chocolate mousse
½ cup sugar
⅓ cup water

4 egg yolks
6½ ounces semisweet chocolate
7 tablespoons unsalted butter
5 egg whites
1 tablespoon additional sugar

Additional powdered sugar, for decoration

For disks Preheat oven to 300°. Butter 2 baking sheets and line them with parchment paper or a brown paper bag cut to fit. Draw 3 ovals, each about 5½ by 10 inches, on the paper.

Sift cocoa with powdered sugar. In another bowl, beat egg whites until firm, adding 1½ tablespoons sugar halfway through. As soon as the egg whites are stiff, turn mixer to low speed and add the remaining sugar. With a spatula, quickly fold in the cocoa-sugar mixture.

Pipe two-thirds of the meringue from a ½-inch plain tip, or spread with a spoon to fill in oval patterns, starting in the center of each oval. Then pipe all the remaining meringue into long strips across one of the baking sheets.

Bake ovals 1 hour, 5 minutes. Check after 15 minutes of baking for premature browning. If meringues brown, lower the heat. The meringue strips will be done first, after about 30 or 40 minutes, and should be removed then, though the large ovals might need 10 more minutes baking. When cooked, the meringues will be hard and will easily detach from the paper.

For mousse   Boil the sugar and water in a saucepan about 5 minutes. Beat the yolks in the top of a double boiler. While beating, slowly add the hot sugar syrup. Cook the syrup-yolk mixture in the double boiler over barely simmering water, stirring constantly, until the yolks are creamy and thick, about 5 to 8 minutes (160°). Immediately transfer to a bowl, straining if lumps occur, and stir to cool down.

Melt the chocolate in a double boiler (or microwave, uncovered, on Medium, stirring every 20 to 30 seconds after the first 2 minutes, until only a small chunk of chocolate remains). Remove from heat and stir until melted and smooth.

Stir butter into chocolate a tablespoon or so at a time. The mixture should have the consistency of very thick cream. Combine the chocolate mixture with the cooked yolks.

Beat the egg whites to stiff peaks, gradually adding the remaining tablespoon of sugar halfway through.

Fold the chocolate mixture into the egg whites with a rubber spatula, making sure the two components are very well blended, with no white streaks showing. Chill 30 minutes or so, to firm up.

To assemble   Stack and frost meringue disks with Chocolate Mousse, covering the entire cake completely with the mousse.

Break the strips of meringue into 1-inch pieces and stud the cake all over with them. It will look like a chocolate porcupine. These meringue pieces can serve to camouflage imperfections in the mousse coating.

Lay a 2-inch-wide strip of newspaper, waxed paper, or foil across the center of the cake, sieve a generous coating of powdered sugar over the cake, and remove the strip.

This cake may be assembled up to 48 hours in advance. In fact, it actually tastes better if made a day ahead.

Makes 16 servings.

Triple Chocolate Polyester Mousse Cake

You've got your French silk, red velvet, and chocolate suede. Why not a nice synthetic?

Triple Chocolate Polyester Mousse Cake got its name when I made chocolate mousse with cooked egg yolks. It was such a radical change from classic mousse with raw yolks that I thought it a sly imposter. Like all fabulous fakes, this mousse is versatile, and some can't tell it from the real thing from France.

In this killer cake, the darkness of the chocolates graduates from the gloss of the mousse on the lower level, to medium brown on the mezzanine, to light beige on a penthouse of chocolate whipped cream.

Chocolate crumb crust
1 round tablet Mexican table chocolate, or 2 ounces (2 squares) semisweet baking chocolate
1 9-ounce box plain chocolate wafers
1 teaspoon cinnamon
3 tablespoons brown sugar
4 tablespoons (½ stick) unsalted butter, melted

Whipped ganache
2 cups heavy cream
6 ounces (6 squares) excellent-quality semisweet chocolate (see Note 1)

Chocolate mousse
10 ounces (10 squares) excellent-quality semisweet chocolate

½ cup sugar
⅓ cup water
4 egg yolks
1 stick (8 tablespoons) unsalted butter, very soft
1 teaspoon pure vanilla extract
5 egg whites

Chocolate chantilly cream
1 tablespoon cocoa
3 tablespoons powdered sugar
1½ cups cream
½ teaspoon pure vanilla extract

Shaved semisweet or bittersweet chocolate (see page 88)

For crust Heat oven to 400°. Chop chocolate and drop through feed tube of an activated food processor or blender. Add wafers and process until fine crumbs form. (Or crush wafers between sheets of waxed paper with a rolling pin.)

Pour crumb mixture into a 9-inch springform pan. Stir in cinnamon, brown sugar, and melted butter and, using your fingers, quickly mash the mixture until the crumbs hold together. Use your knuckles to press up the sides, then press over bottom of pan. Bake 10 minutes. Cool.

For ganache Heat cream to boiling. Meanwhile, finely chop the chocolate and place it in a mixing bowl. Pour hot cream over chocolate, stir, and immediately cover with plastic wrap. Let chocolate melt about 15 minutes.

Remove wrapping and stir mixture until chocolate is completely melted and smooth. Be sure to stir up the bits from the bottom of the bowl. The mixture will resemble thick soup.

Pour into a shallow pan to cool fast. Press plastic wrap directly on surface to prevent a skin from forming. Chill at least 3 hours or up to two days. (Mixture will not set completely.)

For mousse Chop the chocolate evenly, then melt it in a double boiler over barely simmering water (or microwave, uncovered, on Medium, stirring every 20 to 30 seconds after the first 2½ minutes, until only a small solid chunk of chocolate remains). Remove from heat and stir until melted and smooth. Set aside.

Boil the sugar and water about 5 minutes; cool slightly. Beat the yolks in the top portion of a double boiler. While beating, gradually pour in the hot sugar syrup.

Cook the syrup-yolk mixture in the double boiler over barely simmering water, stirring constantly, until the yolks are creamy and thick, about 5 to 8 minutes (160°). Immediately transfer to a bowl, straining if lumps occur, and stir to cool down.

Beat the soft butter until fluffy in an electric mixer (use a paddle attachment, if you have one) about 2 minutes. With mixer on medium, slowly pour the cooked yolks down the side of the mixer bowl into the butter, mixing just until completely blended. By hand, stir in the cooled chocolate and vanilla.

Whip the egg whites to medium-stiff peaks. Fold into chocolate base. Pour into prepared crust and chill about 30 minutes.

For cream Sift cocoa and powdered sugar together. Mix in ¼ cup of the cream until completely dissolved. In a cold bowl and with cold beaters, whip remaining cream to stiff peaks, slowly adding the cocoa mixture and the vanilla.

To assemble Scrape the cold ganache into the bowl of an electric mixer. Beat in quick bursts (use a paddle attachment, if you have one) 30 seconds to 1 minute, or until mixture has the consistency of sour cream. Watch closely, for ganache can "break."

Spread ganache over mousse in crust. Top ganache with Chocolate Chantilly Cream, which you may spread with a spoon or pipe decoratively in garish swirls. Cover and chill 2 to 4 hours (see Note 2).

Remove springform side. Sprinkle cake all over with chocolate shavings. Slice with a knife dipped in a tall glass of hot water, then wiped dry.

Makes 12 servings.

Note 1: This cake really showcases chocolate. Poor-quality chocolate can't hide.

Note 2: This cake should be covered to prevent refrigerator odors from permeating its celly texture, yet a covering would damage any decorative topping you've attempted. If you need to chill until serving, chill cake and Chocolate Chantilly Cream separately and apply cream topping when serving.

Tarts That Make Your Heart Beat

After an afternoon spent working on these tarts, my heart palpitated so hard it tried to push through my bones. I've been told by many pastry chefs that chocolate makes them irritable. I waited for a bad mood, but swooned instead.

Snappy dark chocolate cups secrete a layer of thick buttery caramel that sheets when you tug it with a fork. The caramel is topped with a medium brown filling of milk chocolate. Decorative zigzags form a weave on top, with caramel making lines in one direction and chocolate making lines in the other. The vision is shades of brown, with the twinkling gold of the caramel on top, and a taste inspired by Milky Way candy bars.

Except for the chocolate cups, which require tempering (see Having a Good Temper, page 100), this recipe is of average difficulty.

Chocolate cups
8 ounces (8 squares) excellent quality semisweet chocolate

Stretchy caramel
1½ cups sugar

½ cup water

½ cup cream

4 tablespoons unsalted butter, in pats

Milk chocolate ganache filling
1½ cups heavy cream

10 ounces excellent-quality milk chocolate

Chocolate glaze
2 ounces (2 squares) semisweet chocolate

2 tablespoons unsalted butter

½ teaspoon vanilla

To temper chocolate (See Easy Chocolate Cups, page 100.) Finely chop the entire amount of semisweet chocolate. Place ⅔ of it in a bowl over water heated to 120° (*not* hot enough to simmer!), and melt the chocolate gently and slowly. Have the remaining chopped chocolate in a place convenient to the stove.

When chocolate reaches 90° to 110°, remove from heat and add the reserved chopped chocolate, stirring until the solid pieces disappear into the chocolate mass and the entire mixture is very smooth. Reheat again to a working temperature of 88° to 90°.

To form cups Spray 8 rippled 4-inch tartlet shells (prepare 2 or 3 extras in case of breakage) with nonstick spray. Have ready a cooling rack placed over waxed paper or a cookie sheet to catch any drips (see Note).

Quickly pour tempered chocolate into each shell, swirling to coat, and allowing excess to drip back into bowl. Invert on the rack to drip and dry. Chill 6 hours.

To unmold, cut away any hardened protrusions of chocolate so you can see the metal rims of the shells. Rap inverted shells on a counter once or twice to release chocolate cups. Chill cups until ready for use.

For caramel In a heavy saucepan, bring sugar and water to a boil over medium-high heat. (If crystals form on the sides of the pan, cover the pan for 30 seconds, or as long as 5 minutes, so the steam rinses off the sides.) When the sugar darkens, you may swirl the pan to even the color. Take the caramel to the color of iced tea.

Remove from heat and pour in all the cream—the caramel will sputter, so stand back. Return to heat and cook and stir a minute or two. Keep moving the spoon all over the bottom of the pan until caramel and cream are completely smooth. Remove from heat and stir in the butter until all the butter has melted into the sauce. Pour into a bowl and cool at room temperature.

To store the caramel, chill it, covered, although you must warm it again to use (rewarm in a microwave on High for 30 seconds to 1 minute). Makes 1½ cups.

For filling Heat cream to boiling. Meanwhile, finely chop the milk chocolate and place it in a mixing bowl. Pour hot cream over chocolate, stir, and immediately cover with plastic wrap. Let the chocolate melt about 15 minutes.

Remove wrapping and stir until chocolate is completely melted and smooth. Be sure to stir up the bits from the bottom of the bowl. The mixture will resemble thick soup.

Pour into a shallow pan to cool fast. Press plastic wrap on surface to prevent a skin from forming. Chill at least 3 hours, or up to 2 days.

Scrape the cold ganache into the bowl of an electric mixer. Beat in quick bursts (use a paddle attachment, if you have one) 30 seconds to 1 minute until mixture has the consistency of sour cream. (Watch closely, for ganache can "break" and become gritty.) This ganache should be firm enough to slice, but soft enough to mound in the chocolate cups.

For chocolate glaze Melt chocolate and butter over low heat, stirring, until smooth and completely melted. Remove from heat and stir in vanilla. Makes about ⅝ cup.

To assemble Pour about 2 tablespoons warm caramel into bottom of each chocolate cup. Top with cold milk chocolate ganache. Decorate ganache with zigzags of more caramel going north-south, and swizzles of chocolate glaze going east-west. Chill until serving.

Present on individual dessert plates, surrounded by Crème Anglaise (page 38), with Strawberry Puree (page 24) dotted around the tarts. Draw a card once through each strawberry dab to form a pretty curve.

Makes 8 tarts.

Note: If you don't have tartlet shells, use muffin cups. Pour a scant tablespoon of tempered chocolate into each of 12 to 15 ruffled paper muffin liners. With the back of a spoon, spread chocolate across bottoms and up sides of cups. Set in 2½-inch muffin tins for shape. Chill 3 hours.

Easy Chocolate Cups

You don't *have* to temper the chocolate. You can melt it instead. The chocolate cups won't be snappy and shiny, and fingers will slip and leave prints, but your task will definitely be easier. Here's how to do it.

Chop the chocolate. Melt it in the top of a double boiler over barely simmering water (or microwave on Medium, stirring every 20 to 30 seconds after the first 2½ minutes, until only a small solid chunk of chocolate remains). Stir chocolate until completely melted and smooth. Use paper muffin liners to shape untempered chocolate—you won't get good results using tartlet shells. Peel paper away.

Having a Good Temper

Tempering chocolate can be a hassle. Even the weather can affect how long and how well chocolate melts, cools, and becomes chemically stable enough to make snappy molds or candies. Not all chocolate needs to be tempered, however, but I went to the trouble for this dessert because my vision of sturdy walls in the chocolate cups could not otherwise be attained.

I took my time and remembered:

- Only let the chocolate melt.
- Even if the water under it isn't boiling, the heat beneath it is enough to make the chocolate melt—eventually.
- Don't rush.
- Chocolate is fluid enough for working with at temperatures between 90° and 120°. It performs best for dipping or lining molds if no cooler than 75°.

If properly tempered, chocolate will shrink in the molds as it hardens, making it easy to release cups without too much hard rapping on the countertop. For reassurance, coat molds with nonstick spray.

Chocolate-Peanut Butter Cake

Patricia Murakami, the pastry chef at Chinois East-West in Sacramento, California, has a serious addiction: she loves Reese's Peanut Butter Cups. In their honor, she created this dessert. She calls it a cake, although it is softer and creamier than a cake. Peanut butter, brown sugar, and more butter serve as a base. A thick chocolate layer, something between a custard and a ganache, goes on top and chills.

A customer enjoyed it so much that a request for this recipe was made through *Bon Appétit* magazine. But Patricia had long ago given it to me.

Crust
1⅓ cups crushed chocolate cookies

4 tablespoons unsalted butter, melted

Peanut butter layer
10 double graham crackers (from 1 wrapped package)

½ cup packed brown sugar

2 sticks (½ pound) unsalted butter

2 cups chunky peanut butter

Chocolate layer
11 ounces (11 squares) excellent-quality semisweet chocolate

6 egg yolks

1½ cups heavy cream

For crust Spray a 9-inch springform pan with vegetable-oil coating (such as Pam). Combine chocolate cookie crumbs and melted butter (see Note 1). With your fingers, press mixture around the sides and across the bottom of the pan. Chill crust while you prepare the peanut butter layer.

For peanut butter layer Combine all ingredients in a food processor just until blended. Spoon into the crust-lined pan and smooth the top. Chill while you prepare the chocolate layer.

For chocolate layer Chop the chocolate very fine, place it in a medium mixing bowl, and set aside. Have the yolks ready in the top portion of a double boiler.

Heat the cream just until it comes to a boil. While whisking constantly, slowly pour the hot cream into the yolks. Cook in the double boiler over simmering water, stirring constantly, until thickened enough to coat the back of a wooden spoon (160°). Strain cream mixture into the chocolate and gently blend until the chocolate is completely melted and the mixture is smooth. It will be very thick, almost like pudding. Pour over the chilled peanut butter layer. Smooth the top and chill.

For best results, prepare one day ahead. Slice with a knife dipped in a tall glass of hot water, then wiped dry.

Makes 10 to 12 (very rich!) servings.

Note 1: In place of plain chocolate cookies, you can use Oreo or Hydrox sandwich cookies, filling and all.

Note 2: This freezes well.

Judy's Turtle Pie

Turtle Pie gets its gooey dimension from the same concept that weds chocolate, caramel, and pecans for "turtle" candy. This pie was developed by Judy Parks, a pâtissière who produces felonious pastries and chocolates at Tarts & Truffles in Sacramento, California. The pie is constructed of a chocolate cookie crumb crust, a caramel-pecan layer, a mousse-like layer of whipped chocolate ganache, and a chocolate glaze smoothed on top. Each component may be made several days ahead. Ganache must be made at least several hours in advance so it can cool enough to whip without breaking.

Crust
1 cup chocolate wafer cookie crumbs (from 9-ounce package plain chocolate wafer cookies)

1 tablespoon sugar

Pinch salt

2 tablespoons unsalted butter, melted

Caramel-pecan layer
⅔ cup sugar

1 tablespoon dark corn syrup

2 tablespoons water

¼ cup unsalted butter

⅓ cup cream

¾ cup chopped pecans

Chocolate ganache filling
2 cups heavy cream

¼ cup unsalted butter

6 ounces (6 squares) semisweet chocolate

For crust Preheat the oven to 350°. Mix crumbs, sugar, salt, and butter in the bottom of a 9-inch pie plate or springform pan. Using your fingers and knuckles, press crumbs up sides and over bottom of pan. Bake 10 minutes. Cool.

For caramel layer In a heavy saucepan, bring the sugar, corn syrup, and water to a boil over medium-high heat. If crystals form on the sides of the pan, cover the pan for 30 seconds, or as long as 5 minutes, so steam can rinse off the sides. When the sugar darkens, swirl the pan to even the color. Take the caramel to the color of honey.

Remove from heat and stir in butter. Return to heat and stir in cream. Bring back to a boil, then cool.

Reserve approximately 3 tablespoons caramel for garnish. Pour remaining caramel over the chocolate crust. Press pecans all over the caramel. Cool.

For ganache Bring cream and butter to a boil. Chop 1 ounce of the chocolate and reserve. Chop remaining 5 ounces chocolate and, off heat, whisk into the boiled cream until completely smooth.

Remove ½ cup and stir in reserved 1 ounce chocolate; leave this at room temperature. Refrigerate larger portion of ganache several hours, or until completely chilled. Whip by hand or with an electric mixer (use a paddle attachment, if you have one) about 30 seconds until mixture has the consistency of whipped cream. (Don't overwhip or ganache may break or become stiff and grainy.) Spread ganache over caramel so the top is smooth and level. Refrigerate 15 minutes.

Pour room-temperature ganache on top, tilting the pie to cover surface. Chill 1 to 2 hours before cutting.

Garnish top by striping surface with reserved caramel. (If using a springform pan, remove sides.) Slice into wedges, using a knife dipped in a tall glass of hot water, then wiped dry.

Makes 12 servings.

White Chocolate-Passion Fruit Mousse

Lovers of white chocolate will enjoy the delicate texture and slightly tropical flavor of this mousse. Eat it plain or mound it into individual tart shells garnished with fruit.

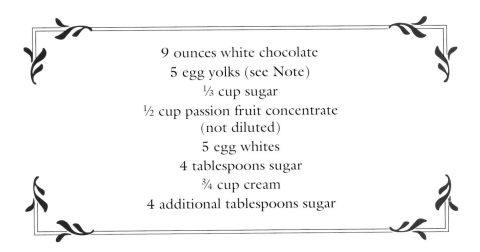

9 ounces white chocolate

5 egg yolks (see Note)

⅓ cup sugar

½ cup passion fruit concentrate
(not diluted)

5 egg whites

4 tablespoons sugar

¾ cup cream

4 additional tablespoons sugar

Chop the white chocolate and melt it in the top of a double boiler over barely simmering water. (White chocolate scorches easily, so make sure you heat it slowly, gently, and patiently.) Stir as it melts to make it smooth. When melted and smooth, leave on top of double boiler, but turn off heat.

In a large bowl, beat the yolks and ⅓ cup sugar until thick and pale, about 45 seconds. Beat in the passion fruit concentrate. Using a wide rubber spatula, scrape the white chocolate into the egg mixture, and whisk well.

Beat the egg whites to medium-stiff peaks, gradually adding 4 tablespoons sugar halfway through. Fold whites into white chocolate base.

In a cold bowl and with cold beaters, whip the cream with the remaining sugar to stiff peaks. Fold into mousse. Cover and chill.

To serve Spoon into goblets, or use to fill Pecan Tart Shells (see page 126) and top with fresh fruit. Or serve spooned into individual dessert bowls or goblets, decorated with bittersweet or semisweet chocolate shavings, and garnished with fresh strawberries soaked in Grand Marnier or other liqueur.

Makes 8 to 10 servings.

Note: This mousse contains uncooked egg yolks.

Caramel Fudge Brownies

You might need a fork to eat these sticky brownies. Be patient and wait for them to cool before removing them from the pan, or you will end up with a gooey chocolate mess.

Perfect.

---

1 stick (¼ pound) unsalted butter
1 cup semisweet chocolate chips
2 eggs
1 cup sugar
½ cup flour
½ teaspoon pure vanilla extract

1 additional cup semisweet chocolate chips
1 bag caramels, unwrapped
½ cup heavy cream
½ cup chopped pecans

Grease an 8-inch square baking pan. Set oven rack in the middle of the oven and preheat oven to 350°.

In the top of a double boiler over barely simmering water, melt butter and chocolate chips (or microwave, uncovered, on Medium, stirring every 20 to 30 seconds after the first minute, until smooth). Set aside to cool.

In a bowl, beat eggs and sugar until pale yellow, about 2 minutes. Thoroughly blend in chocolate mixture, flour, and vanilla.

Pour *half* the batter into the prepared pan and bake 15 minutes. Add the remaining cup of chocolate chips to the remaining batter and set aside.

While the brownies are baking, melt the caramels with the cream over low heat. Spread caramel over baked brownie. Cover caramel with remaining batter. Sprinkle pecans on top.

Return to oven for 20 minutes more. The brownies will jiggle when you remove them from the oven. Don't worry; they will firm up a bit when cool.

Cut the brownies into squares after they're cool.

Makes 16.

Lush Chocolate Sauce

The consistency of this sauce is like that of ganache that isn't whipped. It may be served as hot fudge, poured warm, or cooled to room temperature until it's the consistency of sour cream.

Its best feature is that it won't harden if poured over ice cream. It will keep in the refrigerator for many weeks, or at cool room temperature for a couple of days. Or it may be frozen to meet emergency needs for chocolate sauce.

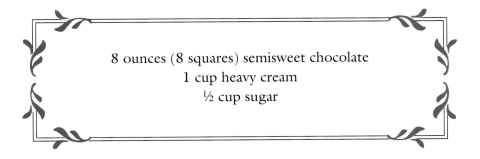

8 ounces (8 squares) semisweet chocolate
1 cup heavy cream
½ cup sugar

Chop the chocolate evenly. In a saucepan, heat half the cream with the sugar until it boils. Remove from heat. Add chocolate and stir until it melts and mixture is smooth. Add remaining cream and stir patiently until thick and smooth.

Yield: 2 cups.

CHAPTER THREE

Great Gooey Pies

Big Banana Cream Pie with Caramelized Bananas and Banana Liqueur

If there were one standard against which all other gooey desserts were measured, it would be banana cream pie. Recipes for banana cream pie are everywhere. But this one is bigger, "gooeyer," and banana-ier than them all.

The buttery crust is sturdy enough to withstand its heavy contents. Where other recipes merely slice bananas plain into the crust, the banana slices here are sautéed in brown sugar, then flamed with banana liqueur. The cream is super-rich from extra egg yolks, added binder, and butter—plus that banana liqueur. I checked with an expert about whether I ought to put banana liqueur in the whipped cream topping. "Go for it," she cheered.

Since this is supposed to be the grandest banana cream pie ever, the ingredient quantities are for filling a 10-inch pie plate. The size alone will shock (see photo plate 2).

Cream pie crust
(For a 10-inch pie plate)
1½ cups flour
Pinch salt
½ teaspoon sugar
6 tablespoons unsalted butter,
very cold, cut in pieces
3 tablespoons solid
shortening, very cold
3 to 4 tablespoons ice water

Banana cream filling
5 egg yolks
2 tablespoons flour
¼ cup cornstarch
⅔ cup sugar
3 cups milk

3 tablespoons butter
1 tablespoon banana liqueur,
such as crème de banana,
or 2 teaspoons banana extract
2 teaspoons pure vanilla extract

Caramelized flamed bananas
2 tablespoons unsalted butter
¼ cup light brown sugar
3 medium-large bananas,
not too ripe
1 tablespoon banana liqueur

Banana-ed whipped cream
2 cups cream
3 tablespoons sugar
2 tablespoons banana liqueur
(or 2 teaspoons banana extract)

For crust   Mix flour, salt, and sugar. Cut in butter and shortening until it looks like flaky meal. Sprinkle in ice water. Work into a ball that cleans the sides of the mixing bowl. (To mix in a food processor, place dry ingredients in work bowl, top with butter and shortening, and pulse until mealy. With machine running, pour in the ice water all at once. When dough forms a ball that knocks around the sides of the machine, stop immediately.)

Flatten dough into a disk, then wrap with plastic film, and chill 30 minutes (or freeze).

Heat oven to 425° for a glass pie plate, 450° for metal. Roll dough to a circle 3 to 4 inches wider than the pie plate. Set in plate and cut overhang with scissors so dough extends ¾ inch beyond the rim. Fold overhang under so it is even with plate's rim and crimp large flutes. Prick the bottom and sides all over with a fork, about 50 times. Cover bottom with foil, fill with rice or beans, and bake 15 minutes. Pour off grains and foil and return crust to oven to bake 5 to 10 minutes more. Crust should be pale.

For filling   Stir yolks and set bowl in a place convenient to the stove.

In a heavy saucepan, whisk flour, cornstarch, sugar, and milk until free of lumps. Set over medium-high heat and bring to a boil, stirring constantly. Boil for 2 minutes, stirring fast and getting into the corners of the pot.

Remove from heat and whisk a little of the milk into the egg yolks, then pour the tempered yolks into the hot milk. Continue to cook another FULL 2 minutes, stirring constantly. If lumps form, strain into a bowl.

Pour into a bowl and add butter, banana liqueur, and vanilla, stirring to cool. Press plastic wrap onto surface to prevent a skin from forming. Set filling aside while you prepare the bananas.

For bananas   Place butter and brown sugar in a large skillet; slice in the bananas. Heat over medium-high heat until butter melts and sugar begins to caramelize, about 3 minutes. Don't over-mush the bananas. Shake the pan to distribute bananas instead of bruising them with a tool. (If you must use a tool, use a rubber spatula.) With heat high, pour in liqueur all at once. Ignite with a match and let flame subside by itself. Pour bananas onto a jelly-roll pan to cool quickly.

To assemble   Line the baked pie shell with cooled bananas. Top with filling (which may still be warm). Wrap pie in plastic and refrigerate until filling sets, about 6 hours.

In a cold bowl, with cold beaters, whip the cream, sugar, and liqueur to stiff peaks. Pipe from a pastry bag fitted with a large star-shaped tip with a wide opening. You will have lots of whipped cream, so the designs can be big, even garish. Make rows, rounds, mounds, or swirls. Chill again, and keep cold until serving.

To slice wedges, use a smooth knife dipped in a tall glass of hot water, then wiped dry.

Makes 8 to 10 servings.

Note: The crust may suffer some shrinkage, but if you've pricked it enough, it will sustain baking better. I have also baked it carelessly without weighting from dry beans, and had it come out fine.

Big Chocolate Banana Cream Pie

Chocolate and banana are a fine flavor pairing. This pie is made like Big Banana Cream Pie—using Caramelized Bananas—with one grand exception. Before anything goes together, the crust is painted with a coating of pure semisweet chocolate.

Cream pie crust
(For a 10-inch pie plate)

1½ cups flour

Pinch salt

½ teaspoon sugar

6 tablespoons unsalted butter,
very cold, in pieces

3 tablespoons solid
shortening, very cold

3 to 4 tablespoons ice water

Chocolate cream filling

2¾ cups milk

5 ounces (5 squares)
semisweet chocolate, divided

5 egg yolks

¼ cup cornstarch

2 tablespoons flour

⅔ cup sugar

2 teaspoons vanilla extract

Caramelized flamed bananas

2 tablespoons butter

¼ cup light brown sugar

3 medium-large bananas,
not too ripe

1 tablespoon banana liqueur

1 tablespoon dark rum

3 additional ounces excellent-
quality semisweet chocolate,
to line pie plate

Kahlua whipped cream

2 cups heavy cream

3 tablespoons sugar

2 tablespoons Kahlua

Chocolate shavings or crumbled
chocolate cookies, for garnish

For crust Mix together flour, salt, and sugar. Cut in butter and shortening until mixture looks like flaky meal. Sprinkle in ice water. Work into a ball that cleans the sides of the mixing bowl. (To mix in a food processor, place dry ingredients in work bowl, top with butter and shortening, and pulse until mealy. With machine running, pour in the ice water all at once. When dough forms a ball that knocks around the sides of the machine, stop immediately.)

Flatten dough into a disk, wrap with plastic film, and chill 30 minutes (or freeze).

Heat oven to 425° for a glass pie plate, 450° for metal. Roll dough to a circle 3 to 4 inches wider than the pie plate. Set in the plate and cut overhang with scissors so dough extends ¾ inch beyond the rim. Fold overhang under so it is even with plate's rim and crimp large flutes. Prick the bottom and sides all over with a fork, about 50 times. Cover bottom with foil, fill with rice or beans, and bake 15 minutes. Pour off grains and foil and return crust to oven to bake 5 to 10 minutes more. Crust should be pale.

For chocolate filling In a saucepan, heat the milk to just under a boil.

Melt the chocolate in a double boiler over barely simmering water. (Or microwave, uncovered, on Medium, stirring every 20 to 30 seconds after the first 2 minutes, until only a small solid chunk of chocolate remains.) Remove from heat and stir until melted and smooth. Cool.

Beat yolks, cornstarch, flour, and sugar in a saucepan until pale and thick, about 1 minute. Stir in melted chocolate. Whisk in the hot milk.

Over medium-high heat, bring mixture to a boil, stirring constantly. Custard will thicken quickly. Let simmer 1 full minute, stirring fast and getting into the corners of the pot. Pour into a bowl and add vanilla. If lumps form, strain into a bowl. Press plastic wrap over surface to prevent a skin from forming. Set aside while you prepare the bananas.

For bananas Place butter and brown sugar in a large skillet; slice in the bananas.

Heat over medium-high heat until butter melts and sugar begins to caramelize, about 3 minutes. Don't over-mush the bananas. Shake the pan to distribute bananas instead of bruising them with a tool. If you must use a tool, use a rubber spatula. With heat high, pour in banana liqueur and rum all at once. Ignite with a match and let flame subside by itself. Pour bananas onto a jelly-roll pan to cool quickly.

To assemble Melt the remaining 3 ounces chocolate (as in chocolate filling). Spread over the cooled crust and allow to cool. Top chocolate with cooled bananas. Top bananas with chocolate filling (which may still be warm). Wrap pie in plastic and refrigerate until filling sets, about 6 hours.

In a cold bowl with cold beaters, whip the cream, sugar and Kahlua to stiff peaks. Pipe from a pastry bag fitted with a large star-shaped tip with a wide opening. You will have lots of whipped cream, so the designs can be big, even garish. Make rows, rounds, mounds, or swirls. Fleck with chocolate shavings. Chill again, and keep cold until serving. To slice, use a smooth knife dipped in a tall glass of hot water, then wiped dry.

Makes 8 to 10 servings.

Note: The crust may suffer some shrinkage, but if you've pricked it enough, it will sustain baking better. I have also baked it carelessly, without weighting from dry beans, and had it come out fine.

Domed Coconut Cream Pie with Coconut Milk

This pie takes the quick route to tropical coconut flavor—without cracking a single coconut. I'll do a lot the long way, but I won't crack coconuts and drain them and scrape them and grate them. Live right: buy a fine can of coconut milk and pick up coconut in a bag already grated for you.

Cream pie crust
(For a 10-inch pie plate)

1½ cups flour

Pinch salt

½ teaspoon sugar

6 tablespoons unsalted butter, very cold, in pieces

3 tablespoons solid shortening, very cold

3 to 4 tablespoons ice water

Coconut milk–rum cream filling

5 egg yolks

2 tablespoons flour

¼ cup cornstarch

⅔ cup sugar

2 cups milk

1 cup canned coconut milk

3 tablespoons butter

2 tablespoons rum

1 cup cream

1½ cups premium-quality shredded coconut

Meringue

6 egg whites

¼ teaspoon cream of tartar

½ teaspoon pure vanilla extract

⅔ cup sugar

⅓ cup premium-quality shredded coconut

For crust Mix flour, salt, and sugar. Cut in butter and shortening until mixture resembles flaky meal. Sprinkle in ice water. Work into a ball that cleans the sides of the mixing bowl. (To mix in a food processor, place dry ingredients in work bowl, top with pieces of cold butter and shortening, and pulse until mealy. With machine run-ning, pour in the ice water all at once. When dough forms a ball that knocks around the sides of the bowl, stop machine immediately.)

Flatten dough into a disk, wrap with plastic film, and chill 30 minutes (or freeze).

Heat oven to 425° for a glass pie plate, 450° for metal. Roll dough to form a circle 3 to 4 inches wider than the pie plate. Set dough in the plate and trim with scissors so it extends ¾ inch beyond the rim. Fold this overhang under so it is even with plate's rim and crimp into large flutes. Prick the bottom and sides all over with a fork, about 50 times. Cover bottom with foil, fill plate with rice or beans, and bake 15 minutes. Pour off grains, remove foil, and return to oven to bake 5 to 10 minutes more. Crust should be pale.

For filling Stir yolks and set aside in a place convenient to the stove. In a heavy saucepan, whisk flour, cornstarch, sugar, and both milks until free of lumps. Set over medium-high heat and bring to a boil, stirring constantly. Boil for 2 minutes, stirring fast and getting into the corners of the pot.

Remove pan from heat and whisk a little of the hot milk into the egg yolks, then pour the tempered yolks back into the hot milk. Continue to cook 1 minute more, stirring constantly. If lumps form, strain into a bowl.

Remove from heat and stir in butter and rum. Transfer to a cool bowl and stir to cool down.

In a cold bowl with cold beaters, whip cream to stiff peaks. Fold into cooled filling and gently fold in shredded coconut. Pour filling into cooled pie shell. Chill at least 2 hours. Filling should be cold and firm.

For meringue Preheat oven to 350°. Beat the egg whites, cream of tartar, and vanilla to stiff peaks. Gradually add the ⅔ cup sugar and beat to stiff peaks again.

Starting at the edge of the pie, pipe or swirl meringue to make a seal with the crust (so meringue won't shrink later). Pipe or swirl the rest of the meringue all over the pie. Sprinkle the ⅓ cup coconut over the swirls. Set in oven 10 to 15 minutes to lightly brown meringue tips. Cool at room temperature.

Makes 8 to 10 servings.

Note: Crust may suffer some shrinkage, but if you've pricked it enough, it will sustain the baking better. I have also baked this crust without weighting with dry beans and had it come out fine.

Big Bouffant Lemon Meringue Pie

The worst thing you can do to a lemon meringue pie is compromise its natural pulchritude. Make it big: dome the meringue. But remember, the meringue top will shrink unless you spread it wide enough to touch the sides of the crust and form a seal.

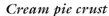

Cream pie crust
(For a 10-inch pie plate)
1½ cups flour
Pinch salt
½ teaspoon sugar
6 tablespoons unsalted
butter, very cold, in pieces
3 tablespoons solid
shortening, very cold
3 to 4 tablespoons ice water

Lemon filling
1⅔ cups sugar
½ cup cornstarch

Dash salt
1⅔ cups water
⅔ cup lemon juice
6 egg yolks
3 tablespoons unsalted butter
4 teaspoons finely
grated lemon zest

Meringue
6 egg whites
¼ teaspoon cream of tartar
½ teaspoon pure vanilla extract
⅔ cup sugar

For crust Mix together flour, salt, and sugar. Cut in butter and shortening until mixture resembles flaky meal. Sprinkle in ice water. Work into a ball that cleans the sides of the mixing bowl. (To mix in a food processor place dry ingredients in work bowl, top with pieces of cold butter and shortening, and pulse until mealy. With machine running, pour in the ice water all at once. When dough forms a ball that knocks around the sides of the bowl, stop machine immediately.)

Flatten dough into a disk, wrap with plastic film, and chill 30 minutes (or freeze).

Heat oven to 425° for a glass pie plate, 450° for metal. Roll dough to form a circle 3 to 4 inches wider than the pie plate. Set dough in the plate and trim with scissors so it extends ¾ inch beyond the rim. Fold this overhang under so it is even with plate's rim and crimp large flutes. Prick the bottom and sides all over with a fork, about 50 times. Cover bottom with foil, fill plate with rice or beans, and bake 15 minutes. Pour off grains, remove foil, and return to oven to bake 5 to 10 minutes more. Crust should be pale.

For filling Combine the sugar, cornstarch, and salt in a heavy saucepan. Gradually add water and lemon juice, stirring until smooth. Beat the yolks and stir into the sugar mixture.

Set the saucepan over medium heat. Add butter and cook, stirring constantly, until mixture thickens and finally comes to a boil. (Just before the boil, mixture will appear to break and curdle, then catch and smooth out again.) Boil 1 minute. Remove from heat and add zest.

Pour the hot filling into the prepared pie shell.

For meringue Preheat oven to 350°. Beat the egg whites, cream of tartar, and vanilla to stiff peaks. Gradually add the ⅔ cup sugar and beat until stiff peaks again.

Starting at the edge of the pie, pipe or swirl meringue to make a seal with the crust, so meringue won't shrink later. Pipe or swirl the rest of the meringue all over the pie. Set in oven 10 to 15 minutes to lightly brown meringue tips. Cool at room temperature.

Makes 8 to 10 servings.

Note: Crust may suffer some shrinkage, but if you've pricked it enough, it will sustain the baking better. I have also baked this crust without weighting with dry beans and had it come out fine.

Elaine's Bluegrass Pie

Here is a pie every cook in Kentucky knows how to make. With its bourbon and corn syrup, it is a hallmark of the Kentucky Derby. But it comes with an advisory.

You can say the actual name of this pie out loud, but you can't print it. Zealous protection of a registered trademark prevents the word "pie" from following the word "derby." A commercial bakery in Louisville has the run on the legal use of Derby Pie.

So . . . this pie must be referred to in print in other ways. Hence, we have Run for the Roses Pie, Thoroughbred Pie, Winner's Circle Pie, Kentucky Oaks Pie (the Oaks being the race fillies run the Friday afternoon before the Derby itself, which is always held on the first Saturday in May), and this—Bluegrass Pie. But we all know what it really is.

I've taken the liberty of using a good buttery crust and adding extra chocolate chips—white ones.

Single buttery pie crust
(For a 9-inch pie plate)

1½ cups flour

½ teaspoon salt

½ teaspoon sugar

1 stick (8 tablespoons) unsalted
butter, very cold, in pieces

2 tablespoons solid
shortening, very cold

About 4 tablespoons ice water

Filling

½ stick (4 tablespoons)
unsalted butter

¼ cup brown sugar

½ cup white sugar

2 tablespoons flour

3 eggs

½ cup dark corn syrup

Pinch salt

1 teaspoon pure vanilla extract

¼ cup bourbon

1 cup chopped English walnuts

½ cup chocolate chips
(or more)

½ cup white chocolate chips
(or more)

Tangy whipped cream

1 cup cream

1 cup sour cream, yogurt
"cream," or crème fraîche
(page 19)

For crust Mix flour, salt, and sugar. Cut in butter and shortening until mixture resembles flaky meal. Sprinkle in ice water. Work into a ball that cleans the sides of the mixing bowl. (To mix in a food processor, place dry ingredients in work bowl. Top with pieces of cold butter and shortening, and pulse until mealy. With machine running, pour in the ice water all at once. When dough forms a ball that knocks around the sides of the bowl, stop machine immediately.)

Flatten dough into a disk. Wrap with plastic film, and chill 30 minutes (or freeze).

Roll dough into a circle 3 to 4 inches wider than pie plate, set in the plate, and trim with scissors so dough extends ¾ inch beyond the rim. Fold this overhang under so it is even with plate's rim and crimp into large flutes. Chill 30 minutes, while you prepare the filling.

For filling Preheat oven to 375°. Cream butter and sugars until fluffy. Add flour and mix until absorbed. Add eggs, one at a time, mixing well after each addition. Add corn syrup, salt, vanilla, and bourbon. Fold in nuts.

Sprinkle both kinds of chocolate chips over the bottom of the pie crust. Immediately pour in batter. Bake 40 minutes.

Remove from oven and let set before serving. The pie should be chewy but not runny. May be rewarmed slightly for serving. Serve topped with vanilla ice cream or Tangy Whipped Cream.

For tangy whipped cream In a cold bowl with cold beaters, whip cream to medium-stiff peaks. Fold in sour cream.

Makes 6 to 8 servings.

Note 1: For the iciest ice water, fill a small bowl with ice cubes and cold tap water. Dip measuring spoon, a tablespoon at a time, into ice water, and pour over the pastry mixture (or through the feed tube of the food processor).

Note 2: You'll probably have leftover scraps of dough. Roll them out, cut them into shapes with a paring knife, place them on a cookie sheet, and set in the oven along with the pie, but remove after 8 minutes. Spread these little "butter cookie" shapes with jam and serve to children or nibble them in the morning with coffee.

French Canadian Maple Syrup Pie

Maple syrup, or *sirop d'érable,* is the mighty river on which the cuisine of Canada floats. It harbors maple syrup dip with thick cream, apple pie with maple syrup, egg in maple syrup, maple mousse, and maple caramel custard. The most astonishing maple dessert is nothing more than bread soaked in maple syrup and topped with the heaviest cream you can find.

Cream is another steady flow. In and around Quebec, the cream bulges with so much butterfat that it will not fall from a spoon. When I had it at L'Arte, a restaurant on the Isle d'Orléans in the middle of the St. Lawrence River, it had been gently lifted off of fresh milk only a few hours before and held its shape without whipping.

You can't get glorious farm cream like this in America, not in public, anyway. If you'd like to come close, make crème fraîche (see below), which is vaguely reminiscent of the cream at L'Arte and whips and pours almost as hesitantly.

This pie is slightly grainy, and is always served with the cream.

Single buttery pie crust
(For a 9-inch pie plate)
1½ cups flour
½ teaspoon salt
½ teaspoon sugar
1 stick (8 tablespoons) unsalted butter, very cold, in pieces
2 tablespoons shortening, very cold
About 4 tablespoons ice water

Maple filling
1½ cups brown maple sugar (see Note)
2 tablespoons light brown sugar
½ cup heavy cream
½ cup pure maple syrup
3 tablespoons unsalted butter
1 egg

Crème fraîche
1 cup cream
1 tablespoon buttermilk

For crust Mix flour, salt, and sugar. Cut in butter and shortening until it looks like flaky meal. Sprinkle in ice water. Work into a ball that cleans the sides of the mixing bowl. (To mix in a food processor, place dry ingredients in a work bowl, top with pieces of cold butter and shortening, and pulse until mealy. With machine running, pour in the ice water all at once. When dough forms a ball that knocks around the sides of the bowl, stop machine immediately.)

Flatten dough into a disk, wrap with plastic film, and chill 30 minutes.

Roll dough into a circle 3 to 4 inches wider than pie plate, set in the plate, and trim with scissors so dough extends ¾ inch beyond the rim. Fold this overhang under so it is even with plate's rim and crimp into large flutes. Chill 30 minutes, while you prepare the filling.

For maple filling Preheat oven to 350°. Place the first five ingredients in a heavy saucepan and cook over low heat for 10 minutes. Beat the egg and add it to the mixture. Pour filling into chilled pie shell. Bake for 30 to 40 minutes.

Slice and serve warm on plates with a thick layer of crème fraîche, or plain cream, poured over and down the sides of each wedge.

For crème fraîche Put 1 cup cream in a jar with a lid. Add 1 tablespoon buttermilk. Screw on the lid and leave the jar at room temperature for 24 hours. Then chill the thickened cream. The cream should thicken. If it doesn't, your room may have been too chilly. In this case, add a little more buttermilk and set jar in a slightly warmer spot.

Quick crème fraîche Use 3 parts heavy cream to 1 part sour cream. Whip 1½ cups cream with ½ cup sour cream just until beaters make a wake in the cream and soft peaks form.

Makes 6 to 8 servings.

Note: If maple sugar is unavailable, use light brown sugar.

Persimmon Cream Pie

I have this brother-in-law, and he has this persimmon tree. In fall, Hachiya persimmons—the big ones with the elongated tips—come from the tree as plentifully as zucchini in summer. To use four or five in a pie becomes a relief, like crossing something off a things-to-do list.

One Thanksgiving, persimmons lay ripening all over my house. I scooped out the pulp, made my usual recipe for cream pie, and folded the persimmon pulp into the cream.

For best results, persimmons must be riper than you think they are. They ripen best at room temperature, points up—no bags, no ripening bowls. When they look rotten, shriveled, and feel like there's jelly under their skins, they're ready. This can take weeks.

Sometimes at farmers markets, folks who sell persimmons will discount the really ripe ones because they're so ugly. But for this pie, they're just right.

Single buttery pie crust
(For a 10-inch pie plate)
1½ cups flour
½ teaspoon salt
½ teaspoon sugar
1 stick (8 tablespoons) unsalted
butter, very cold, in pieces
2 tablespoons shortening,
very cold
About 4 tablespoons ice water

Persimmon filling
1½ cups persimmon pulp
(from 5 or 6 very ripe
Hachiya persimmons)

1½ cups cream
2 tablespoons flour
1 cup sugar
3 tablespoons unsalted
butter, melted
4 egg yolks
1 whole egg
1 teaspoon pure vanilla extract

Sticky pecan praline crumble
2 cups fresh pecan halves
or pieces
1 cup sugar
¼ cup water
⅛ teaspoon cream of tartar

For crust Mix flour, salt, and sugar. Cut in butter and shortening until mixture resembles flaky meal. Sprinkle in ice water. Work into a ball that cleans the sides of the mixing bowl. (To mix in a food processor, place dry ingredients in work bowl, top with butter and shortening, and pulse until mealy. With machine running, pour in the ice water all at once. When dough forms a ball that knocks around the sides of the bowl, stop machine immediately.)

Flatten dough into a disk, wrap with plastic film and chill 30 minutes (or freeze), while you prepare the filling.

Roll dough to a circle 3 to 4 inches wider than pie plate, set in the plate, and trim with scissors so dough extends ¾ inch beyond rim. Fold this overhang under so it is even with plate's rim and crimp into large flutes. Chill while you prepare the filling.

For persimmon filling Set oven rack in the center of the oven and preheat oven to 450°. Scoop persimmon pulp out of skins, discarding seeds and leaves. Puree pulp in a food processor or blender.

Whisk together cream, flour, sugar, and melted butter. Beat together the yolks, the whole egg, and the vanilla and whisk into cream mixture. Fold in persimmon pulp. Pour filling into chilled pie shell. Top with a handful (about ½ cup) of praline crumble.

Bake 10 minutes at 450°. Reduce heat to 350° and bake 50 minutes to 1 hour more. Rotate pie if crust begins to over-brown, or cover rim with a foil strip. Filling will nearly boil when done.

For sticky pecan praline crumble Toast pecans on a cookie sheet at 350° about 10 to 15 minutes, tossing them a few times. (Nuts will start to smell toasted when they need to come out of the oven.) Butter another cookie sheet and set aside.

In a heavy saucepan, bring sugar, water, and cream of tartar to a boil over medium-high heat. (If crystals form on the sides of the pan, cover the pan for 30 seconds or as long as 5 minutes so steam rinses off the sides.) When the sugar darkens, you may swirl the pan to even the color. As caramel turns the color of light hay, remove from heat. Don't let the caramel get too dark, or the sugar will be too brittle to crumble, and it will snap instead.

Using a wooden spoon, stir in toasted nuts, mixing to coat them very well. Spread caramel-coated nuts out on the buttered cookie sheet, cool 1 hour, then chop coarsely with a knife (a food processor causes the caramel to stick and clump).

You can store the surplus in a tightly covered jar at room temperature for 3 months.

Makes 8 to 10 servings.

Mississippi Mud Pie

An eggy chocolate-corn syrup filling puffs as it bakes, then wrinkles and turns crusty as it cools. A mud sauce that doesn't completely set keeps the pie muddy for as long as it lasts.

Chocolatey crust
(For a 9-inch pie plate)

3 ounces (3 squares)
semisweet chocolate

10 to 11 double graham crackers

2 tablespoons brown sugar

4 tablespoons unsalted
butter, melted

Filling

1½ sticks (12 tablespoons)
unsalted butter

3 ounces (3 squares)
unsweetened chocolate

3 eggs

3 tablespoons light or
dark corn syrup

1⅓ cups sugar

1 teaspoon pure vanilla extract

Mud sauce

2 ounces (2 squares)
unsweetened chocolate

2 tablespoons unsalted butter

⅓ cup water

1 cup sugar

1⅓ cups light or
dark corn syrup

1 teaspoon pure vanilla extract

Tangy whipped cream

1 cup cream

1 cup sour cream, yogurt
"cream," or crème fraîche
(see page 19)

For crust Chop up the chocolate. Drop into an activated food processor and chop fine. Add graham crackers and process to very fine crumbs. (Or grate chocolate by hand, then place crackers between two sheets of waxed paper and crush fine with a rolling pin.)

Pour crumbs into bottom of 9-inch pie plate. Stir in brown sugar and warm melted butter. Using fingers, quickly press crumb crust up the sides and over the bottom of pie plate. Freeze while you prepare the filling.

For filling Set oven rack in the center of the oven and preheat oven to 350°.

In the top of a double boiler over barely simmering water, melt butter and chocolate. (Or microwave, uncovered, on Medium, stirring every 20 to 30 seconds after the first minute, until only a small solid chunk of chocolate remains.) Remove from heat and stir until melted and smooth. Cool slightly.

Whip eggs by hand until foamy (see Note). Then whip in remaining ingredients. Stir in melted chocolate. Pour mixture into crust and bake 50 to 60 minutes. The middle will rise and, when done, will appear unset. Cool on a rack, where the filling will shrink and crack, forming a basin for the sauce.

For mud sauce After pie bakes, melt chocolate with butter and water in a heavy saucepan over very low heat. Add sugar and corn syrup. Hold barely at a simmer for 10 minutes, stirring now and then to prevent sticking. Remove from heat and stir in vanilla. Yield: 2⅓ cups sauce.

For tangy whipped cream In a cold bowl with cold beaters, whip cream to medium-stiff peaks. Fold in sour cream.

To assemble Cool sauce a little, then pour 1¼ cups of it into the cooled pie. Cool again, but don't expect sauce to completely set.

When cool, serve each wedge garnished with some of the remaining sauce and a dollop of Tangy Whipped Cream.

Makes 8 to 10 servings.

Note: The pie will have a "muddier" consistency if the eggs are whipped by hand with a whisk.

Butterscotch Tarts in Pecan Shells

From the magic mind of Rick Whitnah, a California pastry wizard who first conceived of a Dessert Diner as a restaurant form, come these sweet butterscotch tarts. His mother used to make them. They're both regal and homespun.

The butterscotch mixture demands a strong arm. Plan on standing and stirring at the stove about 20 minutes.

You may also prepare this recipe as two 9-inch pies.

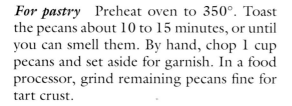

Tartlet pastry
2 cups pecans
3 cups flour
¼ cup brown sugar
2 sticks (½ pound) cold unsalted
  butter, in pieces
1 egg yolk
⅓ cup cream
2 to 3 tablespoons ice water

Butterscotch filling
2¼ cups milk
9 tablespoons unsalted butter
1½ cups brown sugar
¼ cup plus 2 tablespoons flour

12 egg yolks, in a bowl
1½ teaspoons pure
  vanilla extract

Burnt sugar syrup
2 cups granulated sugar
1 tablespoon corn syrup
1 tablespoon lemon juice
1 cup boiling water

**Burnt sugar-whipped
cream topping**
2 cups cream
2 tablespoons brown sugar
½ teaspoon pure vanilla extract
⅓ cup burnt sugar syrup
  (from above)

For pastry Preheat oven to 350°. Toast the pecans about 10 to 15 minutes, or until you can smell them. By hand, chop 1 cup pecans and set aside for garnish. In a food processor, grind remaining pecans fine for tart crust.

To continue by hand: Mix flour and brown sugar in a large mixing bowl. Cut in butter with a pastry blender until mixture resembles coarse sand (see Note 1). Stir in fine-ground pecans. Add yolk and cream and mix until mixture just holds together.

Add enough ice water to make dough moist enough to gather into a ball.

To continue with a food processor: Measure flour and brown sugar into work bowl. Top with butter and pulse until mealy. Add fine-ground pecans, yolk, and cream and pulse once or twice. With machine running, pour in the ice water all at once. When dough forms a ball that knocks around the sides of the bowl, stop machine immediately.

Flatten dough into a disk, wrap with plastic film, and chill 30 minutes (or freeze).

Set oven rack in the center of the oven and preheat oven to 350°. Roll out dough on a floured surface to fit 20 3½-inch rippled tartlet molds. Prick bottoms all over with a fork. (Or use 2 9-inch pie plates.)

Bake pastry 15 minutes, or until golden brown. Cool in molds on a wire rack. When cool, remove pastry shells from molds.

Makes 20 3½-inch pastry shells.

For butterscotch filling   Heat milk to just under a boil. In another saucepan, heat the butter until golden brown but not burned. Over medium-high heat, add brown sugar and flour and, whisking constantly, cook a full 2 minutes.

Whisk a little of the hot milk into the brown sugar mixture and stir until smooth. With heat set at medium-high, add the rest of the milk and cook, whisking well, until mixture starts to thicken. Whisk some of the hot mixture into the yolks, blend well, then whisk yolks back into the main butterscotch mixture. Continue to cook, whisking frequently, until butterscotch is very thick, which may take another 5 minutes. Remove from heat and stir in vanilla.

Scrape butterscotch filling into a bowl, stirring to cool. If lumps occur, pour through a strainer.

When cool, pour pudding into pastry shells (see Note 2).

For burnt sugar syrup   Bring sugar, corn syrup, lemon juice, and a few tablespoons of the water to a boil over medium-high heat. (If crystals form on the sides of the pan, cover for 30 seconds or as long as 5 minutes to allow steam to rinse off sides.) When caramel darkens, you may swirl the pan to even the color. Take the caramel to a medium mahogany. Just as it emits a burnt aroma, remove from heat and pour in the rest of the boiling water. (The mixture will bubble up, so stand back.) Return to heat and boil 1 minute more, stirring until sugar and water are smooth.

Cool a little. Pour into a measuring cup with a pour spout (to make it easier to add syrup to whipped cream later) and cool to room temperature (see Note 3).

For burnt sugar-whipped cream topping
In a cold bowl and with cold beaters, whip cream, brown sugar and vanilla just until cream starts to whip up. Add ⅓ cup burnt sugar syrup, pouring it in a thin stream and beating continuously to incorporate, until medium-stiff peaks form.

To assemble   Spoon on burnt sugar-whipped cream, or spiral it over each tart, using pastry bag with a plain tip with a large opening (see Note 4). May serve immediately.

Makes 20 servings.

Note 1: Set pieces of butter to be used for the crust on a plate and place in freezer while you prepare other ingredients, for maximum chill.

Note 2: This dessert tastes best assembled immediately before serving, without chilling the butterscotch. However, except for the whipped cream topping, the tarts can be put together and refrigerated for about a day. Add the whipped cream at serving time.

Note 3: Syrup will keep several days at room temperature or several weeks in the refrigerator.

Note 4: If you want to spiral the whipped cream from a pastry bag, chill the filled bag about 30 minutes to firm up the cream.

CHAPTER FOUR

Great Gooey Cakes

Gooey Butter Coffee Cake

A much-loved recipe from *Food Editors Hometown Favorites* was contributed by Barbara Gibbs Ostmann when she was food editor of the *St. Louis Post-Dispatch*. She wondered why no one except the people of St. Louis knew about this cake.

The cake's yeast base is a little dry, and so on its own would never be in this book. To compensate, the cake suffocates in gooey butter topping before baking.

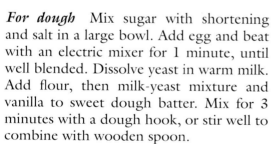

Sweet dough	**Gooey butter**
¼ cup sugar	2½ cups sugar
¼ cup solid shortening	2 sticks (1 cup) unsalted
¼ teaspoon salt	butter, softened
1 egg	Dash salt
1 cake (0.6-ounce) compressed	1 egg
yeast (or 1 package dry yeast)	¼ cup light corn syrup
½ cup warm milk	2¼ cups flour
2½ cups flour	¼ cup water
1 tablespoon pure vanilla extract	1 tablespoon pure vanilla extract
	Powdered sugar
	(to sprinkle on top)

For dough Mix sugar with shortening and salt in a large bowl. Add egg and beat with an electric mixer for 1 minute, until well blended. Dissolve yeast in warm milk. Add flour, then milk-yeast mixture and vanilla to sweet dough batter. Mix for 3 minutes with a dough hook, or stir well to combine with wooden spoon.

Turn dough out on a floured board and knead for 1 minute. Place in a lightly greased bowl, cover with a towel, and set in a warm place to rise for 1 hour.

For gooey butter Combine sugar, butter, and salt. Add egg and corn syrup. Mix enough to incorporate. Add flour, water, and vanilla.

To assemble Divide dough into 2 pieces. Place in 2 well-buttered 9-inch square pans. Crimp edges halfway up sides of pans so gooey butter will not run out and seep underneath. After dough is spread out, punch holes in dough with a fork (to keep the dough from bubbling when baking).

Spread gooey butter equally and evenly over dough in each pan. Preheat oven to 375°, and let cakes stand for 20 minutes.

Bake cakes for 30 minutes. Do not overbake, or topping will not be gooey. After cakes are cool, sprinkle tops with powdered sugar.

Makes 2 cakes.

Quick Gooey Butter Coffee Cake

Here is a version that bypasses yeast dough.

1 box pound cake mix or 1 box mix
for a 2-layer yellow cake
4 eggs, divided
1 stick (½ cup) unsalted butter, melted
1 8-ounce package cream cheese
1½ tablespoons pure vanilla extract
1 16-ounce box powdered
sugar, divided

Preheat oven to 300°. In a bowl, blend together cake mix, 2 eggs, and melted butter. Pour into an ungreased 12- by 8- by 2-inch rectangular baking dish. In another bowl, combine cream cheese, remaining 2 eggs, vanilla, and the powdered sugar minus 2 tablespoons. Mix well and spread over batter in dish.

Bake 15 minutes. Remove cake from oven and sprinkle reserved 2 tablespoons powdered sugar on top. Return to oven and bake 25 minutes longer. Do not overbake or topping will not be gooey.

Note: This coffee cake is good cold, but much better warm. And yes, this coffee cake really does require an entire box of powdered sugar, so don't skimp.

Italian Cream Cake

Very soft butter and cream cheese put the "cream" in cream cake. Rather than frost only three layers, I split each layer in half for a six-layer cake. This shortens the distance from frosting layer to frosting layer, combatting TLCD (Terminal Layer Cake Dryness) with frequently occurring encounters with goo.

Cake

1 stick (½ cup) unsalted butter
½ cup shortening
2 cups sugar
5 egg yolks
1 teaspoon baking soda
1 cup buttermilk
2 cups cake flour
1½ teaspoons pure vanilla extract
1½ cups packed shredded coconut
1 cup chopped pecans
5 egg whites

Italian cream frosting

2 sticks (½ pound) unsalted butter, softened
1 pound cream cheese, softened
2 teaspoons pure vanilla extract
2 1-pound boxes powdered sugar

For cake Grease and flour 3 8-inch cake pans. Set oven rack in the center of the oven and preheat oven to 350°.

Cream butter and shortening until light and fluffy. While beating, gradually add sugar and beat well. Beat in egg yolks, one at a time, until each is completely absorbed. Mix baking soda and buttermilk together and add to batter alternately with the flour. Stir in vanilla, coconut, and pecans.

Beat whites to stiff peaks. Gently fold into batter with wide strokes of a big rubber spatula. Divide batter evenly among the three prepared pans.

Bake cakes for 25 minutes. Cool in the pans, on racks, for 10 minutes. Invert onto racks and cool completely.

For frosting Beat all ingredients together until mixture has the consistency of sour cream.

To assemble Using a serrated knife, slice off browned or hardened areas of cakes, then split each in half horizontally. Fill and frost with Italian cream frosting. Chill frosted cake well before serving and try to eat it the day you make it.

Makes 16 to 20 servings.

Note: The cake is very tall. You might have to remove a rack in your refrigerator to accommodate the tower.

Fluffy Strawberry-Banana Cream Cake

Most children adore the combination of strawberries, bananas, and whipped cream. My nieces, nephews, and son love the flavor of this cake, and possibly find some additional pleasure in its gushiness.

The cake goes together quickly and may be made a day in advance, but wrap it well. You can save time by using a store-bought angel food cake.

Angel food cake
1 cup cake flour (sifted before measuring)

½ cup sugar

1½ cups egg whites (whites from 12 or 13 large eggs), at room temperature

1¼ teaspoons cream of tartar

1 teaspoon salt

1 cup additional sugar

2 teaspoons pure vanilla extract

Filling
2 cups cream

1 to 2 tablespoons sugar (to taste)

1 cup sour cream

2 pints fresh strawberries (or use 1 16-ounce bag frozen berries, thawed), in small dice

1 to 2 bananas, in small dice

For cake Set oven rack in the center of the oven and preheat oven to 350°. Mix flour with sugar and sift three more times.

In another bowl, beat egg whites, cream of tartar, and salt until stiff. (If whites are cold, hold bowl over a pan of hot water to warm them a little.) Gradually add remaining 1 cup sugar and beat until stiff again. Fold in vanilla.

Fold flour mixture, 2 tablespoons at a time, into the whites, using a big rubber spatula and making wide, gentle strokes.

Pour batter into 2 ungreased 9- or 8-inch round cake pans. Bake 25 minutes, or until the place where you press your finger springs back, or until a toothpick inserted in the center comes out clean.

Let cakes cool on a rack, upside down in their pans, for 1 hour. Run a thin knife around the rim of each pan to free any stuck areas. Go around each cake gently lifting up an inch at a time, using a thin frosting spatula. Cake will pull free. Remove layers from pans. Trim, if necessary, to make layers perfectly flat and round.

For filling In a cold bowl with cold beaters, whip cream and sugar to stiff peaks. Fold in sour cream.

To assemble Using a long, serrated knife, split each layer in half horizontally. To 1 cup whipped cream/sour cream mixture, add ½ cup diced strawberries and ½ cup diced bananas. Fill and frost layers. Use remaining whipped cream/sour cream mixture to frost outside of the entire cake. Garnish with leftover strawberries and bananas.

Chill at least 4 hours. You may have to touch up frosted areas as cake firms. At serving, press more bananas around bottom edge of the cake.

Makes 8 to 10 servings.

Beautiful Upside-Down Lemon Meringue Cake

An amazing lightness emanates from this dessert. Amidst whipped cream is a refreshing lemon layer reminiscent of the filling in a lemon meringue pie. But here, the meringue is under, rather than over, the lemon. This pretty cake makes a delightful finish to a luncheon or a summer supper. You'll need an enormous platter if serving it tableside. Otherwise, cut into squares in the kitchen and present on individual plates.

Meringue
6 egg whites
½ teaspoon baking powder
½ teaspoon lemon juice
1¼ cups sugar
½ teaspoon pure vanilla extract

Lemon filling
6 egg yolks
¾ cup sugar
Grated and minced zest
of 1 lemon

⅔ cup fresh lemon juice
(about 3 large lemons)

Whipped cream
2 cups cream
1 tablespoon powdered sugar
1 teaspoon pure vanilla extract

Candied violets, optional,
for garnish
12 to 15 whole strawberries,
for garnish

For meringue layer Set oven rack in the center of the oven and preheat oven to 300°. Line a 10- by 15-inch jelly-roll pan with parchment or waxed paper and grease generously.

Beat the egg whites, baking powder, and lemon juice to stiff peaks. Add sugar and again beat to stiff peaks. Fold in vanilla, then spread mixture in the prepared pan.

Bake 1 hour, or until meringue is light brown and crisp. If not crisp on top, turn off oven and leave meringue inside for an hour. Cool meringue completely, then invert onto another jelly-roll pan or cardboard liner (see Note) or onto a huge platter. Peel off paper. Trim any protrusions or uneven areas with scissors.

For filling In the top of a double boiler, beat the yolks, sugar, and zest until thick, about 1 minute. Add the lemon juice and beat again. Cook, stirring, over simmering water until mixture thickens. Strain into a bowl and cool.

For cream In a cold bowl with cold beaters, whip cream, sugar and vanilla to stiff peaks.

To assemble Spread about a third of the whipped cream over the meringue. Carefully spread the cooled lemon filling over the whipped cream without making streaks, covering the entire surface.

Place remaining whipped cream in a pastry bag with a medium star or plain tip.

Decorate the side of the cake, then the top in a lattice design. (If you like, garnish with candied violets at lattice intersections.)

Cut into squares and present on individual dessert plates, with a strawberry garnishing each serving.

Makes 12 to 15 servings.

Note: Cardboard liners that exactly fit the dimensions of a jelly-roll pan are available wherever cake-baking or wedding-cake supplies are sold.

Tres Leches Cake
(Cake of Three Milks)

Without question, this Nicaraguan dessert is the gooeyest I've ever eaten. A nine-egg cake is puddled in three milks—evaporated, sweetened condensed, and true cream.

The frosting is a form of Italian meringue. It works itself into a consistency that's gloriously sticky, sweet, soft, and swirlable. Long-time home bakers may recognize it as White Mountain Cream, Snow Peak Frosting, or Sweetheart Frosting, which should give you some idea of the visuals.

Because true Nicaraguan cream is thicker and a touch more acidic than American cream, sour cream may be mixed into the three-milk filling to simulate the taste of Latin *crema*. As for the evaporated milk, its taste is not subtle, but is dearly loved and expected by anyone who eats this cake.

The recipe comes from *Miami Herald* food editor Felicia Gressette, who didn't even pause when asked for a gooey dessert. The recipe appeared in the *Miami Herald* with the advice that "This is a very good dessert, but extremely fattening . . ." and that it must be served very cold.

A second advisory is: You must already own (or go borrow or buy), a platter large enough to hold a solid 9- by 13-inch cake with a border and rim wide enough to contain the drizzly filling. I recommend a large oval platter. Otherwise, cut the cake in half and frost each piece (see Note 1).

Cake
9 egg yolks
2 cups sugar
1 teaspoon pure vanilla extract
2 cups flour
½ cup milk mixed with 1 tablespoon baking powder
9 egg whites

Three-milk filling
3 egg yolks
2 cups cream (or combination 1 cup cream and 1 cup sour cream)

1 5-ounce can evaporated milk
1 14-ounce can sweetened condensed milk
1 teaspoon pure vanilla extract
1 tablespoon rum or favorite liqueur

Swirly frosting
½ cup water
1 cup light corn syrup
1½ cups sugar
3 egg whites

For cake Grease or butter a 9- by 13-inch glass baking pan. Set oven rack in the center of the oven and preheat oven to 350°.

Beat yolks and sugar until thick and pale, about 1 minute. Add vanilla. Add flour alternately with milk mixture. Beat egg whites to stiff peaks. Fold about a third of the whites into the batter, to lighten it, then fold in all the egg whites until completely blended. Pour batter into the prepared baking pan. Bake 30 to 35 minutes. Cool on a rack in the pan. When cool, invert onto a large serving platter with a rim (see Note 1).

For three-milk filling Beat the yolks well. Bring 1 cup of the cream to a boil. While beating, slowly pour cream into the yolks and continue beating until foamy and cooled (see Note 2). Add remaining cream and evaporated and condensed milks and beat thoroughly. Mixture will not peak. Add vanilla and rum.

For frosting Bring water, corn syrup, and sugar to a boil over medium-high heat. Cook until it's a clear syrup that can spin a thread (230° to 234°). If sugar browns, it will become too caramelized and frosting will be stiff.

Meanwhile, beat egg whites until stiff. Still beating, add the hot sugar syrup in a slow stream; continue beating about 5 minutes, or until glossy, fluffy, and stiffly peaked, and somewhat cooled.

For assembly When cake has cooled, punch holes in it with the end of a wooden spoon. Slowly pour the three-milk filling over the cake so it can absorb all the filling. Swirl frosting on sides and top of cake in big strokes. Refrigerate at least 3 hours or overnight.

Makes 16 servings.

Note 1: If you don't have a rimmed platter large enough to hold this cake and its oozing cream filling, cut the cake in half after cake cools. Place each half on a dinner plate and cover each with half of the filling and half of the frosting. Set the two cakes at either end of a buffet.

Note 2: The yolks in the filling are partially heated.

Meringue-topped Strawberry Trifle Cake

Baking this European-style cake from scratch is a time-consuming process. The elements are layered as in a trifle, then topped with fluffy meringue and browned; the cherry flavor of kirsch is mingled with cream and strawberries. To cut down on preparation time, use store-bought sponge cake and jam instead of homemade cake and the strawberry-caramel filling.

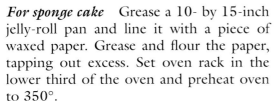

Sponge cake
5 egg yolks
½ cup sugar
1 cup cake flour, sifted
before measuring
1 teaspoon pure vanilla extract
5 egg whites
2 tablespoons sugar

Vanilla custard
2½ cups milk
5 egg yolks
3 tablespoons cornstarch
½ cup sugar
1½ tablespoons kirsch,
brandy, or vanilla extract

Strawberry-caramel filling
3 pint baskets fresh strawberries
(or 6 cups frozen)
1 cup sugar
½ cup water
Thick rind of an entire orange
⅓ to ½ cup kirsch
(brandy, rum, or bourbon)

Meringue
6 egg whites
¼ teaspoon cream of tartar
½ teaspoon pure vanilla extract
⅔ cup sugar

Garnish
¼ cup slivered almonds
2 tablespoons powdered sugar

For sponge cake Grease a 10- by 15-inch jelly-roll pan and line it with a piece of waxed paper. Grease and flour the paper, tapping out excess. Set oven rack in the lower third of the oven and preheat oven to 350°.

Beat the yolks and sugar together until very pale and thick, about 2 minutes (mixture should ribbon back into the batter when dropped from the beaters). Add flour to yolk mixture, beating at slow speed just until combined. Stir in vanilla.

Beat the egg whites to stiff peaks, gradually adding the 2 tablespoons sugar halfway through. Using a big rubber spatula, gently fold about a third of the whites into the yolks to lighten them, using wide strokes. Very gently add the remaining whites, folding until no white lumps remain.

Spread batter in the jelly-roll pan, using a frosting spreader to smooth the top. Don't bang the pan to settle the contents, or you'll lose valuable air cells. Bake 15 to 17 minutes, until lightly browned. A toothpick should come out clean.

Let the cake cool on a rack for 5 minutes, then run a thin knife around the edges to loosen stuck areas. Invert the cake onto another jelly-roll pan and slowly peel off the waxed paper. Invert cake onto a rack, top side up, to cool completely.

For custard   In a heavy medium-sized saucepan, warm the milk. Place a strainer over a large bowl set in a larger bowl of ice.

In a bowl (preferably with a pour spout), beat the yolks, cornstarch, and sugar together until smooth and ribbony, about 1 minute. Slowly whisk half the hot milk into the yolks, then pour the yolks back into the main milk mixture. Set over medium heat and slowly bring to a boil.

Boil, whisking constantly, for 1 minute. Custard will thicken quickly. Immediately strain. Stir in kirsch. Stir to cool.

Press plastic directly onto the surface of the custard to prevent a skin from forming, and chill about 2 hours.

For strawberry-caramel filling   Wash and hull strawberries. Puree half of them. Slice the remaining berries across and reserve.

In a heavy saucepan, bring sugar, ¼ cup of the water, and the orange rind to a boil over medium-high heat. (If crystals form on the sides of the pan, cover the pan for 30 seconds or as long as 5 minutes so steam rinses off the sides.) After sugar darkens, you may swirl the pan to even the color. Take the caramel to the color of pale honey. Off the heat, add remaining water, which will spatter. Return to heat briefly to stir out lumps.

Remove rind, then add strawberry puree and heat through. Add the strawberry slices and heat just until the slices soften, about 30 seconds to 1 minute. Transfer to a bowl to cool.

To assemble   Cube the cake. Arrange some pieces in the bottom of an attractive ovenproof 10- or 12-cup casserole. Sprinkle with half the kirsch. Spoon half the custard over the cake. Spread a good three-fourths of the strawberries over the custard. Layer again with cake, kirsch, remaining custard, and ending with remaining strawberries.

For meringue   Preheat oven to 400°. Beat the egg whites, cream of tartar, and vanilla to stiff peaks, gradually adding the ⅔ cup sugar halfway through.

Starting at the edge of the casserole, pipe or swirl meringue around edges of baking dish, making a seal. Then pipe or swirl the rest of the meringue all over the trifle cake. (This looks especially pretty if piped from a pastry bag fitted with a large star tip.)

Sprinkle with almonds and sift powdered sugar over the meringue. Set in oven 3 to 5 minutes, to lightly brown.

Makes 8 servings.

Crazy Cake

The crazy thing about Crazy Cake is its quaint methodological gimmick. The dry ingredients are combined in a baking dish, and the liquid ingredients are added separately into wells depressed in the dry ingredients—why, I don't know, because everything gets all stirred up anyway. It does bake up into a very moist cake, so moist, that it needs no frosting. One has been added anyway.

Cake batter
1½ cups sifted flour
1 cup sugar
3 tablespoons cocoa
1 teaspoon baking soda
½ teaspoon salt
6 tablespoons vegetable oil
1 tablespoon vinegar
1½ teaspoons pure
vanilla extract
1 cup cold water

Cream cheese frosting
8 ounces cream cheese, softened
½ cup powdered sugar
(or honey)
2 to 4 tablespoons milk,
for thinning
1 teaspoon pure vanilla extract

For cake   Set oven rack in the center of the oven and preheat oven to 350°.

Mix the flour, sugar, cocoa, baking soda, and salt very well directly in an ungreased 8-inch square baking dish. Be sure these ingredients are mixed thoroughly.

Make three depressions in the dry ingredients. Into one pour the oil. In the second add the vinegar. In the third add the vanilla. Pour the cold water over all. Stir all the ingredients together with a fork until nicely blended, but do not beat.

Bake for 30 minutes. Remove from oven and cool.

For frosting   Beat cream cheese and powdered sugar until fluffy. If necessary, thin with milk and beat until smooth. Mix in vanilla.

Spread cooled cake with frosting, cut into squares, and set on a serving platter.

Makes 9 squares.

Brenda's Texas Oatmeal Cake

My friend Brenda Bell calls this the health food of gooey desserts. It's got oatmeal, right? Yes, but it also drowns in an icing so sweet it numbs the imagination.

Oatmeal cake is based on a recipe from one of Brenda's old cookbooks from Mason County, Texas. It has made the rounds throughout most of Texas. Brenda's original instructions say to bake it "in one of those big one-layer cake pans you take to covered-dish suppers."

Cake
1½ cups boiling water
1 cup old-fashioned oatmeal
1 cup brown sugar
1 cup white sugar
1 stick (½ cup) butter or margarine, in pieces
2 eggs
½ teaspoon salt
1 teaspoon baking soda
1 teaspoon cinnamon
1½ cups flour

Icing
1 stick (½ cup) butter
½ cup brown sugar
½ cup cream (or evaporated milk or half-and-half)
1 cup shredded coconut
1 teaspoon pure vanilla extract

For cake Grease a 9- by 13-inch baking pan. Pour boiling water over oatmeal and let stand 10 minutes. Preheat oven to 350°.

Cream the sugars and butter until smooth, 1 to 2 minutes. Add eggs, then soaked oatmeal and remaining dry ingredients. Pour into prepared pan. Bake about 40 to 50 minutes.

For icing Melt butter in a saucepan, then mix in remaining ingredients. Spread on cake when it's still warm from the oven. Slip frosted cake under the broiler for a few minutes to get the topping bubbly and brown.

Makes 16 servings.

Gooey Four-Layer Coconut Cake

I think of this cake as the gang leader of gooey desserts. A custard filling oozes between the layers. Frosting is sticky and gooey all around. And canned coconut milk yields real coconut flavor without requiring the cracking of a single coconut.

Coconut custard filling
1¼ cups milk
1¼ cups coconut milk, shaken well
5 egg yolks
3 tablespoons cornstarch
½ cup sugar
1 teaspoon vanilla extract
1⅓ cups premium-quality shredded coconut

Cake
2⅔ cups cake flour
1½ teaspoons baking powder
½ teaspoon salt
2 sticks (1 cup) butter, in pieces
1¾ cups sugar

4 egg yolks
1½ teaspoons pure vanilla extract
1 cup coconut milk (see page 142)
½ cup premium-quality shredded coconut
4 egg whites

Coconut drizzle
1 cup coconut milk
1 teaspoon sugar

Swirly frosting
½ cup water
1 cup light corn syrup
1½ cups sugar
3 egg whites

For filling In a heavy medium-size saucepan, warm the two milks. Place a strainer over a large bowl set in a larger bowl of ice.

In a bowl (preferably with a pour spout), beat the yolks, cornstarch, and sugar together until smooth and ribbony, about 1 minute. Whisk half the hot milk into the yolks, then pour back into the remaining milk and slowly bring to a boil.

Boil, whisking constantly, for 1 minute. Custard will thicken quickly. Immediately strain. Stir in vanilla, and keep stirring to cool.

Spread shredded coconut on a cookie sheet. Toast at 350° about 15 minutes, or until lightly browned. Reserve ⅓ cup for top of cake. Add remaining coconut to custard. Press plastic wrap directly over the surface of the custard to keep a skin from forming, and chill for about 2 hours.

For cake   Grease 2 9-inch cake pans. Line with waxed paper traced to fit the bottoms of the pans. Preheat oven to 350°.

Sift dry ingredients together 3 times. In another bowl, cream butter with sugar until fluffy. Add yolks, one at a time, beating until each one is incorporated. Add vanilla. Alternately add coconut milk and dry ingredients to butter-egg mixture. Fold in the ½ cup shredded coconut.

Beat egg whites to stiff, glossy peaks, then gently fold into batter. Pour batter into the prepared pans. Bake 25 minutes. Cool in pans set on racks for 10 minutes. Run a knife around pans and turn cakes out on racks to cool completely.

For coconut drizzle   Mix together coconut milk and sugar and pour liquid over cake layers before frosting (see directions for cake's assembly).

For swirly frosting   Bring water, corn syrup, and sugar to a boil over medium-high heat. Cook until mixture is clear and can spin a thread (230° to 234°). If sugar browns, it will become too caramelized and frosting will be stiff.

Meanwhile, beat egg whites to stiff peaks. Adding the hot sugar mixture in a slow stream, beat it into the whites, and keep beating about 5 minutes, until glossy, stiff peaks form, and frosting is cool.

To assemble   Trim any hardened surfaces from cakes, then halve them horizontally, using a long serrated knife. Brush coconut drizzle on the layers with a pastry brush. Fill and frost cake with Swirly Frosting. Sprinkle reserved toasted coconut on top of cake.

Makes 16 servings.

Coconut "Milk"

I went to the store to buy a fresh coconut so I could use its milk and flesh in coconut cake. I pierced the coconut's eyes, and nothing came out—it had dried up! Shake the coconut at the store to make sure it's got all its moving parts. Listen for liquid.

The use of fresh coconut is not imperative. You can make alternative coconut "milk" by either of two methods:

1. Heat 1¼ cups milk with 1 cup shredded coconut to just under a boil. Remove from heat and cover for 30 minutes to infuse flavor. Strain, pressing down on solids, and proceed with recipe.
2. Combine 1¼ cups milk with 1 cup shredded coconut in a food processor or blender. Process 30 seconds to 1 minute. Strain, pressing down on solids, and proceed with recipe.

Easy Swirly Frosting

½ cup sugar

2 egg whites

2 tablespoons water

1 7-ounce jar marshmallow cream

½ teaspoon vanilla

Combine sugar, egg whites, and water in a double boiler. Beat with a hand-held electric mixer over boiling water until soft peaks form. Add marshmallow cream. Continue beating until stiff peaks form. Remove from heat and beat in vanilla.

Easy Chocolate-flavored Swirly Frosting

Melt and cool 2 ounces (2 squares) unsweetened chocolate. Fold into Easy Swirly Frosting.

Lemon Pudding-Cake

For a gooey-on-the-bottom sensation, place this pudding-cake in the oven timed to follow dinner, and eat it warm with whipped cream. The fragrance of lemon drifts from the oven just as this cake nears completion.

Pudding-cake
¼ cup flour
1 cup sugar
½ teaspoon salt
2 egg yolks
⅔ cup milk
2 teaspoons grated lemon zest

⅓ cup fresh lemon juice
(from 2 medium lemons)
2 egg whites

Chantilly cream
1 cup cream
1 tablespoon sugar
1 teaspoon pure vanilla extract

For pudding-cake Set oven rack in the lower third of the oven and preheat oven to 350°.

Sift the flour, sugar, and salt into a bowl. In another bowl, beat the yolks lightly. Stir in milk, zest, and lemon juice, mixing just until blended.

Beat the egg whites to stiff peaks. Fold into batter, which will be light and somewhat runny. Pour batter into a 1-quart baking dish of any shape but with 1½-inch sides. Set dish in a larger pan and fill with 1 inch of very hot tap water.

Bake 50 to 55 minutes or until top is golden brown. Serve warm with Chantilly Cream.

For chantilly cream In a cold bowl with cold beaters, whip cream, sugar, and vanilla at high speed to moderately stiff peaks. Store covered with plastic wrap in the refrigerator until ready for use, up to 24 hours. Yield: 2 cups.

Makes 6 servings.

Camille's Pineapple Upside-Down Cake

My friend Camille Glenn of Louisville, Kentucky, is the country's greatest cook. I say that with absolute conviction. Camille has cooked, taught, catered, and written articles about food for most of her life. Cooking on Louisville's WHAS-TV in the late '40s made her the country's first television chef. She studied at the Cordon Bleu and with James Beard. "I'm really just a country cook," she often says with a teasing self-deprecation. "But you must remember, honey, country cooking calls for the best and freshest of ingredients." The national food community finally caught up with her in 1986, when she wrote *The Heritage of Southern Cooking* at age 78.

Camille's sweet tooth has never been a secret. She loves desserts. Her many gifts to me include permission to use her best pineapple upside-down cake.

Pineapple layer	Cake
5 tablespoons melted butter	1 stick (½ cup) butter
1 cup light brown sugar	1 cup sugar
1 8-ounce can unsweetened pineapple slices, drained (see Note)	2 eggs
	1¾ cups sifted flour
Halved maraschino cherries (or pitted prunes)	1¾ teaspoons baking powder
	¼ teaspoon salt
	½ cup milk
	1 teaspoon pure vanilla extract

For pineapple layer Butter a 9-inch square cake pan and pour in the melted butter. Sprinkle with light brown sugar. Place pineapple slices attractively over the sugar. Place a cherry half (or a cooked, whole prune) in the center of each slice of pineapple. Set pan aside while you prepare the batter.

For cake Set rack in the center of the oven and preheat oven to 350°.

Cream the butter and sugar together thoroughly with an electric mixer. Add eggs and continue beating until the mixture changes to a lighter shade of yellow and falls in ribbons from a wooden spoon.

Sift flour together with baking powder and salt, and add mixture alternately with the milk, turning the mixer very slowly or blending by hand with a whisk (which is best). Add vanilla.

Pour batter over fruit. Bake about 45 minutes, or until cake springs back at once when lightly touched. Remove from the oven and let rest 5 minutes. Loosen the edges with a sharp knife. Put a plate over the pan and invert the cake onto the plate. Serve warm, cut into wedges.

Makes 9 servings.

Note: Canned or cooked dried apricots can be used instead of pineapple.

CHAPTER FIVE

Gooey in the Middle

Individual Caramel Lava Cakes

(From Cover)

A slow flow of caramel from the belly of an individual cake sluices like water over a damaged levee into a pool of chocolate and caramel sauces underneath. To me, this is what a gooey dessert is all about.

When making the cakes, it's important to beat the eggs and sugar for a long time. Turn on the mixer and go make a phone call. The batter will lighten to the color of Marilyn Monroe's hair and thicken like cream. The caramel is frozen into convenient plugs for easy insertion during baking.

If you don't have 1-cup ramekins, don't worry—I don't, either. Instead, I bake these cakes in coffee cups (including the one in the cover photograph).

Caramel plugs
1½ cups sugar
½ cup water
Pinch cream of tartar
½ cup cream
4 tablespoons unsalted butter

Little cakes
8 ounces (8 squares)
semisweet chocolate
1 stick (½ cup) unsalted butter

3 whole eggs
3 egg yolks
⅓ cup sugar
2 teaspoons pure vanilla extract
¾ cup flour

Lush chocolate sauce
8 ounces (8 squares)
semisweet chocolate
1 cup cream
½ cup sugar

For caramel plugs In a heavy saucepan, bring the sugar, water, and cream of tartar to a boil over medium-high heat. (If crystals form on the sides of the pan, cover the pan for 30 seconds or as long as 5 minutes so steam rinses off the sides.) When the caramel darkens, you may swirl the pan to even the color. Take the caramel to the color of iced tea.

Remove from heat and pour in cream. Caramel will spatter, so stand back. Return to heat and stir until smooth. Stir in butter until smooth, then remove from heat.

Pour ⅓ of the caramel into a shallow buttered dish, such as an 8-inch square baking dish. Chill very well. Form this cold caramel into 8 "plugs" about the size of walnuts, then put the pieces on a plate and freeze them. Reserve the remaining ⅔ caramel to rewarm later and use as sauce.

For cakes   Preheat oven to 425°. Heavily butter and then flour 8 1-cup ramekins, or use coffee cups. Set cups on a cookie sheet.

Chop chocolate into small even pieces. Melt with the butter in a double boiler over barely simmering water (or microwave, uncovered, on Medium, stirring every 20 to 30 seconds after the first 1 or 2 minutes, until only a small chunk of solid chocolate remains). Remove from heat and stir until melted, smooth, and cooled.

Beat eggs, yolks, and sugar together at high speed for 6 to 8 minutes. The mixture will turn the color of Marilyn Monroe's hair and become thick like cream. Fold in the cooled chocolate and vanilla. Sift the flour over chocolate and fold in.

Pour batter into prepared cups. Bake 7 minutes. Pull out of oven and tuck a frozen caramel plug deep into the center of the half-baked batter in each cup. Return to oven and bake for 6 to 7 minutes more. Cakes will rise straight over the rims of the cups, and may crack slightly.

Cool, in cups, on a wire rack for 10 minutes.

For lush chocolate sauce   Chop the chocolate evenly. In a saucepan, heat half the cream with the sugar until it boils. Remove from heat. Add chocolate and stir until it melts and sauce is smooth. Add remaining cream and stir again, patiently, until thick and smooth.

Warm the sauce gently for pouring. If allowed to set at room temperature, it will turn the consistency of sour cream and can be used like frosting. Makes 2 cups.

To assemble   Warm the remaining caramel sauce and make Lush Chocolate Sauce. Pour some caramel sauce on each plate, tilting so caramel coats the surface. Drizzle Lush Chocolate Sauce in a north-south zigzag over the caramel. Pull a toothpick, knife, or index card back and forth across the chocolate, going east-west, to create a feathering effect.

Run a thin knife around each cake to carefully loosen, then invert onto the sauce. Top with warm Lush Chocolate Sauce, letting sauce drip down the sides of the cakes. If desired, decorate with fresh berries. Serve warm. When cut, caramel will spill out of the warm cake.

Makes 8 individual cakes.

The Real Tunnel of Fudge Cake

My mother still has the circular paper insert from her first Nordic Ware Bundt cake pan. (The *B* is capitalized because the name is a registered trademark of Northland Aluminum Products.) This insert was really an advertisement for all the cakes a cook could turn out of a Bundt pan. On one side are pictures of the various cakes. On the other side, a recipe accompanies script that implores the cook to "try the recipe that won $5,000 in the Pillsbury Bake-Off!"

That recipe was the original Tunnel of Fudge Cake. But the recipe has evolved over time. The following is the current official version from Pillsbury.

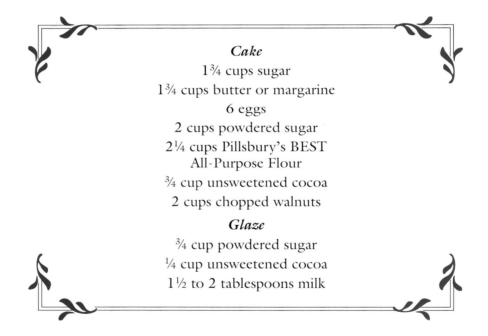

Cake
1¾ cups sugar

1¾ cups butter or margarine

6 eggs

2 cups powdered sugar

2¼ cups Pillsbury's BEST
All-Purpose Flour

¾ cup unsweetened cocoa

2 cups chopped walnuts

Glaze
¾ cup powdered sugar

¼ cup unsweetened cocoa

1½ to 2 tablespoons milk

For cake Heat oven to 350°. Grease and flour a 12-cup Bundt or 10-inch tube pan.

In a large bowl, combine sugar and butter or margarine; beat until light and fluffy. Add eggs, 1 at a time, beating well after each addition. Gradually add 2 cups powdered sugar; blend well. Lightly spoon flour into measuring cup; level off. By hand, stir in flour and remaining cake ingredients until well blended. Spoon batter into greased and floured pan; spread evenly. Bake at 350° for 58 to 62 minutes (see Note 2). Cool upright in pan on wire rack for 1 hour; invert onto serving plate. Cool completely.

For glaze In a small bowl, blend ¾ cup powdered sugar, ¼ cup cocoa, and enough milk for desired drizzling consistency. Spoon over top of cake, allowing some to run down sides. Store tightly covered.

Makes 16 servings.

Note 1: Nuts are essential to this cake.

Note 2: Because this cake has a soft filling of fudge, an ordinary test for done-ness cannot be used. Accurate oven temperature and baking time are essential.

The early Tunnel of Fudge was a cake designed to use many Pillsbury products. It creamed 1½ cups butter; added 6 eggs, one at a time; and gradually added 1½ cups sugar, beaten until light and fluffy. Two cups of Pillsbury's BEST Flour (Regular, Instant Blending, or Self-Rising could be used) were stirred in by hand.

Then came the secret ingredient — 1 package of Pillsbury Two-Layer Size Double Dutch Fudge Buttercream Frosting Mix, which formed the gooey center. Two cups of walnuts finished it off. It all went into a greased Bundt pan and baked at 350° for 60 to 65 minutes.

Things have changed since this recipe first appeared. Pillsbury discontinued Double Dutch Fudge Buttercream Frosting Mix. The cake was reconstituted so the gooey center now forms on its own.

Rothschild Omelet

It isn't really an omelet, and it isn't for rich people, although when it was first created, it was such a luxury that—as the saying went—only a Rothschild could afford all the eggs and sugar.

If you've got eggs and cream in the house, you've got an impromptu dessert. Each of three dinner-plate-size "omelets" is spread with enough jam to produce a gooey middle so rich that it oozes out the edges and melts its way down the omelet's warm sides. Then the whole thing is slathered with whipped cream. Obviously, there's no time to wait. You've got to serve this immediately.

---

7 egg yolks
½ cup flour
⅞ cup sugar
1 cup plus 2 tablespoons whole milk
7 egg whites

1 cup cream
Jam of choice (strawberry or peach—but even one of those boutiquey wine jellies would be great)

Generously grease 3 ovenproof dinner plates. Heat oven to 400°.

Whisk the yolks, flour, sugar, and milk together directly in a medium-size heavy saucepan, whisking until the mixture forms a smooth paste. Cook over medium heat, stirring gently and constantly, until the paste thickens, then remove from heat.

Beat the egg whites to soft peaks. Fold ¼ of the whites directly into the warm yolk base, using a big rubber spatula and making wide strokes. Then, for maximum air, fold the yolk-whites mixture back into the remaining whites, and fold some more.

Put ⅓ of the mixture on each plate, being careful not to let mixture go all the way to the rim. Bake the "omelets" all at once, arranged on all your oven racks, for about 15 minutes.

Meanwhile, in a cold bowl with cold beaters, whip the cream to medium-stiff peaks and keep cold until the batter is baked.

While omelets are still warm, spread one of them with jam. Put another omelet on top and spread it with jam. Repeat with the third omelet. Cover the stack with the whipped cream, which will begin to melt somewhat because of the heat, but in the process yield a luscious sauce.

Serve at once.

Makes 6 to 8 servings.

Poached Pears Stuffed with Cheese and Dried Fruits
(Served with "Apricot" Syrup)

I am at a loss to explain how a poaching liquid made with no apricots boils down to a syrup that develops an unmistakable apricot flavor.

Inside these pears is a lovely, soft center of cream cheese and brandied dried fruits (a deluxe version would use mascarpone cheese). This recipe never disappoints at a dinner party.

The dried fruits
¼ cup golden raisins
¼ cup minced prunes
¼ cup minced dried apricots
⅓ cup brandy

The pears
6 Bartlett pears, just underripe, stems on
2 tablespoons lemon juice

2 cups white wine, such as white table wine
½ cup sugar
Zest of 1 lemon
Zest of 1 orange
1 cup orange juice
¼ cup slivered almonds
½ cup softened cream cheese or mascarpone cheese (see Make Your Own Mascarpone Cheese, page 73)

For dried fruits Soak the raisins and minced fruits in the brandy.

For pears Peel the pears, leaving stems intact. Slice a thin, horizontal piece off the bottoms so pears will sit upright. With a melon baller, scoop out cores from the underside. As you work, place pears in a big bowl of cold water to which 2 tablespoons of lemon juice has been added. You'll be reserving 1 cup of this lemon water.

Stuff the pears' cavities with tin foil, to maintain shape during cooking. Stand pears in a Dutch kettle with a cover. Add wine, sugar, zests, orange juice, and the 1 cup reserved lemon water; liquid should come three-fourths of the way up the pears. (If not, add more wine or water.) Cover and bring to a simmer over medium heat. Simmer 20 minutes, or until a knife can pierce a pear at its thickest part with little resistance.

Using a slotted spoon, remove pears to stand on a plate. Boil down poaching liquid to make 1 cup, about 35 minutes. The liquid will become jammy and begin to taste like apricots. Pour it into a small pitcher and chill.

Meanwhile, toast the almonds on a cookie sheet in a 350° oven for 8 minutes, stirring occasionally. Blend the soaked fruit and the brandy with the cheese until smooth. Stir in the toasted almonds.

To stuff pears For ease, place cream cheese-fruit mixture in a pastry bag without a tip, and force the mixture into the pears' cavities (or use a small spoon to stuff mixture into pears). Stand pears, stems up, on a platter and chill.

To serve, pour cool poaching liquid syrup down the necks of the pears and let it pool on the plate.

Makes 6 servings.

Cream Puffs with Two Creams

When they work, they're easy, quick, and dependable. When they don't, go figure.

Success with this kind of pastry depends on subtle variables: the weather, the season, the degree of dryness of the flour, even the water-to-fat ratio of the eggs. As you can see, many of these are hard to evaluate, so in the end, you must judge your cream puff dough by other observations.

It is important to wait a few minutes before you begin adding eggs. After the last egg is added, the dough should hold its shape but still be sticky.

Watchfulness doesn't end there. The trick to making cream puff dough rise in the oven is bottom heat. When baking sheets are placed close to the heat source, the eggs expand and push the limits of the dough, and after a while, a shell hollow enough to hold a filling will form.

A word of caution. A hot humid day? No way! And don't use black bakeware.

The cream puffs
1 stick (½ cup) butter
½ cup water
½ cup milk
1 cup flour
4 eggs

Chocolate pastry cream
2½ cups milk
4 ounces semisweet chocolate
5 egg yolks
3 tablespoons cornstarch

⅓ cup sugar
2 teaspoons vanilla extract (or use Kahlua, raspberry liqueur, or amaretto, as you prefer)

Brandy pastry cream
1¾ cups milk
4 egg yolks
¾ cup sugar
½ cup flour
6 tablespoons butter, in pieces
2 tablespoons brandy (or vanilla extract)

For puffs Set oven rack in the lower third of the oven and preheat oven to 425°.

In a heavy saucepan, bring the butter, water, and milk to a boil. At the boil, add the flour, all at once; take the pan off the heat and beat the dough with a wooden spoon until it is smooth and leaves the sides of the pan. Set dough aside 3 to 5 minutes.

In the center of the dough, drop an egg. Beat well with the spoon until egg is completely absorbed. Repeat for each egg, beating until each is absorbed before adding another. Dough should be satiny and able to hold a shape.

Drop dough by tablespoons — or pipe quarter-size portions from a pastry bag fitted with a medium, plain tip — onto ungreased baking sheets.

Bake 15 minutes at 425°, then reduce temperature to 400° and bake 15 minutes more. Remove and prick puffs with a toothpick to release steam. If inside is still undercooked, return to 400° oven to dry out (but don't overbrown the puffs).

Make a dent in the side of each puff along its natural seam, through which to add a little of each pastry cream.

For chocolate pastry cream In a heavy medium-size saucepan, warm the milk.

Meanwhile, place a large fine-mesh strainer over a large bowl set in a larger bowl of ice.

Melt the chocolate in a double boiler over simmering water (or microwave, uncovered, on Medium, stirring every 20 to 30 seconds after the first 1 or 2 minutes, until only a small chunk of chocolate remains). Remove from heat and stir until melted and smooth.

In a bowl (preferably with a pour spout), beat the yolks, cornstarch, and sugar until smooth and ribbony, about 1 minute. Whisk half the hot milk slowly into the yolks, then pour yolk mixture back into the main milk base.

Add chocolate and bring mixture to a boil over medium heat, stirring. Allow to boil 1 minute, custard will become instantly thick. Immediately strain, then add vanilla. Stir custard to cool it down.

Chill cream with plastic wrap pressed on the surface to prevent a skin from forming. Makes 2¾ cups.

For brandy pastry cream In a heavy medium-size saucepan, warm the milk. Place a large fine-mesh strainer over a large bowl set in a larger bowl of ice.

In a bowl (preferably with a pour spout), beat the yolks, sugar, and flour together until smooth and ribbony, about 1 minute. Whisk the hot milk slowly into the yolks, then pour yolk mixture back into the main milk base and slowly stir, over medium heat, about 6 to 8 minutes. Custard will become thick and tight; immediately strain. Add butter, bit by bit, then the brandy, stirring to cool the mixture down.

Chill pastry cream with plastic wrap pressed on the surface to prevent a skin from forming. Makes 2¼ cups.

To assemble Through seam opening in each cream puff, add equal amounts of chocolate and brandy pastry cream fillings.

To serve Arrange on an attractive platter and sprinkle with powdered sugar.

Makes 2 dozen cream puffs.

Croquembouche

(Tower of Caramel-coated Cream Puffs)

In this presentation, caramel-coated cream puffs are arranged to form a towering sticky cone like a stylized Christmas tree.

The cream-puff tower is wrapped in spun sugar that picks up light and makes people gawk. Trust me, this isn't difficult. The only hazard is that once you get the feel of the pull-and-drape motion, you won't want to stop. But don't cloak your creation in a tangled web. Keep it looking wispy. And for this special exercise, beware of humidity.

Croquembouche has become a trendsetting showstopper at weddings: each guest gets a filled puff from the cone, surrounded by crème anglaise and a dollop of fruit puree.

The cream puffs

Prepare 1 recipe Cream Puffs as directed (page 157). Fill them with Brandy Pastry Cream (page 157).

4 cups sugar

1 recipe Crème Anglaise
with Cinnamon (page 38)

1 recipe Strawberry Puree (page 24)

For caramel coating   Cover a baking sheet with waxed paper. In a heavy saucepan, bring 2 cups of sugar to a boil over medium-high heat. (If crystals form on the sides of the pan, cover for 30 seconds or as long as 5 minutes so steam can rinse off the sides.) When the sugar darkens, you may swirl the pan to even the color. Take the caramel to a light amber, no darker.

Remove pan from heat. (If sugar cooks too long and turns too dark, it will harden and become an unchewable shell around the puffs.) Pick up a filled cream puff carefully with tongs. Dip top side of puff in the caramel, swirling to coat. Let excess drip back into saucepan. Set each puff on waxed paper, right side up.

Cover a 9-inch cardboard round with foil. Arrange a circle of puffs around the circumference of the cardboard, their shiny tops tilted outward. Fill in with a smaller circle, and then another, until a 12-inch-tall cone is created. Puffs will generally stick together, although you may need a few toothpicks to keep them in place. Save a nicely formed puff for top. The dessert will keep 2 days in a cool place.

For spun sugar   Wait until shortly before serving time, especially if weather is humid. Heat the remaining 2 cups sugar without disturbing, as directed for the caramel coating (above), until sugar is a medium mahogany and hot enough (320°) to spin a hard thread from a fork dipped into it and held up high.

Dip a two-pronged barbecue fork into the caramel. Letting large drips fall back into the saucepan, wait for the threads to form just under the tines; then quickly wrap the entire cream puff tower with spun sugar, pulling fork toward you to stretch out the thread, and draping the thread as you go. When the thread gives out, repeat with another dip of the fork. (You won't want to stop!)

Continue spinning sugar around the dessert until it is veiled in threads of golden sugar. Serve as soon as possible.

To serve   Line individual dessert plates with a ladleful of Crème Anglaise with Cinnamon. Toward one side of this creamy pool, add a dollop of Strawberry Puree. Draw the point of a piece of cardboard through the strawberry dollop several times in different directions, making a red spray design. At the opposite side of the plate, place a cream puff from the Croquembouche.

Makes approximately 24 servings.

Fried Custard

Fried custard comes to me from an Italian friend who serves this after the feast on All Saints' Day. The custard is a tightly whipped pastry cream bound strongly with flour. It is chilled until firm enough for cutting — about the consistency of cream cheese. Cut it into diamonds or squares, or if you're all thumbs, just gather it up any old way. The flavor of this has hints of cinnamon and lemon. You'll need a candy thermometer to know when the oil is the right temperature.

2 ¼ cups milk
1 vanilla bean or 1 ½ teaspoons
pure vanilla extract
1 ¼ cups flour
½ teaspoon ground cinnamon
Pinch salt
½ teaspoon finely grated
lemon zest
2 whole eggs

6 egg yolks
½ cup sugar

3 additional beaten eggs,
for dipping
2 to 3 cups fresh cake crumbs
or bread crumbs

Powdered sugar
Grand Marnier, optional

Butter an 8-inch square pan. In a heavy medium-size saucepan, barely boil the milk with the vanilla bean. Split the bean lengthwise, scrape it with the back edge of a knife, and add it to the cream—seeds, pod and all. (If you're using vanilla extract, add it after the custard has cooked.)

Sift together the flour, cinnamon, and salt. Stir in lemon zest and set mixture aside.

Beat the eggs, yolks, and sugar together in another heavy pot. While whisking, slowly add the hot milk. Then add the flour mixture, whisking well to combine. Switching to a wooden spatula, stir mixture constantly over medium heat until it thickens. When mixture boils, stir hard for 2 FULL minutes: the custard should stand up in peaks. Remove from heat. (If using vanilla extract, add it now.)

Spread custard in the buttered pan. It will look sandy. Chill until set—about 4 hours, or overnight.

Cut cold custard into diamonds or other attractive shapes. Dip each diamond into beaten egg, then roll in crumbs. Deep-fry in oil or shortening heated to 350° on a candy thermometer. The diamonds will sink at first. When they are golden brown and float, they're done. (Fried custard should not be doughy, but smooth inside.)

Drain on paper towels, then arrange on a pretty platter. Sprinkle with powdered sugar and, if you like, a few drops of Grand Marnier.

Makes about 8 servings, depending on the size of your fried custard pieces.

Cream Cheese Baskets with Gloria's Lemon Curd

A soft and passion-inducing basket is a luxurious container for soft and pillowy lemon curd. For speed, prepare the curd ahead so it can chill while you make the baskets.

If you like, you could fill these baskets with something other than lemon curd—something fruity and custardy, such as White Chocolate Passion Fruit Mousse (page 105).

This is a beautiful luncheon dessert.

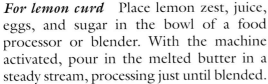

Lemon curd	**Cream cheese baskets**
4 teaspoons finely grated lemon zest	1 8-ounce package cream cheese, very soft
⅔ cup lemon juice	½ cup sugar
5 eggs	1 teaspoon pure vanilla extract
1 cup sugar	1 teaspoon lemon juice
1 stick (8 tablespoons) unsalted butter, melted	1 cup heavy cream
	Raspberry puree (page 24)

For lemon curd Place lemon zest, juice, eggs, and sugar in the bowl of a food processor or blender. With the machine activated, pour in the melted butter in a steady stream, processing just until blended.

Scrape mixture into a small heavy saucepan and cook over medium heat, stirring constantly and fast, about 5 minutes, or just until curd begins to bubble and thicken. Immediately remove from heat. Pour through a large fine-mesh strainer into a bowl.

Cool slightly. To store, press plastic wrap directly onto the surface of the curd and chill.

For cream cheese baskets Beat cream cheese, sugar, vanilla, and lemon juice just to blend.

In a cold bowl with cold beaters, whip the cream to medium-stiff peaks. Fold a scoop of whipped cream into beaten cheese to loosen the cheese so it will blend with the rest of the cream. Fold remaining cream into cheese until smooth. Chill until ready to assemble dessert.

To assemble At serving, place cheese in a pastry bag fitted with a medium plain or rippled tip. Pipe out 1 round "basket" (forming bottoms and sides) directly onto each of 10 small dessert plates.

Fill each basket with lemon curd. Decorate bare spots on plates with raspberry puree.

Makes 10 servings.

How to Can Lemon Curd

Before you prepare the curd, have ready 3 jelly jars (½-pint size) that have been washed and run through the dishwasher or sterilized 20 minutes in boiling water. Prepare caps and screw bands according to the manufacturer's directions. Keep jars hot until ready for use.

Prepare the curd as directed. Remove from heat and ladle hot curd into hot jars to within ¼ inch of rims. Adjust lids and screw bands. Set aside, undisturbed, in a cool place, spacing jars 2 inches apart, to cool. Curd will keep at room temperature for 1 month.

You can also pour the lemon curd into freezer containers, cool, cover, and freeze for several months. If stored in refrigerator, the curd will keep 1 week.

Makes 3 cups curd.

Note 1: I like to use lemon curd as a base for mousse—that is, fold 1 cup cream, whipped, into the curd so it becomes moussey, lighter. Serve this mounded in wine goblets.

Note 2: If you don't want to make your own lemon curd, use store-bought lemon curd. You'll need about 3 cups.

CHAPTER SIX

Sticky Gooey Candy, Bars and Buns

Burnt Sugar Candy

These caramels are the purest of candies. They're made with just two ingredients, but the cook experiences a journey through the precise chemical properties of sugar and heat. Sugar, the first ingredient, is caramelized on its own before it is ever introduced to the half-and-half, the second (and base) ingredient. The result is the ultimate in stretchy, rich caramel.

After cutting the caramel in squares, it is best to roll the pieces between dry palms into balls, then wrap the candy balls in waxed paper. I like to give these out at Halloween, after asking many children to help with the wrapping.

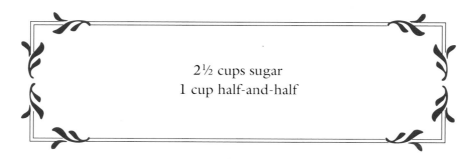

2½ cups sugar
1 cup half-and-half

Generously butter an 8-inch square baking pan.

Place 1 cup of the sugar in a large heavy saucepan such as a 4- to 5-quart soup pot. Heat over medium-high heat, without disturbing, to 300° to 320°, or until amber-colored.

Meanwhile, place the half-and-half and remaining sugar in a heavy saucepan, stir to dissolve sugar, and warm over low heat just to melt the sugar.

Slowly add the hot sugar-cream to the amber syrup. Continue to cook over medium-high heat to the soft-ball stage (235° to 240°). Remove from heat and stir vigorously with a wooden spoon until foam subsides and mixture becomes creamy, about 1½ minutes.

Pour into prepared pan. When cool, cut into 1-inch squares. With dry palms, roll into balls, then wrap each ball in waxed paper. (The end-twist wrap used for taffy is attractive.)

Makes about 5 dozen.

Note: These will keep stored in a dry, cool room for several weeks. Serve with ice cream or with other wrapped candies at Halloween or holiday time.

Creamy Cream Caramels

A difference of just three or four degrees on a candy thermometer can mean the difference between caramel that's soft and pliant and caramel that's firm as a lollipop. I prefer the texture of these caramels when cooking is stopped between 238° and 240°. If the mixture gets hotter, the caramels will be too firm. Please don't try to make these particular candies without a candy thermometer!

Also, because the bubbles of this boiling mixture are of geyser proportions, use a large kettle to ensure that your mixture will not boil over and stick on top of your stove.

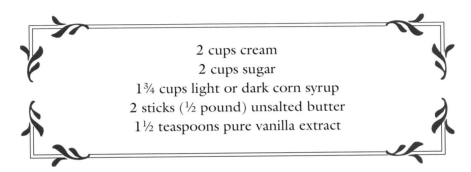

2 cups cream
2 cups sugar
1¾ cups light or dark corn syrup
2 sticks (½ pound) unsalted butter
1½ teaspoons pure vanilla extract

Generously butter an 8-inch square baking pan.

In a Dutch kettle or heavy 4- to 5-quart soup pot, bring 1 cup of the cream, the sugar, the corn syrup and the butter to a rolling boil. Slowly add the remaining cup of cream, making sure that the mixture keeps boiling.

Continue cooking to the soft-ball stage (between 235° and 240°). Off the heat, stir in vanilla. Pour into prepared pan.

Cool and cut into 1-inch squares. Wrap pieces in waxed paper or wrap in the end-twist style, like taffy. For a festive touch, wrap in colored foil.

Makes about 5 dozen.

Persimmon Fudge

In autumn, when an abundant crop of persimmons can challenge your creativity, this homey fudge comes to the rescue. The boiling mixture warms the house. See page 122 for more information on persimmons.

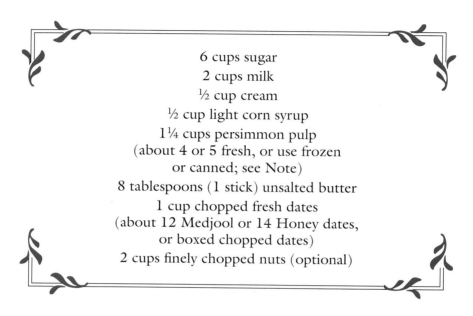

6 cups sugar
2 cups milk
½ cup cream
½ cup light corn syrup
1¼ cups persimmon pulp
(about 4 or 5 fresh, or use frozen
or canned; see Note)
8 tablespoons (1 stick) unsalted butter
1 cup chopped fresh dates
(about 12 Medjool or 14 Honey dates,
or boxed chopped dates)
2 cups finely chopped nuts (optional)

In a large, heavy pot, mix sugar, milk, cream, corn syrup, and persimmon pulp. Cook over low heat, stirring frequently, for 1 to 2 hours, or until mixture reaches the soft-ball stage (235° to 240°). Meanwhile, butter a 9- by 13-inch baking pan.

When fudge is the proper temperature, remove from heat and cool in the pan until barely warm. Using a wooden spoon, beat in the butter. When mixture thickens and butter is absorbed, add dates.

Spread fudge in the prepared pan. When completely cool, cut into small squares. (If desired, squares may be rolled into balls and then rolled in chopped nuts.) Chill 1 day. May freeze 3 weeks.

Makes 10 dozen or more pieces, depending on size.

Note: To prepare persimmons, scoop soft persimmon pulp out of skins, discarding seeds and leaves. Puree in a food processor or blender.

How to chop dates Chop with a chef's knife (with a blade 6 to 8 inches long) dusted with powdered sugar to keep dates from sticking. Or cut dates with scissors.

Self-Made Millionaires

If pecans are arranged in spokes, they become caramel-covered "paws" for Turtles. If they're clustered any old way, they're still a success—as with Millionaires.

Because this is a Texas recipe, these candies go by the name of Self-Made Millionaires. If you want to make your own caramel, use the recipe for Stretchy Caramel and chill (see page 170). But know it's only the nouveau-riche route to millionaire status.

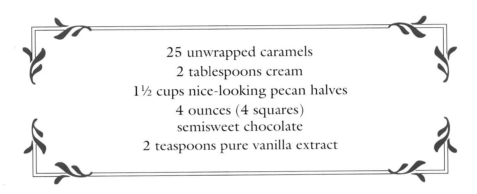

25 unwrapped caramels
2 tablespoons cream
1½ cups nice-looking pecan halves
4 ounces (4 squares)
semisweet chocolate
2 teaspoons pure vanilla extract

In a double boiler over simmering water, melt caramels with cream. Remove from heat and let cool.

Meanwhile, lightly grease a cookie sheet. Arrange clusters of pecans in groups of 4 in rows down the sheet. (For Turtles, arrange pecans in spoke fashion.) Spoon a blob of melted caramel over the center of each pecan group, leaving tips exposed. Let set 30 minutes.

In a double boiler over barely simmering water, melt the chocolate (or microwave, uncovered, on Medium, stirring every 20 to 30 seconds after the first 2 minutes, until only a solid chunk of chocolate remains). Remove from heat and stir until melted and smooth. Add vanilla and cool slightly. Drop chocolate from a spoon over the caramel, again keeping the tips of the pecans exposed. Let set at room temperature. Store in a single layer on waxed paper.

Makes about 2 dozen.

Creamy Tia Maria Penuche

Penuche differs from fudge in two ways: (1) some fudge is cooked, but all penuche is cooked; and (2) some fudge uses brown sugar, but all penuche uses brown sugar. Penuche is taken to the soft-ball stage, at which temperature the sugar becomes highly concentrated.

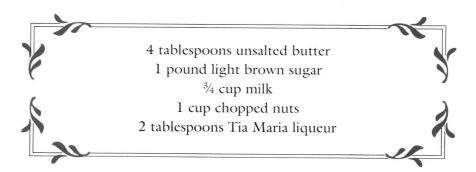

4 tablespoons unsalted butter
1 pound light brown sugar
¾ cup milk
1 cup chopped nuts
2 tablespoons Tia Maria liqueur

In a heavy saucepan, melt 2 tablespoons of the butter. Add sugar and milk and stir well. Cook over low heat, stirring occasionally, until candy reaches the soft-ball stage (235° to 240°).

Remove from heat and add remaining butter *without* stirring. When candy has cooled (sides of pan will be barely warm), add nuts and liqueur. Beat until candy is no longer glossy. Spread in a buttered 8-inch square pan. Cool completely, then cut into squares.

Makes about 5 dozen.

S'mores Bars

I went to two weeks of overnight camp when I was about 8. It was with girls I never really got to know. One night, we were told we would not be sleeping in our cabin. We hiked with sleeping bags to a campsite where we knew there were snakes. Then we were forced to eat from foil tins and sing. When darkness fell, we made that classical campers' distraction, S'mores.

We each pierced a big marshmallow with a straightened coat hanger, held it over a campfire with no sense of timing, and sandwiched burned marshmallows coated in crispy black bubbles between graham crackers lined with chocolate bars. The predicted next utterance was to have been "s'more."

(Can't you just hear the wails of modern advocacy groups opposing the use of coat hangers and taking all the fun out of outdoor camping because children might poke their eyes out? To this day I wish a grown-up had intervened on my behalf about the snakes . . .)

Here, the S'mores of yore have been reinterpreted in a bar made entirely indoors, no camp, no snakes.

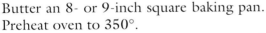

8 tablespoons (1 stick) unsalted butter or margarine
¾ cup packed brown sugar
½ teaspoon pure vanilla extract
1 cup flour
½ cup graham-cracker crumbs (from 4 or 5 double crackers, crushed in a food processor or rolled between 2 sheets of waxed paper with a rolling pin)
8 ounces (8 squares) semisweet chocolate (or 1½ 6-ounce bags or 1½ cups semisweet chocolate chips)
2 cups miniature marshmallows

Butter an 8- or 9-inch square baking pan. Preheat oven to 350°.

Cream butter and brown sugar until fluffy. Add vanilla, flour, and graham-cracker crumbs and mix on low speed, then medium speed, until crumbs form a meal that can be pressed together. Press into prepared pan. Bake 12 to 15 minutes. Cool.

Sprinkle with chocolate chips and marshmallows. Bake 15 to 20 minutes, then run under broiler for 20 to 30 seconds for that campfire-singed look.

Cool and cut into bars with a non-serrated knife.

Makes 16 bars.

Crispy Rice Bars Dipped in Chocolate and Stretchy Caramel

I don't remember ever eating these at night, only after school, in the afternoon. For any stage of childhood (which can coincide with many stages of adulthood), these sticky goodies can't help but bring back those few sunny hours between instruction and supper. With their smudges of caramel and chocolate, they made little hands messy—and, thus, homework impossible.

Bars
4 tablespoons (½ stick)
unsalted butter
4 cups miniature marshmallows
(or 40 big ones, cut into pieces)
6 cups rice cereal
2 cups (1 12-ounce package)
semisweet chocolate chips
3 tablespoons water

Stretchy caramel (see Note)
¾ cup sugar
¼ cup water
¼ cup heavy cream
2 tablespoons butter, in pieces

For bars Butter a 9- by 13-inch pan. Melt butter in a large saucepan over low heat. Add marshmallows, and cook, stirring, until melted and smooth. Remove from heat. Add cereal and half the chocolate chips, stirring gently to coat.

Press the sticky mixture into the prepared pan. Cool completely. Cut into squares.

For stretchy caramel In a heavy saucepan, bring sugar and water to a boil over medium-high heat. (If crystals form on the sides of the pan, cover the pan for 30 seconds or as long as 5 minutes so steam can rinse off the sides.) When the sugar darkens, you may swirl the pan to even the color. Take the caramel to the color of iced tea.

Remove from heat and carefully pour in cream, stirring. The caramel will bubble up. Add butter, stirring until melted. Yield: 1½ cups.

To dip In a double boiler over barely simmering water, melt remaining 1 cup chocolate chips with 3 tablespoons water; stir until smooth.

Dip the top of each square into melted chocolate. Set plain side down, on waxed paper-lined cookie sheet to cool. When cool, drizzle with Stretchy Caramel. Chill.

Makes about 2 dozen.

Note: In place of Stretchy Caramel, melt about 25 caramel candies and mix with 2 tablespoons cream (or milk).

Desperate for Caramel-Walnut Bars

One of the happiest days of my life came when my friend Andrea Litton, a former bakery owner and pâtissière, now a nurse, gave me this recipe—and I don't even like nuts! If anything can make walnuts good, it is the special caramel bedding they're snuggled in here.

The caramel poured over the walnuts comes from a two-step process. First, the base caramel is cooked to the color of iced tea. Second, cream and butter are introduced, and the caramel cooks again—this time achieving a perfect consistency.

The reason I've used the term "desperate" in naming these wonderful bars is because when I served them at a wedding, the guests were desperate to eat them, then became as desperate for the recipe as I had been.

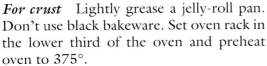

Shortbread crust

⅔ cup sugar

15 tablespoons unsalted butter, at room temperature

2⅔ cups flour

1 pound good-looking walnuts, in large pieces

Andrea's rich and chewy caramel

2¼ cups sugar

¾ cup light corn syrup

¼ cup water

6 tablespoons unsalted butter

¾ cup heavy cream

For crust Lightly grease a jelly-roll pan. Don't use black bakeware. Set oven rack in the lower third of the oven and preheat oven to 375°.

With an electric mixer, cream the sugar with the butter until pale and fluffy. Add flour and combine briefly (use paddle attachment, if you have one) until dough holds together. Finish combining with hands. Press dough over the jelly-roll pan, making a slight rim up the sides. Prick all over (EVERYWHERE!) with a fork.

Bake until barely golden, about 20 to 25 minutes. Cool in the pan. When cool, spread walnuts in an even layer over the dough.

For caramel In a heavy saucepan, combine and stir well the sugar, corn syrup, and water. Cover and boil gently until the color of iced tea, about 35 minutes. Do not let the sugar become dark. Add butter and whisk around until *completely* incorporated.

Stand back, and carefully add cream (caramel will spatter angrily). Whisk until smooth. Continue to cook at a low boil, uncovered, for 10 to 15 minutes.

At this point, check for consistency by dropping a sample of caramel on a cool plate. When cool enough to touch, pinch it between your forefinger and thumb: if it pulls away in a string, it is probably done. Now, taste-test by sampling a cooled drop. If it is chewy, it is done. (But if it sticks hard to your teeth, it's past done and needs more cream to bring it back.)

Remove caramel from heat and cool somewhat. Pour it over all walnuts, filling in corners and crevices. Allow to cool. Do not refrigerate.

When cool, cut in squares and seal air-tight to store.

Makes about 3 dozen.

Sticky Gooey Brownies

The requirements for entering this book are more than met by sticky, gooey brownies, which are swirled with melted marshmallows and droozled (that's a combination of drizzle and ooze) with chocolate sauce. Work the chocolate sauce into the marshmallows after the chocolate has barely cooled. The goal is a swirl, not a blend.

Brownies
4 ounces (4 squares)
semisweet chocolate
½ cup (1 stick) unsalted butter
4 eggs
2 cups sugar
¼ teaspoon salt
1 cup sifted flour
1 teaspoon pure vanilla extract
1 cup chopped pecans, divided

1 6-ounce package
semisweet chocolate chips
12 large marshmallows

Chocolate sauce
2 ounces (2 squares)
unsweetened chocolate
6 tablespoons water
½ cup sugar
3 tablespoons butter
¼ teaspoon vanilla

For brownies Butter an 8- or 9-inch square baking pan. Set oven rack in the center of the oven and preheat oven to 350°.

Melt the chocolate and the butter in the top of a double boiler over barely simmering water (or microwave, uncovered, on Medium, stirring every 20 to 30 seconds after the first minute, until only a small solid chunk of chocolate remains). Remove from heat and stir until melted and smooth.

In a bowl, beat together the eggs, sugar, salt, flour, vanilla, and ½ cup of the pecans. Add melted chocolate mixture, then transfer batter to the prepared baking pan. Pat chocolate chips and remaining ½ cup pecans on top.

Bake for 40 minutes. Meanwhile, halve marshmallows and make chocolate sauce.

Remove brownies from oven and reduce oven temperature to 325°. Place marshmallow halves on top of brownies. Return to oven for 5 minutes, or until marshmallows are slightly browned on top.

Pour chocolate sauce over marshmallows and allow to cool slightly. Swirl sauce lightly into marshmallows, and let set.

For chocolate sauce Melt chocolate with water over low heat, stirring until smooth. Add sugar. Cook, stirring, until smooth and slightly thickened. Stir in butter and vanilla.

Orange-Walnut Squares

This recipe is so rich that the finished product must be cut into small squares.

Bottom layer
8 tablespoons (1 stick) butter
1 cup sifted flour

Sticky walnut layer
1½ cups packed brown sugar
2 eggs, well-beaten
2 tablespoons flour
1 teaspoon pure vanilla extract
½ teaspoon salt

¼ teaspoon baking powder
1 cup chopped walnuts
2 cups flaked coconut

Orange syrup
1½ cups sifted powdered sugar
2 tablespoons melted butter
2 tablespoons orange juice
1 teaspoon lemon juice
1 teaspoon grated orange zest

For bottom layer Set oven rack in the center of the oven and preheat the oven to 350°.

With an electric mixer, combine the butter and flour until a mixture forms that holds together. With hands, press mixture over the bottom of a 9-inch square baking pan. Bake 15 minutes.

For walnut layer Mix brown sugar, eggs, flour, vanilla, salt, and baking powder until thoroughly blended. Stir in nuts and coco-nut. Spread over baked crust, then return pan to oven for 25 minutes. Cool.

For orange syrup layer In a bowl (prefer-ably with a pour spout), stir powdered sugar, melted butter, orange juice, lemon juice, and orange zest until smooth. Pour over walnut layer, spreading smooth. Let topping set 1 hour before cutting into squares.

Makes about 3 dozen.

Lips of the Beauty
(Fritters in Syrup)

In Middle Eastern cooking, dessert often consists of fritters served with a sticky syrup. When the fritters take on shapes explicit enough to cue the imagination, you get names like Lips of the Beauty . . . or Lady's Navel.

This recipe is from Narsai David, the San Francisco radio food host and former Berkeley restaurant owner. He says that Mesopotamian breads and desserts took on such anatomical shapes as a heart or a woman's breast as early as 1700 B.C.

The fritters here are shaped into innocent-looking rounds, but you can use your creativity.

Syrup
1½ cups water
1½ cups sugar
1 teaspoon lemon juice
1 tablespoon orange-flower or rose water

Fritters
1½ cups water
1 stick (½ cup) butter
1½ teaspoons sugar
1¾ cups flour
4 eggs
Light salad oil

For syrup Put the water, sugar, and lemon juice in a small saucepan and boil for a few minutes until the mixture becomes syrupy. Remove the syrup from the heat and cool. Stir in the orange-flower or rose water. Reserve.

For fritters Heat the water, butter, and sugar in a small saucepan until the butter melts and the mixture starts to boil. Add the flour all at once and stir with a wooden spoon until the mixture dries out a bit and starts to pull away from the sides of the pan.

Remove from the heat and add the eggs, one at a time, stirring vigorously with each addition until the batter becomes smooth and glossy. Add the next egg, and continue in the same manner until all 4 eggs have been added to the batter.

Pour about 2 inches of light salad oil into a Dutch oven, a 4- to 5-quart soup kettle, or other deep pot and heat until it reaches 375° on a candy or deep-frying thermometer. While the oil is heating, form the dough into small balls, about the size for hors d'oeuvres, dipping your hands in flour to help shape the dough. (If you prefer, you can shape the dough Turkish-style into a fanciful design instead of into plain rounds.)

When the oil is hot, fry 5 to 10 fritters at a time until they puff up and are nicely browned, 8 to 10 minutes. During the cooking, turn the balls in the oil so that they brown uniformly on all sides. As each batch of fritters comes out of the oil, drain them on paper towels, and immediately put them to soak for 15 minutes in the reserved syrup. Serve in small bowls with a little of the syrup poured over each portion.

Makes 6 servings.

Honey-Pecan Diamonds

I first sampled these jewels at a picnic eaten beneath a starry sky while listening to the strains of Strauss. They were so gooey I couldn't wait to get my hands on the recipe.

The recipe comes from Lina Fat, who runs two restaurants in Old Sacramento, a restored part of town that looks like a set from "Bonanza." The original basements were built during the Gold Rush, and the basement under Lina's restaurants are no different. A warren of subterranean rooms is now offices and the place where she has stashed thousands of recipes.

An insistent urge for something extremely gooey and rich can be answered forever with these diamonds.

Shortbread crust	Honey-pecan filling
10 tablespoons (1¼ sticks) unsalted butter	2 sticks (½ pound) unsalted butter
⅓ cup solid shortening	1⅓ cups brown sugar
½ cup sugar	¼ cup white sugar
1 egg	½ cup honey
1 teaspoon pure vanilla extract	4 cups (1 pound) good-looking pecans
2¼ cups flour	⅓ cup heavy cream
1 teaspoon baking powder	

For crust   Butter a 9- by 13-inch baking pan. Set oven rack in the center of the oven and preheat oven to 350°.

Cream butter, shortening, and sugar (with the paddle attachment of an electric mixer, if you have one) until smooth and fluffy. Beat in egg and vanilla. Sift flour and baking powder together, then add, all at once, to butter and mix slowly with mixer first on low speed, then medium, until a meal forms that will hold together if pressed. Don't overmix.

Press into bottom of pan, forming a slight rim. Prick a million times with a fork. Bake 15 minutes, until baked but still colorless. (Crust will bake a second time with filling.) Cool *completely* (see Note 1).

For honey-pecan filling   In a large heavy saucepan, stir the butter, brown sugar, white sugar, and honey together over medium-high heat. Bring to a boil and boil exactly 3 minutes (about 254°). Mixture will foam, but crystals won't form on the sides of the pan (see Note 2).

Off the heat, use a clean wooden spoon to stir in pecans (see Note 3). Return to heat to soften a bit, then stir in cream until smooth. Pour into the prebaked crust, pouring into the corners first.

Set baking pan on a cookie sheet to keep bottom from overbaking. Bake at 350° for 25 minutes, rotate pan, and bake 15 to 20 minutes more—a total of 40 to 45 minutes.

The middle may jiggle slightly, but will set up when cool. Cool overnight; do not refrigerate. Cut into 1-inch "diamonds." Will keep 2 weeks at room temperature, covered.

Makes about 2½ dozen diamonds.

Note 1: If crust has not cooled completely before hot pecan mixture is added, the heat from the caramel will turn it soggy.

Note 2: Caramel made with honey is timed rather than determined by a thermometer reading. The use of honey creates a soft-ball stage at a temperature that may vary from that required to bring white sugar to the soft-ball stage.

Note 3: Use a clean spoon to stir in the pecans. The spoon originally used for stirring the caramel's ingredients may have sugar crystals clinging to it.

Hello Dollies

I remember this sticky concoction from dorm life at the University of Texas in Austin. Our culinary skills extended to "pour." And that's all you need to do for this adolescent favorite. With the addition of a 6-ounce package of butterscotch chips, you've got Seven-Layer Bars.

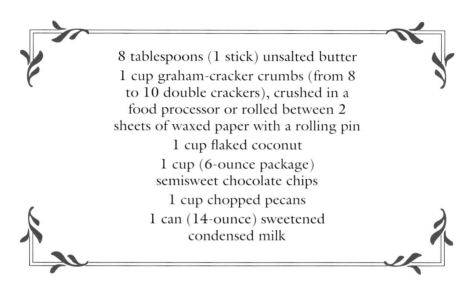

8 tablespoons (1 stick) unsalted butter

1 cup graham-cracker crumbs (from 8 to 10 double crackers), crushed in a food processor or rolled between 2 sheets of waxed paper with a rolling pin

1 cup flaked coconut

1 cup (6-ounce package) semisweet chocolate chips

1 cup chopped pecans

1 can (14-ounce) sweetened condensed milk

Place the butter in a 9-inch square baking dish and set it in the oven as oven preheats to 350°.

When butter is melted, remove the pan from the oven and top butter with crumbs, coconut, chocolate chips, and pecans. Pour condensed milk over all. Bake at 350° for 30 minutes. Cool and cut into squares.

Makes 16.

Orange Glory Pecan-Cinnamon-Raisin Sticky Buns

Who says you can't have dessert at breakfast, and who says you can't have a sticky bun for dessert?

These beautiful buns look like products from a professional bakery. Better yet, they're as gooey as a bun can get. Not only does the orange-flavored syrup meld with the raisins and pecans while seeping into the dough, but a thick cream glaze coats the top.

Make the dough the night before, or even three days before. If you also have ready the assembly for filling the buns—the raisins, pecans, and cinnamon-sugar—all you'll have to do the next morning is make the syrup, roll the dough, sprinkle the fillings, cut, rise and bake. At least that's how it worked in the good old days.

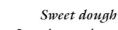

Sweet dough
2 packages dry yeast
½ cup warm water
¾ cup milk
½ cup sugar
2 teaspoons salt
1 stick (½ cup) unsalted butter
2 eggs, beaten
4 cups flour
2 tablespoons very soft butter

Sticky syrup
1 cup water
8 tablespoons (1 stick) butter
Grated zest from 1 orange
(about 1 tablespoon)

1 cup orange juice
2 cups sugar

To assemble
1 cup raisins
1 cup water
4 tablespoons very soft butter
1 tablespoon EACH
cinnamon and sugar
1 cup coarsely chopped pecans

Sticky bun glaze
1 cup powdered sugar
2 tablespoons cream or milk

For dough In a small bowl, stir the yeast with the warm water. Set aside until bubbly.

Heat milk, sugar, salt, and butter together until butter melts. Pour into a large bowl to cool to lukewarm.

Add yeast to the cooled milk mixture. Add eggs and 2 cups of the flour and beat well by hand, about 2 minutes. Add the remaining 2 cups flour 1 cup at a time, beating well until smooth, about 2 minutes. Dough will be soft and smooth and should pull cleanly away from the sides of the bowl.

Turn into a buttered bowl, then generously butter the surface of the dough with the softened butter, top and bottom.

Cover with plastic wrap. Refrigerate as little as 2 hours, or overnight, or up to 3 days. Dough will rise in refrigerator. It will be ready for rolling and shaping the next morning.

For syrup Bring water, butter, orange zest, orange juice, and sugar to a boil and simmer 10 minutes.

To assemble buns Simmer raisins in water for 10 minutes, then drain. Grease 2 9-inch round cake pans. Pour syrup equally into pans.

Set out 4 small bowls to hold an assembly line of the softened butter, sugar-cinnamon mixture, pecans, and drained raisins.

Divide dough in half. Place first section on a surface lightly sprinkled with flour and roll it into a 10- by 12-inch rectangle. Spread surface with half the butter, then sprinkle with half the cinnamon-sugar, pecans, and raisins.

Roll up from long side into a snug log. With a sharp knife, cut into 8 sections. Place spirals, cut sides down, into the syrup in one of the pans, placing 1 spiral in the center and 7 around. Repeat with remaining dough and second pan.

Cover buns with a cloth and let rise 1 hour. After 40 minutes, preheat oven to 375°.

Bake buns 25 to 30 minutes. Remove and immediately invert onto a rack with waxed paper underneath to catch drips. Let cool 10 minutes before icing with the glaze.

For glaze Do not mix until ready to use. With a fork, mix sugar and cream until smooth. Pour over buns.

Makes 16 sticky, gooey buns.

Maple-Pecan Sticky Buns with Cinnamon-Chocolate Centers

Chocolate is tucked in the folds of these sticky breakfast buns. The dough is the same as for Orange Glory Pecan-Cinnamon-Raisin Sticky Buns.

Maple caramel
1 cup brown sugar
½ cup maple syrup
8 tablespoons (1 stick) unsalted butter

To assemble
4 tablespoons very soft butter
1 cup (6-ounce package)
semisweet chocolate chips
1 tablespoon *each* cinnamon and sugar
1 cup coarsely chopped pecan halves
1 recipe sweet dough (page 180)

For syrup Grease 2 9-inch cake pans. In a heavy saucepan, heat the sugar, maple syrup, and butter until butter melts, then simmer very gently 10 minutes. Pour maple caramel equally into the greased pans.

While caramel simmers, set out 4 small bowls to hold an assembly line of the soft butter, chocolate chips, cinnamon-sugar, and pecans.

To assemble Divide prepared dough in half. Roll first section into a 10- by 12-inch rectangle on a surface lightly sprinkled with flour. Spread with half the soft butter, then sprinkle with half the chocolate chips, cinnamon-sugar, and pecans.

Roll up from long side into a snug log. With a sharp paring knife, cut into 8 sections. Place spirals, cut sides down, into the syrup in one of the pans, placing 1 spiral in the center and 7 around. Repeat with remaining dough.

Cover buns with a cloth and let rise 1 hour. After 40 minutes, preheat oven to 375°.

Bake buns 25 to 30 minutes. Remove from oven and immediately invert onto a rack with waxed paper underneath to catch drips. Let cool 10 minutes before icing with Sticky Bun Glaze (page 180).

Makes 16 buns.

CHAPTER SEVEN

Great Gooey Classics

(Only in America)

Incredible Banana Pudding

The importance of this dessert is underscored by its inclusion by *Louisville Courier-Journal* writer C. Ray Hall in the Four Food Groups of Kentucky—chili, Pepsi, gravy, and banana pudding.

In its mundane form, the recipe mixes up instant vanilla pudding, slaps it over some bananas and vanilla wafers, and tops it with not very many beaten egg whites, which are then browned. Banana pudding is in need of an upgrade.

What follows is the extraterrestrial of banana puddings. The pudding is homemade, with whipped cream folded in. This is real vanilla pudding, made from scratch. (I've never understood the big deal about packaged pudding mixes. What are you saving yourself—the time spent measuring a couple of tablespoons of flour and some sugar?) Vanilla wafers are soaked in bourbon. A huge meringue goes atop.

Banana pudding inspires awe when presented in a round bowl with sloping sides, like the type used for pasta.

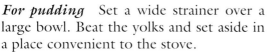

Vanilla pudding
6 egg yolks
1 cup sugar
½ cup flour
4 cups milk
1 tablespoon pure vanilla extract
3 tablespoons unsalted butter

For assembly
1½ cups cream

1 box (7½ ounces) vanilla wafers
6 bananas, thinly sliced
Bourbon, for sprinkling
over wafers

Meringue
6 egg whites
¼ teaspoon cream of tartar
½ teaspoon pure vanilla extract
⅔ cup sugar

For pudding Set a wide strainer over a large bowl. Beat the yolks and set aside in a place convenient to the stove.

Whisk the sugar, flour, and milk in a heavy saucepan until free of lumps. Set over medium heat and cook, stirring constantly with a wooden spatula, just to a boil.

Remove from heat and whisk a little of the hot, thick pudding into the beaten yolks, then pour the yolk mixture back into the main pudding mixture, whisking really well. Continue to cook 1 to 2 minutes more, stirring constantly until thick.

Strain, then stir in vanilla and butter until butter melts.

To store, press plastic wrap directly onto the surface of the pudding and refrigerate 3 hours.

To assemble In a cold bowl with cold beaters, whip the cream to stiff peaks. Fold into cold pudding.

Line an attractive ovenproof dish (8- to 10-cup volume) with half the vanilla wafers and sprinkle lightly with bourbon. Top with one-third of the pudding, then half the bananas. Add another layer of wafers and bourbon, the next third of pudding, and then the remaining bananas. End with a final layer of pudding.

For meringue Preheat oven to 350°. Beat the egg whites, cream of tartar, and vanilla to stiff peaks. Gradually add the ⅔ cup sugar and beat until stiff again.

Starting at the edge of the pudding, pipe or swirl a border of meringue around circumference of the dish to make a seal. Pipe or swirl the rest of the meringue all over the pudding. Heat in the oven 10 to 15 minutes to brown meringue tips. Cool at room temperature.

Makes 16 servings.

An Old, Quick Recipe for Banana Pudding

1 package instant vanilla pudding
48 vanilla wafers
6 bananas
2 egg whites
4 tablespoons sugar

Prepare pudding according to package directions. Line bottom and sides of a deep dish with a thick layer of wafers. Top with alternating layers of bananas, pudding, and coarsely crumbled wafers.

Preheat oven to 400°. Beat egg whites until stiff; gradually add sugar and beat until stiff again. Spread over pudding. Bake 10 minutes, to brown meringue.

Makes 6 servings.

The Ultimate Vanilla Pudding Dessert

Standard vanilla puddin' with vanilla wafers has always been primed for an upgrade. The basic arrangement whips up a box of instant vanilla pudding, layers it with vanilla wafers, and tops it all with whipped cream.

Ultimate Vanilla Pudding, elevated to the status of a capitalized Proper Noun, is nearly a trifle. With vanilla pudding made from scratch, wafers dipped in bourbon, and Sticky Pecan Praline crumbled throughout, it leers its gooey excess from the bowl.

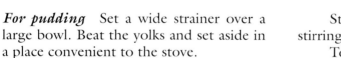

Vanilla pudding
6 egg yolks
1 cup sugar
½ cup flour
4 cups milk
1 tablespoon pure vanilla extract
3 tablespoons unsalted butter

Sticky pecan praline crumble
2 cups fresh pecan halves
or pieces

1 cup sugar
¼ cup water
⅛ teaspoon cream of tartar

For assembly
1 box (7½ ounces)
vanilla wafers
2 or 3 tablespoons bourbon
1 cup cream
2 tablespoons sugar

For pudding Set a wide strainer over a large bowl. Beat the yolks and set aside in a place convenient to the stove.

Whisk the sugar, flour, and milk in a heavy saucepan until free of lumps. Set over medium heat and cook, stirring constantly with a wooden spatula, just to a boil.

Remove from heat and whisk a little of the hot, thick pudding into the beaten yolks, then pour the yolk mixture back into the main pudding mixture, whisking really well. Continue to cook 1 to 2 minutes more, stirring constantly until thick.

Strain, then add vanilla and butter, stirring until butter melts.

To store, press plastic wrap directly onto the surface of the pudding and refrigerate 3 hours.

For sticky pecan praline crumble Toast pecans on a cookie sheet at 350° about 15 minutes, tossing them a few times. When they smell toasted, they need to come out of the oven.

Butter another cookie sheet and set aside. In a heavy saucepan, bring sugar, water, and cream of tartar to a boil over medium-high heat. If crystals form on the sides of the pan, cover the pan for 30 seconds or as long as 5 minutes so steam rinses off the sides. When the caramel darkens, you may swirl the pan to even the color. As caramel turns the color of hay, remove from heat. Don't let the caramel get too dark, or the sugar will be too brittle to crumble (it will snap instead).

With a wooden spoon, stir in nuts, coating them well. Spread out on the buttered cookie sheet and cool 1 hour. Chop coarsely with a knife (see Note).

To assemble Layer vanilla wafers on the bottom of an 8-cup soufflé dish or glass bowl. Top with one-third of sticky pecan praline crumble, then sprinkle with half the bourbon. Top with half the pudding. Repeat layers of wafers, crumble, bourbon, and pudding, then top with crumble.

In a cold bowl with cold beaters, whip the cream and sugar to stiff peaks. Spoon or pipe enormous swirls of cream over the crumble. Chill very well.

Makes 8 servings.

Note: A food processor causes the crumble to stick and clump rather than break. If you like sticky pecan praline crumble, make a double batch. You can store the extra in a tightly covered jar at room temperature for 3 months.

Viennese Vanilla Wafers

To carry a classic to an extreme it deserves, make homemade vanilla wafers in the Viennese style.

Remember the thin, plain, light cookies decorated with nothing more than a browned edge? These are as much a vanilla wafer as the cookies that come out of a box, and they're easy to make. It's nice to know there's a a classy option to the store-bought variety.

4 eggs
⅔ cup sugar
½ of vanilla bean
1 cup sifted flour

Butter as many cookie sheets as you have. Do not use black bakeware.

In a saucepan, beat the eggs, sugar and vanilla bean, which has been split, scraped, and added to mixture—pod, seeds, and all —just until well blended. Set the saucepan over low heat. Beat and heat eggs, sugar, and vanilla bean just until past lukewarm. The eggs will begin to thicken slightly. When they do, remove pan from heat and keep beating to cool the mixture somewhat.

With a large rubber spatula, fold in the flour until no lumps remain. Drop batter by teaspoonfuls onto the buttered sheets, using the back of the spoon to spread to about 1½ inch diameter.

Set cookie sheets aside at room temperature for 3 hours.

Preheat oven to 275°. Bake cookies about 12 minutes, or until ⅛-inch circle around the edges browns. Cool on racks.

Makes 4 dozen.

Ambrosia

To remove Ambrosia from the "whipped topping" category involved digging deeply into cookbooks printed before imitation whipped cream came along. From about four decades ago comes this refreshing fruit combination mixed with one version of cream or another—plus sherry.

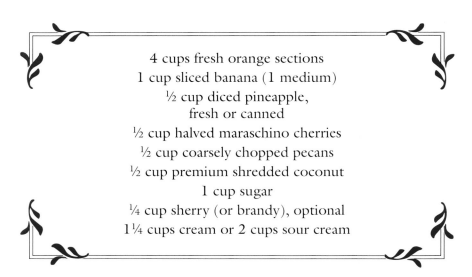

4 cups fresh orange sections
1 cup sliced banana (1 medium)
½ cup diced pineapple,
fresh or canned
½ cup halved maraschino cherries
½ cup coarsely chopped pecans
½ cup premium shredded coconut
1 cup sugar
¼ cup sherry (or brandy), optional
1¼ cups cream or 2 cups sour cream

Combine all ingredients except cream in a large bowl. Whip the cream to stiff peaks (or use sour cream) and fold into fruit. Chill very well.

Makes 10 servings.

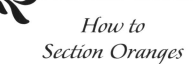

How to Section Oranges

Slice top and bottom off the orange so it stands flat. With the orange standing on the countertop and a sharp knife poised at the top, saw off skin between pulp and peel, using downward slices, all around the orange. Holding the peeled orange over a bowl (to catch the juices), cut along both sides of each membrane to free sections. Mix the captured juice with the orange sections.

Five-Cup Dessert

Here is a classic shortcut for Ambrosia.

1 cup pineapple pieces or fruit cocktail
1 cup mandarin oranges
1 cup sour cream
1 cup miniature marshmallows
1 cup premium shredded coconut
Sugar to taste

Drain pineapple (or fruit cocktail) and mandarin oranges. Mix in a bowl and fold in sour cream. Add marshmallows and coconut and sweeten to taste. Refrigerate until serving time. You may make this 24 hours in advance.

Makes 6 to 8 servings.

Date Pudding
(Another Food for the Gods)

The gods aren't crazy. Why resort to burnt offerings when what they truly crave are gooey desserts?

This dessert was given to me by a Nebraskan. It is along the lines of a Texas creeping cobbler. The batter on the bottom bubbles to the top, and the "filling" on top oozes to the bottom. It is disgustingly rich and gooey. If you keep it chilled, it will keep for two weeks. It's supposed to be thin.

Batter
1 cup flour
½ cup sugar
2 teaspoons baking powder
1 egg
¼ scant cup milk
1 cup chopped fresh dates, about 12 Medjool or 14 Honey dates (see Note) or boxed chopped dates
1 cup coarsely chopped pecans or walnuts

Filling
2 cups sugar
2 cups boiling water
2 tablespoons unsalted butter, fairly soft
1 teaspoon pure vanilla extract

Chantilly cream
½ cup cream
1 tablespoon sugar
½ teaspoon pure vanilla extract

For batter Preheat oven to 350°. Combine flour, sugar, baking powder, egg, and milk in a medium bowl. Add dates and nuts. The batter will be very stiff. Spread in a thin, even layer across the bottom of a lightly buttered 9- by 13-inch baking pan.

For filling Combine sugar and boiling water in a pour-spout bowl, stirring until sugar dissolves. Whisk in butter and vanilla. Pour mixture over date batter.

Bake 45 minutes, until golden brown. The pudding will rise to the top and the "filling" will sink to the bottom.

For chantilly cream In a cold bowl with cold beaters, whip cream, sugar, and vanilla to moderately stiff peaks. Chill, covered, until ready for use.

Cool the Date Pudding thoroughly. Cut into big squares. Top each square with a dollop of chantilly cream.

Makes about 8 servings.

Note: To keep dates from sticking, chop with a chef's knife (with a blade 6 to 8 inches long) dusted with powdered sugar. Or cut dates with a scissors.

Mississippi Mud Cake

From the South, this cake varies little from cook to cook, even from book to book. Requiring little more effort than a simple sheet cake, it gathers its luster from two important additions—marshmallow cream straight from the jar, and frosting heavier than a river bottom.

Cake
4 eggs

2 cups sugar

2 sticks (1 cup) unsalted
butter, melted

1½ cups flour

⅓ cup cocoa

1 cup premium
shredded coconut

1 cup chopped pecans

1 jar (7-ounces)
marshmallow cream

Mud frosting
1-pound box powdered sugar

⅓ cup cocoa

1 stick (½ cup) unsalted
butter, melted

⅓ cup milk

1 teaspoon pure vanilla extract

Garnish
Coconut, optional

For cake Grease a 9- by 13-inch baking pan. Set oven rack in the center of the oven and preheat oven to 350°.

In a large bowl, beat the eggs and sugar until pale and thick, about 1 minute. Add the melted butter, and beat well. Sift the flour and cocoa together, then add to batter, beating until thick and very smooth, about 1 to 1½ minutes. Stir in coconut and pecans. Bake 25 minutes.

Immediately spread with marshmallow cream, carefully moving the cream evenly across the warm cake with a frosting spatula but not pulling on the cake's top skin. Cool 1 hour.

For mud frosting Combine sugar and cocoa in a mixing bowl. Add melted butter and beat mixture on low speed until crumbly. Slowly add milk, beating on high until smooth. Add vanilla and continue to beat 2 minutes until completely smooth and frosting is no longer granular. Frost cake, smoothing frosting to edge.

To serve, cut cake into large squares. Decorate with sprinkled coconut, if you like.

Makes 12 to 16 servings.

Gloria's Meringue Bridge Torte

Sacramento Union food editor Gloria Glyer responded perfectly to the call for a gooey dessert. The meringue disks in this torte are left to absorb a whipped cream-toffee bar filling for at least 8 hours. They soften as they do. This is very rich, very sweet, and, says Gloria, "very delicious . . ."

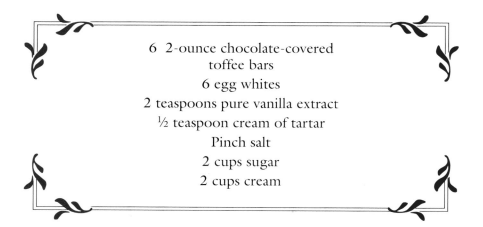

6 2-ounce chocolate-covered
toffee bars
6 egg whites
2 teaspoons pure vanilla extract
½ teaspoon cream of tartar
Pinch salt
2 cups sugar
2 cups cream

Put toffee bars in the refrigerator. Line two 10- by 15- by 2-inch jelly-roll pans (or cookie sheets) with parchment paper. Draw a 9-inch circle on each paper. Preheat oven to 275°.

Beat egg whites, vanilla, cream of tartar, and salt to stiff peaks, gradually adding sugar halfway through. Spread meringue, or pipe in spirals, to fill up the circle patterns, starting in centers.

Bake 1 hour. Turn off heat and let the meringue disks dry inside the oven with the door closed at least 2 hours.

Meanwhile, crush the chilled toffee bars into fine pieces. You should have about 1½ cups.

In a cold bowl with cold beaters, whip the cream to stiff peaks. Fold in the toffee pieces.

To assemble Frost one meringue disk with the toffee-cream. Top with second meringue disk. Frost the torte completely with remaining toffee-cream. Chill at least 8 hours, or overnight. Garnish with additional crushed candy, if desired.

Makes 10 to 12 servings.

Note: For a perfect circle, trace the outline of a 9-inch round cake pan.

Coca-Cola Cake

A classic unimaginable without Coke Classic—no diet beverages desecrating this cake! Coca-Cola Cake runs along the lines of Mississippi Mud Cake. The procedure and ingredients aren't too sophisticated as cakes go, but it's fun, sweet, and—with its rich fudge brownie flavor—better-tasting than dessert snobs would ever admit.

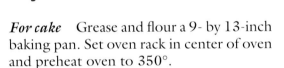

Cake
2 cups sugar
2 cups flour
½ cup vegetable oil
3 tablespoons cocoa
1 stick (½ cup) unsalted butter
1 cup Coke Classic
½ cup buttermilk
1 teaspoon baking soda
1 teaspoon pure vanilla extract

2 eggs
1½ cups miniature
  marshmallows

Coke icing
1-pound box powdered sugar
1 stick (½ cup) unsalted butter
2 tablespoons cocoa
⅓ cup Coke Classic
1 teaspoon pure vanilla extract
½ cup chopped nuts, optional

For cake   Grease and flour a 9- by 13-inch baking pan. Set oven rack in center of oven and preheat oven to 350°.

Mix sugar and flour in a mixing bowl. In a saucepan, heat oil, cocoa, butter, and Coke, stirring to dissolve mixture; then bring to a boil. Remove from heat and pour hot mixture over dry ingredients. Beat well.

Add remaining ingredients and beat well again. Marshmallows will not dissolve, and batter will be rather thin. Pour into prepared pan and bake 30 to 35 minutes. Don't worry if cake bakes unevenly. Frost while warm.

For icing   Place sugar in a bowl. In a saucepan, bring butter, cocoa and Coke to a boil. Pour butter mixture over sugar, and beat in vanilla and nuts. Spread immediately on warm cake.

Dump Cake

This novel bit of Americana embodies everything that horrifies purists. I believe it to be a legitimate example of the gooey popular culture. Its name alludes to the method required to make it. Good luck.

1 large can crushed pineapple
1 can cherry pie filling
1 box yellow cake mix
½ cup chopped pecans or walnuts
2 sticks (1 cup) unsalted
butter or margarine

Grease a 9- by 13-inch baking pan. Preheat oven to 350°.

Dump undrained pineapple into baking pan and spread evenly. Dump and spread pie filling. **Don't you dare mix!** Dump, or rather, sprinkle, cake mix over cherries. Top cake-mix layer with nuts. Slice butter into pats and distribute over nut layer.

Bake 1 hour, or until brown. Serve with ice cream.

Makes 8 to 10 servings.

Dirt Cake

You'll need a flower pot and a party of children with good imaginations. Susan Puckett, who heads up the food section at the *Atlanta Journal & Constitution*, gave me this recipe, as is, with the following tips from a reader:

- Scrape frosting from the Oreo cookies to make good, rich-looking "dirt."
- Put Gummi Worms in the "dirt" and a few on top.

1 large bag Oreo cookies
½ stick (¼ cup) unsalted
butter, softened
1 cup powdered sugar
1 8-ounce package cream cheese, softened
3⅓ cups milk
2 small packages instant
French vanilla pudding
1 8-ounce package frozen
whipped topping, thawed

Process cookies into crumbs in a food processor or blender, or place in a large plastic bag and crush with a rolling pin.

Cream together butter, powdered sugar, and cream cheese. In another bowl, beat the milk, instant pudding, and whipped topping. Blend cheese and pudding mixtures to form a custard-like mixture.

In a clean flower pot, alternate layers of custard and cookie crumbs, starting and ending with the cookie crumbs. Chill (or freeze) until serving.

Makes 10 to 12 servings.

Holiday Cranberry Refrigerator Cream Cake

Glistening from the deep red of cranberries, this cake falls into a category of American sweets known as icebox desserts. The novelty of having cold storage available in one's own house inspired a generation of cooks to prepare desserts absolutely dependent on refrigeration. Desserts swirled with cream, layered with cheese, or bound with gelatin are hallmarks of the icebox age.

This is a pretty layering of cranberry pastry cream with cream cheese and sour cream, finally decorated with billows of whipped cream.

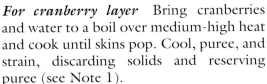

Cranberry layer
4 cups fresh cranberries
1½ cups water
3 egg yolks
1½ cups sugar
¼ cup flour
Finely grated zest of 1 orange
Juice of 1 orange
2 tablespoons unsalted butter

Cream cheese layer
1 8-ounce package cream cheese, soft
½ cup powdered sugar
1 cup sour cream

For base
3 3-ounce packages store-bought ladyfingers

For garnish
1 cup cream

For cranberry layer Bring cranberries and water to a boil over medium-high heat and cook until skins pop. Cool, puree, and strain, discarding solids and reserving puree (see Note 1).

In a medium-size saucepan, beat egg yolks and sugar by hand or with a portable electric mixer until thick, about 1 minute. Add flour, zest, and orange juice and beat until smooth. Add cranberry puree. Place over medium-high heat and bring to a boil, stirring constantly. Remove from heat and add butter a bit at a time.

For cream cheese layer Beat cream cheese and powdered sugar until fluffy. Fold a "scoop" of sour cream into the beaten cheese to lighten it so it's easy to blend with the sour cream. Fold in remaining sour cream.

To assemble Line the bottom of an 8- or 9-inch springform pan with a round of waxed paper. Split ladyfingers lengthwise into halves, then halve them crosswise. Stand some ladyfinger halves around sides of pan, rounded side out, and rounded tips up. Trim the cut ends of remaining ladyfingers to a V-shape so each ladyfinger looks like a flower petal. Arrange like a daisy in the bottom of the pan, flat sides up, making sure these ladyfingers are flush with those around the sides. Cut a circle from ladyfinger scrap or use pieces as needed to fill in center and any gaps. Make this attractive, because what's on the bottom will become what you see on the top.

To fill pan Pour half of the cranberry mixture into the springform pan. Chill 30 minutes. Spread half the cream cheese mixture over cranberry layer. Top with another layer of ladyfingers and cover with remaining cream cheese. Fill with remaining cranberry mixture. (You could use a tube pan or other mold without waxed paper.) Chill at least 6 hours (or wrap well and freeze).

To serve, run a thin knife around ladyfingers to loosen any stuck areas. Invert pan onto a serving platter, remove springform collar, and carefully remove pan bottom and waxed paper. (If frozen, thaw in refrigerator.)

For garnish In a cold bowl with cold beaters, whip cream to stiff peaks. Pipe big swirls, using a pastry tip with a large opening, into center of cake, or pipe huge stars around edge. Cut into wedges with a knife dipped in a tall glass of hot water, then wiped dry.

Makes 10 servings.

Note 1: If you can't find fresh cranberries, use dried cranberries. Cook 2 cups dried cranberries in 1½ cups water for 5 minutes, drain, and proceed with recipe.

Note 2: For a decorative effect, alternate chocolate and vanilla ladyfingers around the rim of the dessert.

Note 3: Instead of cream cheese, use mascarpone cheese.

Hawaiian Refrigerator Dream Cake

Marshmallows. Sweetened condensed milk. Maraschino cherries. Cream. What more could a gooey-substance lover want? With store-bought ladyfingers, this is a quick make-ahead that both children and adults have loved every time I've made it.

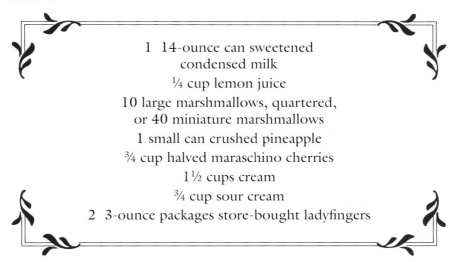

1 14-ounce can sweetened
condensed milk
¼ cup lemon juice
10 large marshmallows, quartered,
or 40 miniature marshmallows
1 small can crushed pineapple
¾ cup halved maraschino cherries
1½ cups cream
¾ cup sour cream
2 3-ounce packages store-bought ladyfingers

Combine condensed milk and lemon juice in a mixing bowl. Add marshmallows, pineapple, and cherries.

In a cold bowl with cold beaters, whip cream to stiff peaks, then fold in sour cream. Fold *half* the cream mixture into the fruit mixture. Chill remaining cream for decoration later.

To assemble Split ladyfingers lengthwise into halves, then halve them crosswise. Stand ladyfinger halves around sides of pan, rounded sides out, rounded tips up.

Trim cut ends of remaining ladyfingers to a V-shape so ladyfinger looks like a flower petal. Arrange "petals" like a daisy in the bottom of the pan, flat sides up, making sure these ladyfingers are flush with those around the sides. Cut a circle from ladyfinger scrap or use pieces as needed to fill in center and gaps.

To fill pan Fill springform pan with fruit mixture. Cover with remaining whipped cream mixture, smoothing to edge. (Or use a tube pan or other mold without waxed paper.) Chill at least 6 hours, or wrap well and freeze.

To serve, run a thin knife around ladyfingers to loosen any stuck areas. Remove springform sides. Serve cut in wedges.

Makes 10 servings.

Better Than Better-Than-Sex Cake

This dessert is a long version of the original Better-Than-Sex Cake quickies, an only-in-America phenomenon (see photo plate 3).

For anyone who has never collected community club cookbooks, know that Better-Than-Sex Cake is a mainstay with two possible origins (see below).

Desserts in the entire Better-Than-Sex genre are constructed like flat trifles. Mine is, too, but with different body parts. It is very gooey and lush, and made from scratch.

Even so, *Better Than* Better-Than-Sex Cake may be as poor a substitute for real sex as its Better-Than-Sex predecessors, despite recipe titles that arrive at such a drastic conclusion. This is so good I nearly named it "After Sex Cake," or, in honor of the '90s, "*Instead*-of-Sex Cake."

Crust
2 sticks (1 cup) unsalted butter
2 tablespoons sugar
2 cups flour

Cream cheese layer
1 8-ounce package
cream cheese, very soft
½ cup sugar
1 teaspoon pure vanilla extract
1 teaspoon lemon juice
1 cup cream

Vanilla pudding layer
3 egg yolks
½ cup sugar
¼ cup flour
2 cups milk
2 teaspoons pure vanilla extract

2 tablespoons unsalted butter

Whipped cream layer
1½ cups cream
3 tablespoons powdered sugar
1 tablespoon vanilla extract

Pineapple caramel layer
1 8-ounce can crushed
pineapple, drained
1 jar caramel sauce or
chocolate sauce (optional)

Chocolate glaze
2 ounces (2 squares)
semisweet chocolate
2 tablespoons unsalted
butter (or margarine)
½ teaspoon vanilla extract

Butter a 9- by 13-inch baking pan. Set oven rack in the center of the oven and preheat oven to 350°.

For crust   Beat butter and sugar until fluffy. Add flour and, with mixer on low, blend until mixture is pebbly and can be pressed together. Press mixture on bottom of buttered baking pan, then bake 20 minutes, or until golden. Cool completely (see Note 1).

For cream cheese layer   Beat cream cheese, sugar, vanilla, and lemon juice just to blend. In a separate bowl, whip cream to medium-stiff peaks. Fold a "scoop" of whipped cream into beaten cheese, then fold remaining cream into cheese.

For vanilla pudding   Beat the yolks and set aside in a place convenient to the stove.

Whisk the sugar, flour, and milk in a medium saucepan until free of lumps. Set over medium heat and cook, stirring constantly with a wooden spatula, just to a boil.

Remove from heat and whisk a little of the hot, thick pudding into the beaten yolks, then pour the yolk mixture back into the main pudding mixture, whisking really well. Continue to cook 1 to 2 minutes more, stirring constantly until thick.

Pour pudding into a bowl and add vanilla and butter, stirring until butter melts. If pudding has lumps, pour through a large fine-mesh strainer.

Chill, with plastic wrap pressed directly on the surface of the pudding, until ready to use.

For whipped cream   In a cold bowl with cold beaters, whip the cream, sugar, and vanilla to stiff peaks.

To assemble   Spread crust with cream cheese mixture. Top with pineapple, then optional caramel or chocolate sauce (see Note 3). Spread pudding over pineapple. Spread whipped cream evenly over pudding.

Chill well before serving. At serving, make chocolate glaze.

For chocolate glaze   Melt chocolate and butter over low heat, stirring until smooth and completely melted. Remove from heat and stir in vanilla. Drizzle over dessert in zigzags back and forth across the cake to decorate the surface.

Makes 12 servings.

Note 1: You may use a food processor for crust: Process all crust ingredients until a coarse mixture.

Note 2: Using commercial or homemade mascarpone cheese (see page 73) in place of cream cheese would really 'luxe up this cake.

Note 3: Make your own Stretchy Caramel Sauce (see page 170) or Lush Chocolate Sauce (see page 107). Caramel may also be drizzled *with* the chocolate glaze on top, and in pineapple layer.

The Original Better-Than-Sex Cake

Lots of people talk about Better-Than-Sex Cake, which you might say gives it an oral tradition. It also has more than one origin, if this is possible. The most widely circulated recipe uses yellow cake mix and a syrup with crushed pineapple. Another uses German chocolate cake and Mrs. Richardson's fudge sauce.

Subsequent concepts may be imposters, but they've been passed around as promiscuously as the original(s).

1 box yellow cake mix
1 8-ounce can crushed pineapple
½ cup sugar
1 small package instant vanilla pudding
2 cups milk
1 16-ounce tub Cool Whip
Coconut, shredded

Bake cake according to package directions, in an oblong baking pan. Bring pineapple and sugar to a boil. Pour over warm cake. Cool.

Beat pudding and milk and spread over cake. When pudding is firm, spread Cool Whip over cake and top with coconut. Chill until serving.

Makes 10 to 12 servings.

Another Parent of Better-Than-Sex Cake

1 box German chocolate cake mix
1 14-ounce can sweetened condensed milk
1 jar Mrs. Richardson's fudge sauce, or other brand
1 8-ounce tub Cool Whip
2 Heath toffee bars, crushed

Bake cake according to package directions, in an oblong baking pan. As soon as the cake comes out of the oven, poke holes in it with the end of a wooden spoon. Pour sweetened condensed milk over the cake. Cool for about 20 minutes. Spread fudge sauce (you may warm sauce slightly, with lid off, in the microwave, or use bottled caramel sauce) over the cake. Top with Cool Whip and sprinkle with crushed Heath bars.

Sons of Better-Than-Sex Cake

Too much unprotected consumption of sex cake gave birth to more cakes traced to the same DNA—layers of pudding upon layers of pudding.

Better-Than-Robert Redford Cake

Crust

2 cups flour
2 sticks unsalted butter or margarine
2 tablespoons sugar

Cream cheese layer

12 ounces cream cheese, softened
1¼ cups powdered sugar
1 16-ounce container Cool Whip

Pudding layer

2 packages instant pudding (any flavor)
3 cups milk

Preheat oven to 350°. Mix first three ingredients and press into an oblong baking pan. Beat cream cheese and powdered sugar, fold in one-third of the Cool Whip. Spread mixture over crust.

Beat pudding with milk. Spread over cream cheese layer. Top with remaining Cool Whip.

Makes 10 to 12 servings.

Better-Than-Tom Selleck Cake

Crust

1½ sticks unsalted butter
1 cup flour
½ cup brown sugar
¾ cup chopped pecans

Cream cheese layer

8 ounces cream cheese, softened
1 cup powdered sugar
1 cup Cool Whip
1 large (6¾-ounce) package instant chocolate pudding
3 cups milk
1 large (6¾-ounce) package instant vanilla pudding

Preheat oven to 325°. Mix first four ingredients and bake in a pan for 25 minutes, stirring several times. Remove ½ cup of the baked mixture. Spread remainder in a 9- by 13-inch baking pan. Cool.

Mix cream cheese and powdered sugar. Fold in Cool Whip. Spread over first layer. Beat chocolate pudding mix with 1½ cups milk and spread over second layer. Beat vanilla pudding mix with 1½ cups milk and spread over chocolate layer. Sprinkle with reserved mix. Chill until serving time.

Makes 16 to 20 servings.

Zelda's Chocolate Icebox Dessert with Maraschino Cherry Angel Food Cake

Here is your basic icebox dessert. Nothing cooks. Nothing bakes (unless you make your own cake). Heat is applied to chocolate so it melts, and that's it for the stove. I like to serve desserts of this kind in large, attractive serving bowls rather than in oblong baking pans. Stash this in the freezer until you want to serve it. Let it thaw, and it looks as though you went to a lot of trouble.

Zelda is my neighbor. When I made this and took it down the street to her husband, apparently I'd done everything right. The chocolatey mass jiggling in my bowl was instantly recognized as a rendition of the family favorite.

Angel food cake
1 cup sifted cake flour
½ cup sugar
1½ cups egg whites (12 to 13 whites from "large" eggs), room temperature
1¼ teaspoons cream of tartar
½ teaspoon salt
Additional 1 cup sugar
2 teaspoons pure vanilla extract
1 cup halved maraschino cherries

Chocolate mousse
¾ cup sugar
½ cup water
4 egg yolks
6½ ounces (6½ squares) semisweet chocolate
7 tablespoons unsalted butter
3 egg whites
1 cup cream

For cake Set oven rack in the lower third of the oven and preheat oven to 375°.

Mix flour with the ½ cup sugar and sift three times. In another bowl, beat egg whites, cream of tartar, and salt until stiff. (If whites are cold, hold the bowl over a pan of simmering water to warm them a little.) Gradually add the remaining 1 cup sugar and again beat until stiff.

Fold in vanilla. Fold in flour mixture, 2 tablespoons at a time. Fold in cherries. Pour batter into an ungreased tube or angel food cake pan and bake 35 minutes, or until the place where you press your finger on top of the cake springs back.

Cool cake upside down in the pan for 1 hour. (Set pan on its legs, or place on the neck of a bottle or funnel.) Run a spatula around the rim of the cake to release it, then place it, upturned again, on a rack. Allow it to fall gently out of pan in its own sweet time.

Cut into cubes with an angel food cutter or serrated knife.

For mousse Boil the sugar and water in a saucepan about 5 minutes. Beat the yolks in the top of a double boiler. Slowly beat the sugar syrup into the yolks. Cook, stirring, in a double boiler over simmering water until the yolks are creamy and thick, about 5 to 8 minutes (160°). Pour through a strainer into a bowl sitting in ice. Stir to cool faster.

Melt the chocolate in a double boiler (or microwave, uncovered, on Medium, stirring every 20 to 30 seconds after the first 2½ minutes, until only a small solid chunk of chocolate remains). Remove from heat and stir until melted and smooth.

Add the butter to the chocolate a tablespoon at a time, stirring with a rubber spatula. Allow the mixture to cool completely. It should be the consistency of very thick cream. Combine cooled chocolate mixture with the cooked yolks.

Beat the egg whites to stiff peaks. With a large rubber spatula, fold the whites into the chocolate, using wide strokes, until no white streaks show.

In a cold bowl with cold beaters, whip the cream to stiff peaks. Fold into mousse until completely blended.

To assemble Fold cake cubes gently into mousse. Scoop into an attractive serving bowl or dish. Wrap well and refrigerate or freeze.

Makes 24 servings.

Coffee Crunch Cake

You may recognize this as a likeness of a cake sold at the famous old Blum's location on Union Square in San Francisco, near where Macy's now stands. It fulfills many gooey criteria. The cake is creamy and soft from whipped cream, and sticky and sweet from crushed coffee candy you make yourself.

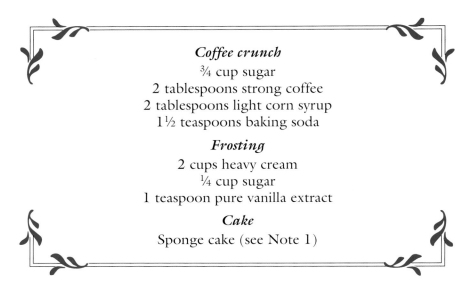

Coffee crunch
¾ cup sugar
2 tablespoons strong coffee
2 tablespoons light corn syrup
1½ teaspoons baking soda

Frosting
2 cups heavy cream
¼ cup sugar
1 teaspoon pure vanilla extract

Cake
Sponge cake (see Note 1)

For coffee crunch Lightly grease a baking sheet and set aside. Do not use black bakeware.

Combine sugar, coffee, and corn syrup in a heavy, deep saucepan, such as a Dutch kettle, over medium-high heat (see Note 2). Bring to a boil and take to the hard crack stage (300° to 310°).

Remove from heat at once. Add baking soda, free of lumps. Stir the foaming mixture until it thickens and pulls away from the sides of the pan (overbeating will break down the foam). Pour immediately onto the prepared baking sheet. Cool thoroughly. When cool, knock out of the pan and break up into very small pieces—½ inch or smaller. Store Coffee Crunch in an airtight container to prevent it from becoming too sticky.

For frosting In a cold bowl with cold beaters, whip the cream, sugar, and vanilla to stiff peaks.

To assemble Frost bottom cake layer with ½ inch of whipped cream. Top with remaining cake layer and frost entire cake with remaining cream, swirling. Chill until ready to apply the Coffee Crunch.

No more than 4 hours before serving, generously decorate the top of the cake with Coffee Crunch (see Note 3). Assail the sides with Coffee Crunch by grabbing handfuls and quickly plopping them onto the sides (see Note 3). If not serving immediately, refrigerate.

Makes 10 to 12 servings.

Note 1: You may purchase two 9-inch layers of sponge or chiffon cake (or any other plain white or yellow cake), or prepare the the sponge cake in Strawberry Trifle Cake (page 139), made in two 9-inch cake pans.

Note 2: A deep saucepan for the Coffee Crunch is specificied with good reason. The mixture *quadruples* in size.

Note 3: The candy will get sticky if left on the cake too long before serving.

CHAPTER EIGHT

Gooey Fruit Desserts Ice Cream and Beverages

Nectarine Parfait with Almond Zabaglione

California grows almost all the nectarines in the world. Most have been bred for thin skin, which makes peeling optional. It also makes nectarines the easiest stone fruit to prepare. If the skin is reddish, it will give a deep hue to your presentation.

Nectarines can sustain large doses of the companion flavor of almonds. Adding almond-flavored liqueur to a zabaglione with whipped cream elevates the flavor of the fruit.

Nectarines
2½ pounds nectarines
3 tablespoons unsalted butter
⅔ cup packed dark brown sugar
1½ tablespoons amaretto

Amaretto zabaglione
6 egg yolks

¾ cup sugar
¾ cup amaretto
1 cup cream

Buttered almond topping
4 tablespoons butter
½ cup slivered almonds

For nectarines Wash, pit, and thinly slice the nectarines. In a wide, heavy skillet, melt the butter and brown sugar. When bubbly, add nectarines and sauté over medium-high heat until the liquid from the fruit thickens, about 10 minutes.

With heat high, sprinkle amaretto over fruit, and quickly ignite. Let flames subside. Immediately pour nectarines onto a cookie sheet to cool.

For zabaglione In a deep mixing bowl, beat yolks and sugar until pale and thick, 1 to 1½ minutes. Set bowl over a pan of simmering water.

Add amaretto and whisk mixture with a balloon whisk (or portable electric mixer set at medium speed) until it is thick and foamy and has tripled in volume, about 12 to 15 minutes. The yolks should be very fluffy and soft, like a whipped custard.

Remove from heat. Cool completely, stirring the zabaglione now and then for the next 15 minutes to hasten cooling.

In a cold bowl with cold beaters, whip the cream to stiff peaks. Fold into zabaglione, leaving no lumps. Cover and chill 2 hours.

For topping In a medium skillet over medium heat, melt the butter. When bubbly, add the almonds, swirling them around the pan to coat completely. Toss and cook until a toasty smell comes from the pan.

Buttered almonds will keep 1 week covered or in a zip-style plastic bag at room temperature.

To assemble Fill sundae or parfait glasses in alternating layers of fruit and zabaglione, starting with fruit and ending with zabaglione. Top each with buttered almonds and, if you have one handy, a mint sprig. May chill up to 2 days.

Makes 8 1-cup parfaits.

Lemon-Blackberry Parfait with Zabaglione Mousseline

Traditional zabaglione, made with sweet Marsala and whipped until tripled in volume while being heated over simmering water, is fluffed up and aired out with whipped cream folded in just before assembly. I've got blackberries in my yard incapable of eradication, so every summer, I pull out the parfait glasses and deal with them like this.

Blackberries
3 cups blackberries

3 tablespoons brown sugar

½ teaspoon cornstarch mixed with
1 tablespoon water

Zabaglione
5 egg yolks

⅓ cup sugar

¾ cup sweet Marsala (or brandy, rum,
or fruit-flavored liqueur)

Zest of 1 lemon,
very finely grated

½ cup cream

Mint sprigs

For blackberries Rinse the blackberries (see Note). Toss in a bowl with brown sugar and let sit 5 minutes. Puree ½ cup of the blackberries, including any accumulated juice, and bring to boil in a small saucepan. At the boil, stir in cornstarch mixture and boil 20 seconds, stirring. Pour over whole berries, stir, and set aside.

For zabaglione In a deep mixing bowl, beat the yolks and sugar until pale and thick, 1 to 1½ minutes. Set bowl over a pan of simmering water.

Add Marsala and lemon zest, and whisk mixture with a balloon whisk (or portable electric mixer set at medium speed) until it is thick and foamy and has tripled in volume, about 12 to 15 minutes. The yolks should be very fluffy and soft, like a whipped custard.

Remove from heat. Cool completely, whipping up the zabaglione now and then over the next 15 minutes to hasten cooling.

In a cold bowl with cold beaters, whip the cream to stiff peaks. Gently fold into zabaglione, leaving no lumps. Cover and chill 2 hours.

To assemble   Fill sundae or parfait glasses in alternating layers of fruit and zabaglione, starting with fruit and ending with zabaglione. Garnish each with a mint sprig. Will keep, assembled, 2 days.

Makes 4 1-cup parfaits.

Note: If you've picked your own blackberries, they may harbor spider webs or bugs. Please be sure to wash them.

Judy's Caramel Apples

Long before caramel candies were invented, apples were being dunked in hot, thick caramel homemade by a much-appreciated cook. No child can turn these down.

6 small Granny Smith apples

Judy's caramel
1 cup sugar
1 cup dark corn syrup
½ cup butter
1 cup cream
½ teaspoon vanilla

Wash apples and remove stems. Insert popsicle stick or dowel into stem end of apple so that 1½ inches of stick is inside the apple. Set aside so apples are room temperature for dipping. Line a cookie sheet with buttered foil.

For caramel In a saucepan, combine all caramel ingredients except the vanilla. Cook, stirring constantly over medium-high heat to bring mixture to 240° to 244° on a candy thermometer. (The temperature here is critical. This range produces a soft caramel that is perfect for dipping. If the caramel gets up as high as 250°, it will become too firm.) To stop the cooking, place the saucepan of caramel into a bowl of water. Cool to 175°.

To dip apples Hold each apple by the stick and dunk it completely into caramel; carefully pull up at a slight angle so the stick won't dislodge. Gently twirl stick so excess caramel will drip off. Place apple on buttered foil. Caramel will harden completely within a few minutes. If caramel cools to below 150°, it will become too thick to cover apples easily; in this case, reheat it in a double boiler.

Makes 6 caramel apples (recipe doubles easily).

You will want to use the leftover caramel in a constructive manner. Here are some possibilities:

1. Pour into a square buttered mold or pan. When cool, cut with a sharp knife dipped in hot water. Individually wrap for plain caramel candies.

2. Roll caramel into balls, then roll balls in chopped pecans or walnuts. Individually wrap for caramel-nut candies.

3. Reheat caramel in a double boiler, thin to desired consistency with hot milk or cream, and use as caramel sauce over ice cream.

Peach Cloud

The most beautiful stone fruits in America must come from the mountains east of Sacramento. Hot days and cool nights characterize a growing season that allows fruit to reach dimensions usually reserved for jokes about Texas.

When perfectly cut by Marcy Friedman, a friend who has worked on this recipe for most of her adult life, curvy peach slices arrayed in tight rows form waves over an elegantly gooey cloud of meringue, cream cheese, and marshmallows. The peaches glisten in a passion fruit glaze, a delicious souvenir of Marcy's life in Hawaii.

Meringue crust
6 egg whites
¼ teaspoon salt
1¾ cups sugar

Cream-and-cheese layer
6 ounces cream cheese, very soft
½ cup powdered sugar
1 teaspoon vanilla
2 cups cream
2 cups miniature marshmallows

Peach layer
5 or 6 large freestone peaches, such as O'Henry

Glaze
⅓ cup undiluted frozen passion fruit juice
2 to 3 tablespoons water
1 teaspoon arrowroot or cornstarch

For meringue   Lightly butter a 9- by 13-inch baking pan. Set oven rack in the center of the oven and preheat oven to 250°.

Beat egg whites and salt to glossy, stiff peaks, gradually adding sugar halfway through. Spread meringue evenly in the prepared pan. Bake 1½ hours. Turn the oven off and leave the meringue inside the oven 12 hours or overnight (see Note 1). It will get a hint of color.

For cream-and-cheese layer   Beat cream cheese, powdered sugar, and vanilla until

smooth. In a cold bowl with cold beaters, whip cream to medium-stiff peaks. Fold a "scoop" of whipped cream into beaten cheese, to loosen the cheese and make it easier to fold with the cream. Fold remaining cream and marshmallows into cream cheese. Spread over meringue crust and refrigerate 8 to 12 hours.

For peaches   Drop peaches into a large pot of boiling water for 30 seconds to 1 minute. Test readiness by piercing one with a knife tip: if skin curls back, peaches are ready to peel. Do not boil longer than 1 minute, or peach pulp will begin to cook. Remove peaches from water with a slotted spoon or wide Chinese strainer, place them in a colander, and immediately rinse in cold water. Keep in a bowl of ice water until all peaches are peeled and pitted. Skins *should* slip off. If skins stick to flesh, peel with a knife.

Slice peaches evenly into ¼-inch slices and place in neat lengthwise overlapping rows over the cream-and-cheese layer. Or cut squares from pan and decorate individually (see photo plate 4).

For glaze Boil all glaze ingredients together until clear (see Note 3). Immediately brush onto all surfaces of peaches. Chill until serving. To serve, cut into squares.

Makes 10 to 12 servings.

Note 1: Start this recipe the night before. But beware the damp humid day in summer and the damp rainy day in summer or fall: in such weather, temperamental meringue won't cooperate.

Note 2: If you cannot find large (I'm talking enormous) freestone peaches, buy a few extra medium-size ones. Peaches are juiciest toward the final phase of peach season—around August.

Note 3: Passion fruit juice, which is not that easy to find, is most often sold frozen in cans. If you find it bottled, boil down ½ cup of bottled juice until it measures ⅓ cup, then proceed with recipe. Or substitute strawberry or red currant jam in the glaze.

Schubert's Ooey Gooey Sundaes

Family friend Carl Schubert loves food, and he likes it fast and fantastic. Here is his short week of Ooey Gooey Sundaes.

1. French vanilla ice cream with apple slices sautéed in butter and about 2 to 3 tablespoons Calvados, then covered with hot caramel sauce (store-bought or homemade; see Quick Caramel Sauce, below) and sprinkled with toasted pecans or other nuts.
2. French vanilla ice cream with sliced bananas and strawberries spooned over with store-bought orange marmalade and topped with nuts.
3. Rich chocolate ice cream with fresh raspberries or sliced strawberries topped with hot caramel or chocolate sauce (store-bought or homemade), with nut sprinkling optional.
4. Brownie square set on plate coated with warm caramel sauce, topped with a large scoop of French vanilla or mocha ice cream, which is then topped with whipped cream and (optional) nuts.
5. Drop biscuits, split, with whipped cream and sliced bananas inside, like a sandwich, and a scoop of French vanilla ice cream on top, sprinkled with strawberries, nuts, and white raisins.
6. A large wineglass containing (1) 1 tablespoon of blueberries, (2) 2 quarters of a drop biscuit, (3) French vanilla ice cream, (4) sliced bananas, (5) nuts, (6) 2 more biscuit quarters, (7) caramel sauce, (8) strawberry ice cream, and (9) ½ ounce Grand Marnier. Nuts are optional.

Carl's Tip: Dieters, omit whipped cream.

Quick Caramel Sauce

1 stick (8 tablespoons) butter
½ cup sugar
½ cup brown sugar
½ cup cream (or evaporated milk)

Melt the butter, sugar, and brown sugar over medium heat until bubbly. Pour in cream and heat until no longer gritty. Use over ice cream.

Note: This sauce is not intended to replace caramel sauce made with sugar cooked to an advanced stage of caramelization. This is a little gritty and lacks flavor depth. However, it is wonderful over ice cream.

Martha's Answer

Ice cream cake made to the specifications of my agent, Martha Casselman, came after a verbal agreement reached over the phone. It would be mocha. It would be gooey. And it would have extra chocolate. Here is Martha's Answer.

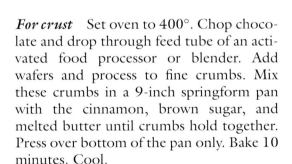

Chocolate crumb crust

2 ounces (2 squares)
semisweet baking chocolate

1 box (9-ounce) plain chocolate
wafer cookies (see Note 1)

1 teaspoon cinnamon

3 tablespoons brown sugar

4 tablespoons (½ stick)
unsalted butter

Chocolate-caramel layer

1½ cups sugar

½ cup water

Pinch cream of tartar

½ cup cream

4 tablespoons (½ stick)
unsalted butter

⅔ cup Lush Chocolate Sauce
(recipe, which makes
2 cups, follows)

1 quart good-quality coffee
ice cream, softened

1 quart good-quality chocolate
ice cream, softened

Lush chocolate sauce

8 ounces (8 squares)
semisweet chocolate

1 cup cream

½ cup sugar

For crust   Set oven to 400°. Chop chocolate and drop through feed tube of an activated food processor or blender. Add wafers and process to fine crumbs. Mix these crumbs in a 9-inch springform pan with the cinnamon, brown sugar, and melted butter until crumbs hold together. Press over bottom of the pan only. Bake 10 minutes. Cool.

For chocolate-caramel layer (for Quick Version, see page 216). In a heavy saucepan, boil sugar water and cream of tartar over medium-high heat. (If crystals form on the sides of the pan, cover the pan for 30 seconds or as long as 5 minutes so steam can rinse off the sides.) When the sugar darkens, you may swirl the pan to even the color. Take the caramel to the color of iced tea.

Remove from the heat and pour in all the cream. The caramel will sputter, so stand back. Return to heat and cook and stir a minute or two. Keep moving the spoon all over the bottom of the pan until caramel and cream are completely smooth. Remove from the heat and add the butter, stirring until the butter has completely melted into the sauce.

Pour caramel into a bowl. Cool slightly. Stir in ⅔ cup Lush Chocolate Sauce until blended, reserving rest for top.

For lush chocolate sauce Chop the chocolate evenly. In a saucepan, heat half the cream with the sugar until it boils. Remove from heat. Add chocolate and stir until it melts and mixture is smooth. Add remaining cream and stir patiently until thick and smooth.

Pour while warm or at room temperature (in which case, sauce will turn the consistency of sour cream).

To assemble Pour 1½ cups of chocolate-caramel sauce over crust, tilting to coat. Freeze until firm. When chocolate-caramel layer is firm, mash soft ice creams, swirling in remaining chocolate-caramel sauce, leaving streaks. Spread ice cream over chocolate-caramel layer in crust, then freeze again to harden. Top with remaining 1⅓ cups Lush Chocolate Sauce. Wrap well and store, frozen, up to 1 month.

To serve Partially soften. Cut cake into wedges with a knife dipped in a tall glass of hot water, then wiped dry.

Note 1: Chocolate wafer cookies appear erratically in stores. If you can't find them, you can make an alternate crust with 1½ cups ground Oreos—cookies, filling, and all.

Note 2: For ease in serving later, line springform pan with a cardboard liner (sold at stores that specialize in cake decorating) before preparing the crust.

Quick Version

Prepare crust as above. Melt 2 ounces (2 squares) of semisweet chocolate and blend it into the contents of a store-bought jar of caramel sauce. Spread over crust. Top with ice cream flavors, as above. Top ice cream with store-bought chocolate sauce.

Meager Attempt at Calorie/Fat Reduction
Use favorite yogurt flavors instead of ice cream.

Boozey Rich Eggnog from a Cooked Base

From the beginning, my eggnog would knock your socks off. In the end, it might have knocked you off. A dozen raw egg yolks were beaten with a sea's worth of froth from egg whites and cream. There they resided in this recipe, most gloriously in the American South, for perhaps a century. Today's Boozey Rich Eggnog steers clear of raw eggs. With premeditated potency, it makes you smile . . . and smile. And it gives you a moustache.

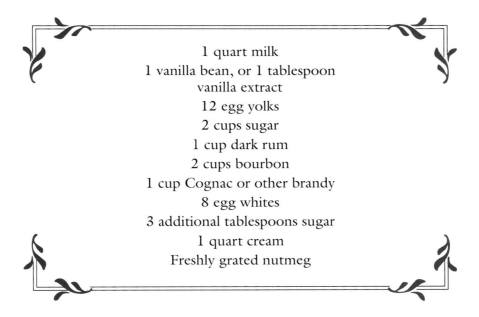

1 quart milk
1 vanilla bean, or 1 tablespoon
vanilla extract
12 egg yolks
2 cups sugar
1 cup dark rum
2 cups bourbon
1 cup Cognac or other brandy
8 egg whites
3 additional tablespoons sugar
1 quart cream
Freshly grated nutmeg

For base In a heavy medium-size saucepan, barely boil the milk with the vanilla bean, which has been split lengthwise, scraped with the back edge of a knife and added to the milk—seeds, pod, and all (if using vanilla extract, you'll add it after eggnog base has cooked).

Meanwhile, place a large fine-mesh strainer over a bowl set in a larger bowl of ice.

Beat the yolks and sugar together in the top of a double boiler, by hand or with electric beaters, until thick and smooth, about 1 minute. Whisk in the hot vanilla milk. Cook in the double boiler set over simmering water, stirring constantly all around the bottom and corners with a rubber or wooden spatula. In time, foam will subside. The eggnog base is done when it coats a wooden spoon without bare spots, 12 to 15 minutes.

Immediately pour through strainer, stirring to cool. When cool to the touch, slowly whisk in all liquors (if using vanilla extract instead of vanilla bean, add this now, too). Store eggnog base in refrigerator overnight or up to three days, to ripen.

To complete eggnog At serving, remove vanilla bean and pour eggnog base into a large punch bowl.

Beat egg whites with 3 tablespoons sugar to stiff peaks; fold into eggnog mixture. Beat cream to stiff peaks and fold it in, too. Let some lumps of the cream and egg whites float on surface. Sprinkle with nutmeg. Serve immediately, using a ladle.

Makes 25 to 30 servings.

An Old, Slurpy English Syllabub—But Not Too Old

Really old recipes for syllabub date to the 1600s. It was the norm to create a beaten froth of sherry, Rhine wine, sugar, and cream; pour it into glasses; and leave it out a day—or two—in a cold English home at Christmastime. After a while, a clear drink formed below and a thick curd floated on top.

A sprig of rosemary or a bruised lemon peel was often mentioned as garnish. Or sprinkle each syllabub with cinnamon or nutmeg. Mostly, this is a dreamy way to drink sherry.

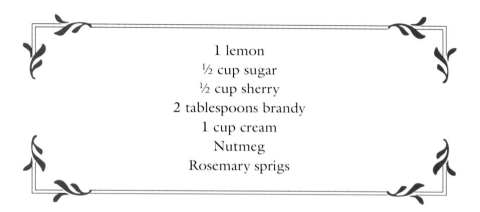

1 lemon
½ cup sugar
½ cup sherry
2 tablespoons brandy
1 cup cream
Nutmeg
Rosemary sprigs

Grate the rind off the lemon, then halve and squeeze out the juice. Mix the lemon juice with sugar and sherry until sugar is dissolved. Stir in brandy.

In a cold bowl with cold beaters, whip the cream to soft peaks. Fold cream into sherry mixture and pour into 6 4-ounce glasses. You may leave the drink at room temperature for a couple of hours before guests arrive, or refrigerate overnight (see Note).

At serving, dust with nutmeg and garnish with a sprig of rosemary. Serve with Almond Paste Macaroons (page 58).

Makes 6 servings.

Note: For a mellow flavor, combine all ingredients except the cream, and leave at room temperature overnight. Whip and add cream the next day.

CHAPTER NINE

Getting the Goo without the Gotcha'

"Cream" and Sugar Slave

The wicked recipe of straight cream and sugar (see Cream and Sugar Slave, page 18) can retrench fat and calories with the help of defatted dairy products. The mild flavor of ricotta and the subtle tang of yogurt produce an enjoyable mixture rounded out with sugar and vanilla.

2 cups ricotta cheese
1 cup Yogurt Cream (recipe follows)
or low-fat sour cream
1 teaspoon pure vanilla extract
½ cup brown sugar
Sliced bananas, strawberries,
or peaches, or other berries
or fruit of choice

Whip the ricotta and yogurt cream with a portable electric mixer at high speed, or in a food processor, until smooth. Add vanilla. Spoon half the mixture into dessert bowls or goblets. Top each with sieved brown sugar, then a final layer of cheese mixture. Chill well. Serve garnished with fresh fruit. The brown sugar will form a faux caramel.

For yogurt cream Place 2 cups plain natural low-fat yogurt (without gelatin or gum) in a colander lined with cheesecloth or white paper towels. Set colander in a pan (such as a round cake pan), cover the entire apparatus with a cloth, and set in the refrigerator to drain for several days (up to 4 days). Discard whey and use thick yogurt as you would sour cream. Yield: About 1 cup.

Makes 4 to 6 servings.

Pears Poached in Spiced Red Wine

The longer this syrup cooks down, the more candylike and sticky it becomes. Use a deeply colored wine, such as a Zinfandel or Cabernet Sauvignon, to produce a beautifully ruby-colored syrup. Avoid burgundies, such as Pinot Noir, because they tend to go pale and can contribute a gray color to the pears. Avoid cast iron; it, too, will turn pears gray.

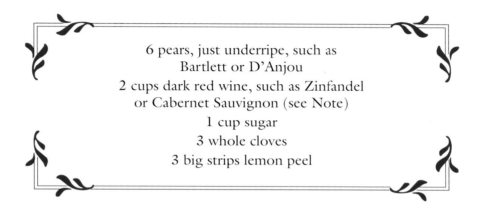

6 pears, just underripe, such as
Bartlett or D'Anjou
2 cups dark red wine, such as Zinfandel
or Cabernet Sauvignon (see Note)
1 cup sugar
3 whole cloves
3 big strips lemon peel

Peel pears, leaving stems intact. Halve (through the stems) and scoop out cores with a melon baller. As you peel them place pears in a big bowl of water to which 2 tablespoons lemon juice have been added.

In a wide skillet, bring the wine, sugar, cloves, and lemon peel to a boil. Add pears, flat sides down and necks toward the center of the skillet. Return liquid to a simmer, cover, and poach 15 to 20 minutes, or until a thin knife can easily be inserted into the thick part of the pear. Using a slotted spoon, transfer pears to a dish.

Remove the peel and cloves from the syrup. With heat high, boil syrup until it measures about 1½ cups. Pour over pears. Serve hot or cold. (Store in syrup in the refrigerator.)

Makes 6 servings.

Note: Or use white wine—a Riesling, Sauvignon Blanc, or any white table wine. In either case, instead of sugar, use honey; and instead of lemon peel, try orange peel.

Blueberries Baked in Phyllo

Using water instead of butter to annoint sheets of phyllo dough would seem to remove some of the meltingness of this paper-thin dough. But the thick blueberry filling more than compensates for this loss. If you must, brush every other sheet with melted butter. Or save the butter for brushing on top before baking. (Could it hurt that much?)

1 box phyllo dough
4 cups fresh blueberries
5 tablespoons sugar
2 tablespoons cornstarch
¼ teaspoon grated lemon zest
1½ teaspoons lemon juice

Thaw phyllo according to package directions. Pick over blueberries, then rinse and drain.

In a large bowl, stir the sugar, cornstarch, and lemon zest together. Gently stir in berries, crushing some of them to release some juice and force the sugar to stick to the fruit. Mix until well combined. Sprinkle with lemon juice and stir a few times more.

Use 2 9-inch pie plates (or disposable tins). Line one with a sheet of phyllo. Add blueberry mixture. Brush the overhanging phyllo with water and flap over berries to form a package.

Line the second pie plate with a second sheet of dough. Now, invert the berry package into the second pie plate. Brush the overhang with water and flap it over the package. Keep flipping in this manner four more times, using a total of 6 sheets of dough. Set oven rack in the center of the oven and pre-heat the oven to 350° for a glass plate, 375° for metal.

Wash out the remaining pie plate, or use a cookie sheet. Spray with nonstick spray or brush with a little butter. Make a large rectangle using 4 phyllo sheets that overlap in the middle and are laid out so there is a separate sheet for each of the four corners of the rectangle. Brush all over with water.

Finally, flip the berry package into the center of the rectangle and gather up the corners into a twisted ruffled topknot in the center of the package.

Bake for 30 to 35 minutes. Serve dusted with powdered sugar.

Makes 6 servings.

Note: You may create 4 individual packages (see photo plate 5), using 4 sheets of phyllo per package, and 1 final sheet for the topknot. Bake 30 minutes.

Orange Freeze Chiffon Pie

It's not really frozen. The flavor is reminiscent of the soda fountain drink, Orange Freeze. And it's not *that* virtuous. It's got sugar and sweet orange juice concentrate. But if you can get past the butter in the crust, you've got to admit this refreshing pie is rather short on fat.

Crust
(For a 9-inch pie plate)

10 graham crackers (processed in a food processor or crushed with a rolling pin between 2 sheets of waxed paper to form 1½ cups fine crumbs)
1 teaspoon cinnamon
3 tablespoons brown sugar
3 tablespoons melted butter

Orange filling
1½ tablespoons (2 envelopes) plain gelatin
¼ cup water
½ cup sugar
¾ cup water
2 cups Yogurt Cream (see page 224)
1 6-ounce can orange juice concentrate, thawed, undiluted
½ teaspoon pure vanilla extract
3 egg whites
¼ cup additional sugar
Orange slices, from a peeled orange, for garnish

For crust Preheat oven to 350°. Pour crumbs into bottom of a 10-inch pie plate. Stir in cinnamon and brown sugar. Add melted butter and, using fingers, quickly mash the mixture until the crumbs hold together. Press mixture up the sides and over the bottom of pie plate. Bake 10 minutes. Cool.

For filling Combine gelatin and ¼ cup water and set aside to soften for 5 minutes.

Heat sugar and ¾ cup water in a saucepan and cook 2 minutes. Cool.

In a bowl, whisk the yogurt cream to aerate it. Add the orange juice concentrate a little at a time. Combine gelatin mixture and sugar syrup, and stir until gelatin is completely dissolved; then add to orange mixture, stirring until smooth. Stir in vanilla and chill 30 minutes, until mixture will mound if picked up with a spoon.

Beat the egg whites to stiff peaks, gradually adding the ¼ cup sugar halfway through. Fold a little of the whites into the orange mixture to pre-lighten it, then fold in all the whites, using wide, gentle strokes, until no lumps remain. Pour filling into the prepared crust and chill. Garnish with thin slices of fresh orange around the edge.

Makes 10 servings.

Lemon-Yogurt Pudding Cake

Puddly on the bottom, moist and almost squishy throughout, this cake has high-fat allure and reduced-fat reality. Yes, you'll get cholesterol from the egg yolks and the tablespoon of butter, but the total indignity diminishes when divided among 8 people.

Don't be misled by the term "cake." When this comes from the oven, be ready with a very large spoon, and serve out portions by the juicy mound, like soufflé. For drama, bake in a soufflé dish.

⅔ cup sugar
¼ cup flour
1½ teaspoons grated lemon zest
2 tablespoons lemon juice
1 tablespoon butter, melted

3 egg yolks
8 ounces plain nonfat (or low-fat) yogurt
½ cup low-fat or skim milk
3 egg whites

Set oven rack in the lower third of the oven and preheat oven to 350°.

Sift together the sugar and flour. Stir in lemon zest, lemon juice, and butter. In a large bowl, beat the yolks until fluffy, about 30 seconds. Beat in the yogurt and milk until no lumps of yogurt remain. Add flour mixture and beat mix until thoroughly combined.

In another bowl, beat the egg whites to soft peaks. Fold ⅓ of the whites into the yolk-flour base, to pre-lighten the mixture. Fold in the remaining whites, using a wide rubber spatula and making wide strokes. Pour the batter into an ungreased, deep, 8-inch soufflé dish. Set this into a larger roasting pan, and fill with an inch of very hot tap water.

Bake 30 minutes, just until top is set. After removing from oven, cake will sink slightly and remain gloriously "undone" on the bottom.

For maximum texture and flavor, serve warm.

Makes 6 servings.

Note: If you don't have a soufflé dish, use any other 8-inch round pan or an 8-inch square baking pan.

Five Minutes and Counting
(Broiled Sour Cream and Grapes)

Imitation sour cream provides results similar to (but not exactly like) the rich flavor of the Five Minutes and Counting recipe on page 26. To mask the off-taste of imitation sour cream, add vanilla and a little cinnamon—just enough to throw off the taste buds.

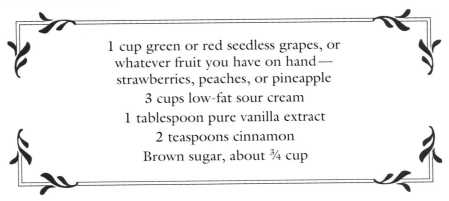

1 cup green or red seedless grapes, or whatever fruit you have on hand—strawberries, peaches, or pineapple

3 cups low-fat sour cream

1 tablespoon pure vanilla extract

2 teaspoons cinnamon

Brown sugar, about ¾ cup

Line 6 ramekins or a baking dish with the fruit. Mix sour cream with vanilla and cinnamon. Spoon over fruit. Sprinkle with brown sugar. Chill until serving, then run under broiler until sugar is mostly melted. Serve immediately.

Makes 6 servings.

Slightly Virtuous Crème Anglaise

You won't get the rich mouth feel, body, or thickness of crème Anglaise made with sturdier milk products, such as cream, half-and-half, or whole milk. You will get a dessert sauce you can pour over fresh fruit. The technique is the same as for full-fat Crème Anglaise (page 38).

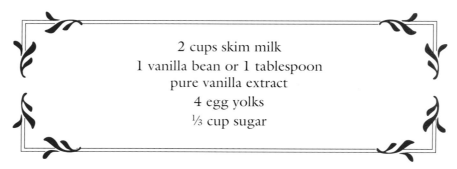

2 cups skim milk
1 vanilla bean or 1 tablespoon
pure vanilla extract
4 egg yolks
⅓ cup sugar

In a heavy, medium-size saucepan, barely boil the milk (see Note 1) and the vanilla bean, which has been split lengthwise, scraped with the back edge of a knife, and added to the milk—seeds, pod and all. (If you're using vanilla extract, add it after crème Anglaise has cooked.)

Meanwhile, place a large fine-mesh strainer over a bowl set in a larger bowl of ice.

In the top of a double boiler, beat the yolks and sugar by hand or with a portable electric mixer until thick and smooth, about 1 minute. Slowly pour the hot milk and vanilla bean over the yolks, whisking as you pour.

Cook in the double boiler set over simmering water, stirring constantly all around the bottom and corners with a rubber or wooden spatula. In time, foam will subside. The crème Anglaise is done when it coats a wooden spoon without bare spots, 12 to 15 minutes.

Immediately pour through the strainer. If using vanilla extract, add it now (see Note 2). Remove, wash, and save the vanilla bean. Keep stirring to cool the custard.

To store, cover with plastic wrap pressed directly onto surface of the crème Anglaise, and refrigerate.

Makes 2 cups.

Note 1: You may warm the milk and vanilla bean in a glass quart-measure, uncovered, in the microwave on High for 3 to 5 minutes, or until bubbles form around the edge.

Note 2: Flavor crème Anglaise with ½ teaspoon cinnamon or 2 teaspoons brandy, rum, amaretto, Grand Marnier, or Kahlua.

Note 3: To keep crème Anglaise warm for serving, place in a bowl or pot set in a larger pot of hot water.

Pairing Dessert with Coffee

The preferred accompaniment to a fine dessert is more often than not a steaming cup of coffee. While we struggle with wine pairing, we seldom ponder the sensory qualities of coffee.

Pairing coffee with dessert is like pairing any other food with wine. The heartier the dessert, the more robust the coffee needed to enhance its taste. When a dessert coats the mouth with fat from such components as cream, chocolate, or butter, the coffee should be considered for what it can add to the entire dessert course.

To begin, coffee should be brewed fresh. Percolated coffee isn't even mentioned when the subject of good coffee is brought up. A good drip coffee maker is a must. Alternately, the French plunge-brewing process is preferred by many coffee experts because it extracts more flavor from the coffee without making it bitter. It's also a ceremonial way of making coffee: the plunging takes place at the table, and is an elegant end to a meal.

Cappuccino, at its source—Italy—is a morning beverage. I find it too greedy a scene-stealer when served at night after dinner, particularly when a dessert is being showcased. Plain coffee in the form of espresso may be too strong for many tastes. I often welcome the fine American tradition of a simple cup of coffee after a meal—black, or with cream and a little sugar. It signals closure, more talking, and it always defers to dessert.

Here is a simple guide to help you match dessert categories with appropriate coffees.

Creamy desserts   Brew a dark roasted coffee of medium body, such as Mocha Java, Italian Roast, or Vienna Roast. Or try a lighter roasted coffee varietal, such as Guatemalan, Costa Rican, or Mexican. Creamy desserts are enjoyed for texture and viscosity. The acidity in a single varietal can balance the creaminess without a distracting sharp flavor.

If you usually drink coffee black, you might want to try a little cream and sugar in your cup when also eating a creamy dessert. Flavored coffees work well with simple creamy desserts. Cinnamon or hazelnut coffee pair well with custard, or French vanilla coffee with tapioca.

Chocolate   Because chocolate is very strong, it will always star. In the midst of chocolate a light-bodied or light-roasted coffee will get lost. French Roast is the strongest, most robust coffee, and can stand up to the concentrated flavor of chocolate. A simple chocolate cake with sauce is nicely rounded out with a coffee flavored with raspberry, almond, vanilla, or mint.

Meringue   Coffee with a winey, berry-fruit background complements meringues well. You'll find these characteristics in light-roasted Kenyan or Zimbabwe beans (which are also good with fruit desserts).

Caramel The strong taste of caramel needs a heavy-bodied coffee with a dark component, such as Sumatra-French blend, Ethiopian-French blend, or Mocha Java French blend. The term "French blend" is a clue that the coffee will have backbone.

Fruit As much as I hate to admit it, flavored coffees work nicely. I was such a purist I hadn't given flavored coffee a chance. Coffees flavored with mint, raspberry, or amaretto make fine companions to fruit desserts.

Index